THE YOU CODE

What your habits say about you

Judi James and James Moore

Vermilion
LONDON

1 3 5 7 9 10 8 6 4 2

Published in 2010 by Vermilion, an imprint of Ebury Publishing
Ebury Publishing is a Random House Group company

Copyright © Judi James and James Moore 2010

Judi James and James Moore have asserted their right to be identified as
the authors of this Work in accordance with the Copyright, Designs and
Patents Act 1988.

The Random House Group Limited Reg. No. 954009

Addresses for companies within the Random House Group can be found at
www.rbooks.co.uk

A CIP catalogue record for this book is available from the British Library

The Random House Group Limited supports The Forest Stewardship
Council (FSC), the leading international forest certification organisation.
All our titles that are printed on Greenpeace approved FSC certified paper
carry the FSC logo. Our paper procurement policy can be found at
www.rbooks.co.uk/environment

Printed and bound in Great Britain by
CPI Cox & Wyman, Reading, RG1 8EX

ISBN 9780091929541

Copies are available at special rates for bulk orders. Contact the sales
development team on 020 7840 8487 for more information.

To buy books by your favourite authors and register for offers, visit
www.rbooks.co.uk

CONTENTS

'Observe all men; thy self most.'
– *Benjamin Franklin*

'. . . a strong "brand" is what makes the people you want
to influence choose you over someone else.'
– *branding consultant Louise Mowbray*

'What do you wear on the running machine? I can't
bear to wear flat shoes.'
– *Victoria Beckham*

INTRODUCTION

WHAT IS THE YOU CODE?

How long does it take for other people to sum you up? A minute? Ten seconds? Recent research shows that, incredibly, it takes just one tiny tenth of a second for someone to make huge judgements – right or wrong – about what we're like. And the clues they pick up mean they are making decisions about everything from attraction and status to employability, along with assessments of our entire personality and future behaviour.

Exactly how those assumptions are made is a complex process. But one thing is for certain: these first impressions will often result from the hundreds of seemingly superficial or subliminal choices that you yourself have made. And every day your brain is making thousands of them, from the pen you take to a meeting, to the ring tone you download to your phone, to the coffee you order from your friendly barista – even your decision to read this book. Each decision adds up to the overall image known as 'You'.

In this book you will discover that although these little choices, some made consciously, others subconsciously, may *seem* trivial they are never without meaning. Every decision sends out clear signals about your personality traits and makes a profound difference to how other people think about you.

The modern pace of life means we sum people up as swiftly as possible based on small amounts of evidence. And, as our attention spans get shorter and populations get larger, we turn to processes like speed-dating to find partners, or websites like Facebook to find friends. How many people have you seen today already? If you live or work in a city you could have commuted with or walked past thousands of individuals and if you work in a large company you could have seen hundreds more. Like any other animal tuned into survival mode your brain will have assessed each one of these people, making decisions to ignore, be attracted to, be alert to, or even be frightened of, which can range from real fear in the case of the menacing-looking guy on the train and perceived fear when you find yourself alone in the lift with the chief executive.

Fortunately for you and your intellectual well-being you made most, if not all, of these judgements without thinking, or at least without conscious thought. Because let's face it: you'd have neither the time nor the energy to start picking over the bones of each and every trans-action. You're probably too busy buying your sandwich for lunch and getting back to work on time to start analysing the other people in the check-out queue. And during that meeting in the afternoon or in that bar or club in the evening you probably got an impression of people around you through what you likely call your 'gut reaction'. You will have liked, disliked, trusted, distrusted, listened to or ignored those around you with-out once asking yourself why you felt the way you did. Because, in the process known by psychologists as cognitive algebra, our brains tend to cut straight to the solution without bothering to study the sums involved in getting to it.

But even in this era of spin, hype and performance where the phrase 'style over substance' is applied with boring regularity to everything from breakfast cereal to politicians, doesn't it make sense to delve deeper into why you present yourself the way you do to other people? It's time to make a few small incisions into your overall impact and peek beneath the surface to discover exactly what it is you're happily telling other people about yourself and your psyche. Because even if you're a lifelong member of that cult called 'being myself' it can only add value to your personal stock to be aware that your messy desk or gnarled old ballpoint are telling your boss that you're unreliable, or that the mountain of cuddly toys on your bed led that new date to believe you're a bunny boiler.

And while we're tripping down the analytical route, how about trying a bit of psychological sat-nav when you're sussing out other people, checking their tattoos to discover what they reveal about them or looking in their bathroom cabinet for clues to their personality rather than just checking out their star sign? Or maybe even figuring out the best way to get a pay rise based on your boss's car colour, rather than his or her apparent mood when you walk into the office?

Still hoping that your own first impressions will dissolve like sugar in coffee once people get to know you for longer? That all their initial prejudices or unfair assumptions will vanish once they stick around long enough to discover the worth of the real you?

Well, the bad news is that they won't. Or at least it's very unlikely.

Psychologists who have studied the science of first impressions have discovered that our initial preconceptions are not easily changed. Though you might argue that they are based on visual stereotype and assumption, and attempt to make balanced and fair appraisals based on long-term knowledge and experience, you'll find evolution is standing in your way. As the human animal we're programmed to make snap decisions on other people as part of our survival programming. Your initial, instinctive assessments will be over fight or flight, safety or danger, but after that your brain will find itself bombarded with a stream of complex information that is often based on the subtlest and subliminal non-verbal signals, so getting your own signals right first time will be vital. The good news is that once you know the rules you can use these telling signals to manage the impression you give other people by making subtle changes in your habits. This is the technique known as 'impression management' and it's our ability to tailor and flex our verbal and non-verbal messages that create success in the modern world. In this book you will get the tools to unlock the secret code of your everyday decisions, uncovering the precise kinds of messages you're sending out about yourself, often without realising it. It gets to the nub of how you really appear and may tell you more about yourself than you ever wanted to know, as well as providing an intriguing insight into the other people around you. But it will also enable you to use what we call The You Code – the secret language behind our choices and habits – to manipulate the message, presenting the best of yourself, without changing the core of who you are.

Part One of *The You Code* is the scary section, because you get to investigate all your inner thoughts and emotions via your foibles and everyday choices. Did you know that the coffee you order tells all about your sociability and attitude to life, while the way you eat your lunch reveals your sexual tastes, preferences and style? Can you bear to discover what your untidy desk really means about your thinking and working processes? Or exactly what your wardrobe behaviour or the mess beneath your bed means?

In Part Two you'll get help analysing others. And we'll include all the most important people in your life from your boss to prospective lovers. We'll show you what their personal choices and behaviours mean and even encourage you to have a cheeky pry into other people's bathroom cabinets in a bid to understand them better.

In Part Three you'll read all about impression management as we show you how to become strategic, making small but effective changes in your impact and image to ensure more success in your career or in the dating and mating game.

But let's start by studying the 'You' in The You Code . . .

PART ONE: WHAT YOUR HABITS REVEAL ABOUT YOU

1

HOW CHOICE AND TASTE DEFINE YOU

Each of your daily choices has a raft of factors behind it. Some factors are conscious but many are subliminal, and all reveal things about your personality that even you aren't aware of. Take a simple choice that you make regularly, like your daily newspaper, for instance. Here's a list of the psychological factors that might be involved in that one choice, versus the reasons you would probably give for buying it:

You:
- 'I like it best'
- 'I buy it for its sports coverage'
- 'I agree with its politics'
- 'It's cheap'
- 'It's the one I always buy'

In reality:
- Historical: you will be affected by the choices made by your parents and the newspaper you saw when you were growing up.
- Muscle memory: you buy the same paper every day

3

without making a decision. Habit helps you avoid the pressure and stress of multiple choice.

- Class and aspiration: your choice of tabloid or broadsheet will be partly, if not fully, based on where you position yourself in terms of class. By moving from tabloid to broadsheet you could be seeing yourself as upwardly mobile.
- Eye familiarity: your eye has been trained to accept information from this print style more readily than any other.
- Tactile familiarity: you find comfort in the way the paper feels and moves when you turn the pages.
- Trust: familiarity has created what is often a false sense of trust for the writers and the information they present.
- Empathy: either you agree with many of their views or you have been brainwashed into believing you do.
- Delegation: you allow the newspaper to make many of your key decisions for you.
- Social acceptance: you buy the paper that fits in with your pack to create a uniformity of thinking.
- Listing skills: your paper takes all your daily information and prioritises and organises it for you, like a PA.
- In-group approval: it helps you present views that will gain approval (if not agreement) of the group you inhabit.
- Mood: the paper you read affects your mood on a daily basis. Some are cheering, others sobering, some worrying, some actively stoke personal anxieties about things like health and safety. Choose your paper, choose your mood.

YOUR REGULAR CHOICES: NATURE OR NURTURE?

It's easy (and lazy) to assume your choices were something pre-determined in your genes; that the things you like and the things you don't are such an intrinsic part of your personality that you have no control over them; that, in other words, you have no choice about your choices! But all choice is variable and relatively open to change. The first step is looking at your current reality and deciding if it's presenting the 'You' that you want other people to see.

Habits can take roughly 12 to 20 days to knock into touch if you have the willpower and focus to change. Ever take sugar in your tea? When you try your first cup without sugar it will taste repulsive, even to the point of making you shudder and grimace, signals of disgust and rejection that animals normally reserve for poisonous substances. But persevere and that unsweetened tea will taste less repellent as the cups go down. After about 20 cups you'll have reached a stage of acceptance that means putting sugar back into your tea would now induce those symptoms of disgust.

Even strong likes and dislikes can be challenged relatively easily and by doing so you might find you release some extra facets of your personality. If someone else likes something there's almost no concrete reason why you shouldn't. The only contradictions to this rule would be instinctive dislikes based on the survival response, like a dislike of pain or loud noise. Nearly everything else is up for grabs if you can only bypass your belief systems.

So even though your choices and tastes can be hugely revealing in terms of your inner psyche, there's no reason why you can't change those habits to present yourself in a way that might make your life more successful.

LOGIC V EMOTION: I HATE SPIDERS

Do you feel that your decisions are simply logical choices, the result of your brain weighing up the possible alternatives, even when it comes to who to date or what clothes you wear?

Belief systems are all to do with links that you have stored in your subconscious, and which will often bypass logical thought. For instance if, as a small child, you watched your parent display acute fear when he or she saw a spider then it's likely your brain will have made an instant 'learned' link between a spider and fear. This memory and link will be stored for future reference so that every time you see a spider you remember to be scared, even though your conscious mind is aware that, in most cases, spiders are incapable of harming you. Your 'consciousness bypass' would mean your reaction of horror appears spontaneous and instinctive when all it's really down to is wonky programming.

Some people experience a lesser version when asked to eat a Brussels sprout or smell a certain perfume. But if you have the urge and desire to change you can just as easily employ positive bypassing. Foods like smelly cheeses, hot chillies, oysters and even beer have a high repulsion factor when you first taste them, but we often persist because we know other people enjoy them and that they are an acquired taste.

So likes and dislikes tend to be totally down to personal choices that can fluctuate. Clothing styles you found the height of taste and fashion a few years ago can look ridiculous and embarrassing once that fashion has changed. Favourite films or books can be puzzlingly disappointing when revisited later, and even a favourite perfume or aftershave can seem to stink once your tastes have moved on. The only sense that seems to be resilient to being 'fooled' is that of hearing, which of course relates to your appreciation of music. Songs and tunes that you loved years ago often retain that appeal in the present day, even if trends have moved on. Why? Mainly because the set of rhythms and patterns of notes trigger pleasure in different parts of the brain and body, and because most music we have heard becomes stored away in individual memories that are amazingly enduring. Hearing one note or just the title of a song will mean we can access nearly all of it at will, playing it over in our head in a way that will give almost as much pleasure as the real thing.

Our emotions play a big part in our daily decisions too. When you make a choice that pleases you your brain gets programmed to make the same sort of decision next time, creating a habit.

So let's take a look at some of those little decisions. And where better to start than with modern society's most popular little daily pleasure: the working-day cup of coffee.

2

HIDDEN MESSAGES IN YOUR IMAGE

Prepare to step back and take a long hard look at YOU. Not the you that you see from the inside, but the external, projected you that is seen by and reacted to by others. This is the you that is the sum of many parts, and the you that is defined by all those everyday decisions. We're going to investigate some of your most telling traits, habits and choices, showing what they say about you and your psyche.

Think you know yourself inside out? Then you're in for a shock because you're about to meet many different facets of you that you probably never knew existed. We'll be showing you how your animal side can emerge when you make apparently simple lunchtime choices, how your handbag or man-bag sends signals about your self-esteem and how you allow your sexual side to hang out on display in simple things like the type of tie you wear or the height of your heels.

WHAT THE COFFEE YOU DRINK
SAYS ABOUT YOU

As you walk off to work carrying that paper cup of over-priced take-away coffee clad in its own little brown cardboard jacket you're taking part in a reward ritual that is as much about self-esteem and social posturing as it is about energising yourself with a cuppa. The act of carrying your coffee through the streets and into work is every bit as important as drinking it. It's effectively a luxury purchase, and therefore a mini-trophy that affirms your status and sense of achievement and success.

Anyone living or working in a town or city will be aware of the 'coffee revolution' that's occurred over recent years. Over 400 billion cups of the stuff are now consumed across the world every year, with 70 million drunk in the UK daily. In the middle of this decade there was a £50 million rise in coffee sales nationally in just three years. A three-year study by the University of Glasgow found that its effects are universal – all classes and age groups have taken up this new obsession with coffee. This has created a new kind of socialising, which means that coffee houses have taken a huge role in our daily 'hunt–kill' reward rituals; not only does a luxury coffee purchase symbolise a reward for a day spent hunting the 'kill' of work success, the coffee house itself can provide the venue for group get-togethers for planning, discussing and celebrating that 'kill'.

The staggering amount of coffee outlets will also make your coffee a signal of both individualism *and* pack conformity. You chose your outlet because it becomes your 'pack' – or the pack you would like to join, but then the opportunity to customise means you retain your feelings of individuality within that pack. We see newspaper shots of celebrities clutching their branded coffee and the gap between ourselves and an American superstar is somehow breached. The brand you choose is like a club you join.

But what about the type of coffee you order and consume? Coffee choices are based on more than mere taste. With their foam, cream and sprinkle-topped options these drinks have been created to appeal on a much deeper psychological level, relating to self-esteem, stress levels and search for the comforts of childhood. Could you expect a rampant, no-holds-barred sex life from a man who orders a decaf soya latte? Could you envision sophisticated leadership from a woman sucking a caramel frappuccino, liberally festooned with sprinkles and marshmallows, through a jumbo-size straw?

The Espresso Drinker

The implied instant gratification 'hit' of this drink suggests lone consumption for a quasi-medicinal purpose (getting that caffeine burst asap!) rather than the altogether more tactile pleasures of the foam, cream and slow-sup of a cappuccino or latte. Espressos are the unfiltered cigarette of the coffee world and imply hard-living, night-time shenanigans followed by a rather louche attempt at daytime repair. This is the most grown-up of all the coffee options, suggesting a rather cynical view of the universe that borders on sarcasm or even aggression. Espresso drinkers tend to wince as they swallow, which suggests they have a 'no pain – no gain' attitude to most pleasures in life. Espresso Man/Woman has left childhood way behind and is now a devotee of all things cool.

If you're an espresso drinker, you laugh in the face of a healthy lifestyle while the caffeine highs and lows can mean you are moody and don't suffer fools gladly. In work you tend to set yourself high standards; sometimes so high that they're impossible for you to achieve. You're into leadership and fast goals; wafflers, time-wasters, small talk and office gossip can make you irritable. You tend to work long hours and expect others to do the same. When there's a task to be done you have strong focus and direction. You're also susceptible to stress and anxiety. When it comes to sex keep the 'instant hit' theme in mind. Espressos tend to be experienced, exciting and consummate lovers but you're not known for your reliability or unswerving loyalty.

The Black Coffee Drinker

Although similar in tone to espressos, plain old black coffee lacks the biting hit that makes the drinker wince. It is also devoid of any the trappings of self-comfort and flirtatiousness that frothy milk or cream adds, meaning that Black Coffee Drinker is no-frills, into minimalism and very adult 'cool', preferring to be direct when it comes to all person-to-person transactions, be it business, conversation or seduction.

You're a Black Coffee Drinker? Indulgence is not a word you'll tend to use and although you're not exactly pious you're closer to being driven and competitive than to pampering and prevarication. Quiet and moody but with brief bursts of extroversion (usually booze-fuelled), as a Black Coffee Drinker you make a difficult but potentially rewarding friend, colleague or partner.

The Latte Drinker

Cosy, reliable and thorough. This is an infantile drink for infantile people who like to pretend they're up there with the cool big kids but who will tend to roll over and display their sweeter side when placed under pressure. This drink is low on flavour but high on security blanket. By taking a dark and dangerous drink like coffee and turning it into a comforting, milky bedtime beverage Latte Drinkers want to come across as hot-shot contenders, but undermine this by baring their immature side at the same time. It's an attempt to turn danger into safety and is the preferred drink of 'pleasers', those who have an overwhelming compulsion to be liked. If your boss is a Latte Drinker, they will use a baby voice or act cute even when they're telling you off.

If you're a Latte Drinker you tend to avoid direct confrontation but that doesn't mean you won't get someone else to do the dirty for you. This is because your fluffy, loveable front can easily hide a stubborn and determined business side that might find political or strategic behaviours useful. However being liked is a priority for you so why jeopardise popularity by fighting your battles yourself when there are henchmen you can delegate to? This 'milk-with-a-dash' preference shows you're not one for grasping life with both hands. Essentially loyal to your family or partner, Latte Drinker is no firework. You tend to like comfortable surroundings and long chats with people you trust. You fear that others find you boring and, to be blunt, sometimes they probably do. But deep down they know Latte Drinker is a good egg, and your sense of fun, often self-effacing, makes you a joy to be around.

If you're a Latte Woman you tend to be the type who has cuddly toys strewn on her bed; if you're a Latte Man you've embraced your metrosexuality with arms stretched wide. You're both likely to have a coyly passive attitude to sex, preferring to be seduced rather than do the seducing, and your ideal romantic evening will include snuggling on the sofa with your partner while you watch a good movie. Sex is probably about play-fighting, fun and pet names rather than anything more adult or extreme.

The Cappuccino Drinker

An extrovert with an optimistic outlook, the Cappuccino Drinker is all about style over substance and is just as happy giving a presentation in the boardroom as poring over *heat* or *Nuts* or drooling over the latest Gucci courier bag. The bulk of the cappuccino's appeal lies with the froth and Freud would have a field day here, with the milky spume remaining largely unconsumed, having little function apart from the tactile pleasures of licking, sucking and even wearing that milk moustache. Cappuccino froth gives the tongue the mother of all workouts and is all to do with the physicality of the experience, rather than the basic consumption of beverage.

A cappuccino is your drink of choice? You like to be surrounded by nice material objects and nice people but you aren't obsessed with them. Touchy-feely toward friends and family you're someone who enjoys sex, but who needs a partner who is always going to be thinking of ways to make it that little bit more exciting. The chocolate and froth on this coffee is more important to you than what lies beneath, and this could very well be true of your lifestyle. You're a starter rather than a finisher and tend to get bored by research, logic and detail.

The Instant Coffee Drinker

A no-frills type who takes life on the chin. At least that's the way you want to be seen. Yes, you're a cheerful, seemingly straightforward type who likes a laugh, but you also have a tendency to procrastinate and some see you as downright shallow. You get a lift easily, but you get depressed and melancholy just as easily. You aren't that adventurous in your career and tend to spend a lot of time reflecting on making any changes or pursuing any new jobs.

To the opposite sex you can be an enigma and while you think you're loyal you need to try hard to show there's some depth to your personality. Your lack of conformity shows in the way you stick to your instant brew while the rest of the world embraces a Gaggia lifestyle and it might also pop up in your career and your sex life. 'If it ain't broke why fix it?' is your motto, and the Missionary position rules okay. You're probably allergic to any behaviour you see as pretentious and that includes leaving the seat down, scraping ground biscuits off the shag pile, or taking your socks or tights off before sex.

The Decaf Soya Milk Drinker

Forget the healthy living and recycling connotations, this coffee option smacks of eco-worrier rather than eco-warrior. If caffeine gives you palpitations and cow's milk brings you out in spots there's little hope for you in cockroach society that is city dwelling. This is a self-righteous option that implies you think you're just too precious for the real world. Allergy-envy is a condition that is on the increase but is your dairy dread and wheat intolerance actually just a ploy to get attention? By advertising your fragile side you're warning the world to back off, like a driver with a 'baby on board' sticker in the rear window but no sign of kiddie passengers. The very faux-ness of your selection (why drink coffee if you don't want caffeine and why pick milk if you're allergic to dairy?) implies you want what you shouldn't have and suggests that you're disguising your true personality: what you see might not be what you get with the Decaf Soya Drinker.

If you're Decaf Soya Man you're signalling that you're trouble from the word go. Picky, fussy and pernickety you're likely to be squeamish in the bedroom too, rushing off to shower as soon as the exchange of bodily fluids is over. If you're Decaf Soya Girl you're pretentious and high maintenance. You repeat the 'my body is a temple' mantra, and you're likely to be just as demanding in bed as you are in your lifestyle. And the Decaf Soya Drinker does have a tendency to be self-obsessed. If you're a Decaf Soya Drinker you're the sort of person who spends half an hour answering the question 'How are things' without ever realising that your colleague was only being polite.

The Frappucino Drinker

What the hell is frappucino? This slush-puppy for sophisticates is like the ultimate coffee poseur's joke, except it only seems to be ordered by people with no sense of irony. In many ways it's part of a reassuring ritual for the average townie: in winter drink cappuccino, and in summer frappuccino. The only problem with the UK weather is it's easy to frap too early and get caught sucking slush in the middle of a June downpour!

As a Frappuccino Drinker you like to stay at the cutting edge, but the problem is that you don't know when to jump on a bandwagon or when to get off it. You might see yourself as a trendsetter but in fact you're sending out the message that you're someone who favours style over substance. Your relationships therefore often only last as long as your drink choice. You can appear flighty and very 'easy come, easy go' when it comes to friendships and relationships. You'll try anything once but especially if you've seen a celebrity do it first.

The No Coffee Drinker

Never has a phrase been so shocking, show-stopping and strangely alienating as 'I don't drink coffee'. Tell people that you don't do sex or drink booze or that you never watch TV or rarely wear knickers or wash your hair and you'll get empathy, sympathy or even respect. But no coffee? In animal terms this is like an ape that 'doesn't do grooming'. In body language terms you'll see people who don't even try to mask the fact that they think you're a freak. So what's your problem? If it's medical ('I find it repeats', 'it makes me hyper') then unless you are the wrong side of 90 years old you are a complete wuss. If you are frightened of coffee you are frightened of life, as Dr Johnson should have said. In the grand spectrum of available drug options, coffee has to tick all of the boxes: it's legal, of some medical benefit, and is only mildly addictive. If it's taste that puts you off then you really are a child. Coffee tastes *wonderful*. Get over it. Twenty-one days is all it will take to break your cycle of disgust and then you'll be back in the real world with all the other grown-ups, rather than sipping herbal tea with all the wimps.

WHAT YOUR TEA SAYS ABOUT YOU

Tea is an interesting option, especially drunk outside the home. Whereas indoor coffee is always sadly inferior to the take-away variety (hence the knacker's yard of home cappuccino-makers on display at car boot sales), home-brewed tea is invariably better than take-away tea, meaning that whereas coffee drinkers are aspirational, motivated and ambitious, those who drink tea outside the home will settle for second rate. Tea drinkers only really shine when it's an option between canteen coffee and canteen tea because stewed tea is far less lethal than stewed coffee.

So what about the tea perfectionist? Someone who brings their own pot to work and goes through the rituals of warming and stirring? There's a whiff of the maiden aunt about this behaviour, suggesting a pedantic character who is very unlikely to be married. (Tea after a restaurant dinner for two will suggest that sex is unlikely to be on the menu.)

Earl Grey
. . . drinkers do have an air of superiority but they're also those who prefer their gratification delayed, rather than

instant because the 'delicate' flavour of this tea can take several samplings before it can be enjoyed. Earl Grey without milk suggests that you are pretentious but with milk hints you're a snob without portfolio, someone trying to look posh but without really 'getting it'.

Builders' Tea

. . . is the drink *du jour* of everyone in the media. This option suggests you're jolly and creative and spontaneous but of course it's all a bit of a front. Your working-class credentials are blown out of the water by the fact that no builder ever called this 'builders' tea'.

Chai

. . . is the trendy tea option, having only appeared on coffee-bar menus in recent years. It singles you out as someone who likes to embrace change and try all things new, but not as heroically as you might hope, as this sweet, milky option is very akin to a sugary, caffeine-free latte, i.e. the drink of very small kiddies.

Lapsang Souchong

. . . how precious are you? How special? Not very is the likely answer but you clearly like to think so.

We've got you to a 'tea'

Drinking tea and coffee is such a ritualistic process that it even tastes better quaffed from your favourite cup according to psychologists at the University of Sheffield. Nearly two thirds of us own a favourite cup or mug.

While we're on the subject of liquids it's worth taking a look at your choice of water too.

WHAT YOUR WATER SAYS ABOUT YOU

Since the day eau de Perrier made its way to these shores and onto our dinner tables the stuff you drink and wash in has become an über-elitist liquid with water snobs cropping up everywhere. Want to show you have a palate that is refined beyond that of most mere mortals? Then claim you can do a blindfold taste test to recognise brand, region and vintage. Of course, this is never possible but hopefully no one you know has a life that is dreary and mind-numbingly dull enough to take you up on your challenge and if they do you can always claim it was the type of glass it was served in that polluted the taste.

Like any other of our modern-day, multiple-choice affectations then, the water you choose to quaff and the way you choose to quaff it will speak volumes, if not gallons . . .

Tap Water

If you live in the city and drink water straight from the tap without running it for half an hour beforehand you're clearly the sort of person who adds a sugar cube to champagne ('To get rid of some of the bubbles and help it go down') or ketchup to a dish of curry; that is, you're someone with no sense of either taste or decorum or you have a depressive personality and a nice taste in chemical additives.

You're unpretentious, unaffected and a bit of a salt-of-the-earth type who drinks like kids do: because they're thirsty rather than to impress. This 'down the hatch' behaviour could also indicate that you're not the world's healthiest eater as basic thirst like yours tends to stem from consumption of copious amounts of salt.

If you order tap water in a restaurant you're either a very thrifty snob or something of a champagne socialist, that is someone who will pay £19 for a fishcake but who takes a stand akin to the people's popular front when it comes to being charged for what God/nature supplied for free. And there's the added bonus of showing that uppity waiter you're nobody's fool at the same time. The louder you ask for tap water at a restaurant table the more stubborn, opinionated and sanctimonious you're likely to be. Yes, it's more environmentally friendly. But you probably drive a car. It proves, not so much that you're green, but that you're frankly a bit of a show off.

Carbonated Water

You're a bit of a kid at heart but not so much of a kid that you'll refer to a drink as 'fizzy', preferring instead euphemisms like 'carbonated' or even 'sparkling'. In fact, it's the fizz you like as it means that the non-existent olfactory experience of water is made up for by the tactile one, buzzing around in your mouth and throat and causing suppressed burps for the rest of the meal.

You're someone who likes to pretend their body is a temple but who falls from grace regularly because fun overrules denial every time in your book. You're sometimes silly, often fun or funny and borderline unreliable, although in a charming way. You like to take risks that are often uncalculated and struggle with planning, theorising and discussing. If you don't get on with the things in your life straight away your short attention span means you'll get bored and move on quickly.

Still Water

You're quietly elitist although with a complete horror of being seen as flashy. You like to do things the right way for the right reasons and if that means some form of denial or even suffering then so be it because you live by the mantra 'no pain, no gain'. This means you'll put up with things in your life that you dislike just to allow yourself to enjoy the things you do like without feeling guilty about them. So it could be your job is less than wonderful but you know it means your holidays and days off will be three times as pleasurable when they do arrive. You're a sensible person deep down and more reliable than you like to let on.

Designer Water

Oh, how finely tuned your palate, how wide your wallet that you have to insist on a certain brand of water when you know they all taste roughly the same? You are the original princess (or prince) and the pea.

You're into success and flaunting that success, but more via displeasure than through having fun. For you money means grumbling: you insist on the best and become bitchy when the best doesn't measure up to your standard. For you fussiness is an art form rather than an affectation and you believe your ability to recognise what you see as 'quality' makes you very, very special. You probably take the same pose with booze ('I can only drink a Mouton '97') and even loo paper ('No quilting please, it gives me piles').

So you prepare to hit the streets with your cardboard cup of self-endorsing cappuccino in one hand and the 'my body is a temple' bottle of designer spring water stuffed in one pocket of your DKNY jeans. Already you're defining yourself as an über-cool urbanite with an income that far outstrips your intellect. But what's next in line for image enhancement? Well, if you're a woman it's your handbag and if you're a chap then it's your man-bag. But these aren't just indicators of how fashion forward (or not) you are, they are yet another pointer to your psychological leanings . . .

WHAT YOUR HANDBAG SAYS ABOUT YOU

The relationship between a woman and her handbag has an unmistakable aura of secrecy and mysticism about it. And though a woman might appear casual about what is ostensibly a carrier for tissues, comb and cash, attempt to touch it, or – God forbid – peer into it and watch her go! If any woman allows her man access, even temporary access, to her handbag he may assume that this is no female he's dating but some sort of well-disguised lady boy. A woman's handbag is so sacrosanct that even closest female friends aren't allowed to peek within, not that they ever would, as women respect the sanctity of the handbag. The contents (on average worth a staggering £577 according to a recent study) are as private as the external signals emitted by the size, cost and style of it are public. Women own an average of 111 bags in a lifetime and this object is both a temple of secrecy and a symbol of status, taste, social bonding and success, according to its design, cost and designer label.

The fashion for bags is equally remarkable. Women will happily spend mini-fortunes on a bag they secretly find disgusting, just because the statement it makes is right for them. There is very little in the way of genuine bonding with a bag design, it is nearly all to do with the signal you want to send out, like battle dress during warfare. Your bag shows which battalion you fight for, your rank and your levels of courage and commitment. And women work hard for their bags – to say their thinking behind which bag to buy is superficial is like saying to a football fan 'it's only a game'.

Birkin Bag Woman

If you're Birkin Bag Woman you can be as cute as a Popsicle one minute and a living nightmare of assertive, high-status principles the next. You're a 'history woman', with a lean towards the continuity of fate and fashion. This bag has some practical attributes that reflect a Mary Poppins 'no-nonsense' approach to life although the fact it has to be uneasily hand- or arm-held means that, for you, style will win out over practicality when push comes to shove.

Courier Bag Girl

You're fully in touch with your masculine side, so much so that you will happily suffer a bag that has been designed with the male body in mind just to underline your equality to men. You're setting out your personality stall as someone refreshingly honest and carefree, but because the courier bag requires broad shoulders (which means you're constantly adjusting or grabbing your shoulder strap so that it doesn't slide off, creating a hula-hoop effect) and you delve inside infrequently (the long flap opens up into your face, making you root through your bag like a blind squirrel), you're clearly a girl who will be in frequent bad moods as you search in vain for your train ticket and lipgloss.

If you're dating a Courier Bag Girl, she'll happily go halves on dinner with you, but only if you hang around long enough for her to find her credit card.

Clutch Bag Woman

Über-girlie but misleadingly so, Clutch Bag Woman emits an aura of old-fashioned charm and good manners. This bag is high maintenance, requiring the attention of one hand all the time, but petite enough to suggest delicate contents like a lace hankie and a rouge brush. Clutch Bag Woman can be a bit of a control-freak though. Your bag can be a mini-Tardis, containing a toothbrush, condoms and a change of underwear and can be inserted under armpit, between teeth when necessary or even brandished as a weapon during moments of conflict. It also frequently serves as a receptacle of vomit during taxi rides home after hen nights. One thing about Clutch Bag Woman is that you know how to party.

Designer Sack Woman

The trend for huge handbags was started when celebs were seen lugging bags that could carry approximately ten times their own body weight. These huge bags were ugly enough and outrageous enough to be an instant hit. Designer Sack Woman might look prepared for every emergency but you're as impractical as a giddy stoat – that shoulder-to-floor bag you're lugging around probably contains nothing more useful than a dead chihuahua and a can of spray paint. This bag is primarily for camouflage because you can hide behind it in emergencies, conceal half your body bulk if you're pre-liposuction, and/or it can be an emotional prop because the huge size of it makes you feel smaller, almost as if you're a child playing at being grown-up, and means, in adult emotional terms, you're not the full shilling.

When it comes to new relationships, one good thing about this bag is that it's an excellent litmus test for your guy's patience. See his smirk when you turn up lugging it (he'll think it's an overnight bag full of sex toys) but then watch his response as you spend three hours rooting in it for one small lipgloss. If he hasn't eaten his own arm with frustration, marry him.

Organiser Bag Woman

The one thing you can assume about Organiser Bag Woman is that she's *not* well organised. Your desire to create order out of the chaos that is your life is genuine but buying a bag that contains more pockets and folders than a shoplifter's coat means you'll be constantly rooting within it and panicking as precious items like passports, loyalty cards and the only draft of your novel/ten-year business plan hunker down into the depths of the lining. You're a borderline hysteric who suffers near-fatal bouts of stress, especially in supermarket queues.

Across-the-body Satchel Girl

The hands-free effect of this bag *should* imply a girl who's a free spirit, unfettered by girlish fashion and as tactile as an orphaned koala. In actuality, Satchel Girl's hugely practical approach to life is that of a head girl or hockey captain. You'll wear berets and mittens which you think is an ironic statement but in fact you are locked in your own little Enid Blyton world – and that is part of your charm.

Cloth Bag Woman

It has to be said that some women are not of the bag sisterhood and will happily carry bags made of cloth, hessian or straw, often with embroidered detail and/or sequins. Cloth Bag Woman will appear charming and whimsical with a streak of eccentricity that men often find refreshing and adorable. In reality you often come with immense emotional baggage, like brutal ex-husbands or protracted divorces followed by unsuitable liaisons with Spanish waiters or Masai tribesmen. You are a difficult woman who can be generous, loving and loyal but will tend to break down in tears after one and a half cocktails, and it's a pretty safe bet to say you'll have the film *Mamma Mia* playing on a loop in your DVD player.

No-bag Bag Lady

In fact, this woman has more in common with a bag lady than you might think at first. A woman with no bag is like a woman with no home, meaning she's forced to use her clothing to carry all her necessities around in much the same way a homeless person trails everything about in a battered supermarket trolley.

No designer of class or note makes clothing for women that has useable pockets, meaning you'll stuff business cards and money in your bra, hankies up your sleeves and even bus tickets in your shoes. Grim, unhygienic and clearly lacking in any sense of social perspective or decorum, if you're a No-bag Bag Lady you'll probably stuff your things in your friends' bags.

Man-bag mania

It's not just the girls. Eight out of ten men now carry a 'man-bag' according to research from More Than.

Man-bags

Like women wear thongs to please themselves so no man has ever bought a man-bag because it singles him out as a stud-muffin to the laydees. Man-bags actually make gallons of sense on a practical level. They should mean that a guy doesn't just stuff everything in his trouser pockets as usual. Though actually, most still do. However, in body-language terms these bags are a bit of a liability.

Courier Bag Man displays the nearest thing to cool and straightforward sexuality in bag terms, although a man-bag on a date would still be viewed with some suspicion. Blokes are still bag novices, insofar that they tend to leave them well out of view in pubs and cafés – a field day for bag snatchers – and they still struggle during the rooting process, often smacking themselves in the face with the flap while searching for pens or chapstick. Get too adept though and they'll receive an old-fashioned look from most women so it's a no-win situation in the bags-for-blokes department.

Rucksack Man manages to blend the traits of a hill-walker, schoolboy and corporate man in a way that is borderline sinister and fetishist. What is the essence that he has tried to pluck out of these three very contrasting options? In reality he is probably just a natural-born herder, sticking with his school-bag because all the other big boys at his City company seem to have done the same, despite the fact that they're knocking into other commuters like bull-elephants with cataracts and impressing no one at client meetings as they pull their laptop out of what looks like an over-grown plimsoll bag.

Briefcase Man is creating a statement of corporate blandness although, like the handshake ritual, there are many visual or aesthetic subtleties that denote status and corporate attitude. The elderly leather briefcase is the weapon of choice for the high-status work snob, but the plastic version implies chaotic working, especially if it is carried hanging half-open. The zip-top A4 folder design that tucks under the arm should set off warning bells to anyone who prefers to stay awake during conversations as it's only ever toted by the terminally dull and ferocious, picky and meticulous.

If women buy bags to lift their mood and enhance their self-perception by using them to display their status and standing, then both men and women use hairstyles to announce to the rest of the world how they want to be treated, perceived and accepted. One shocking fact about hairstyles is that we tend to make much less change to it than we think. Most of us sport the same cut, colour and hair parting that we wore in infant school. Don't believe us? Take a look at an old school photo. No matter how hard you try, that basic style is one you'll keep gravitating back to throughout your life. (Unless, of course, nature steps in and makes it all fall out.)

WHAT YOUR HAIR COLOUR SAYS ABOUT YOU

Your hair colour and style is inextricably linked to your personality, so much so that it will often be the way someone – even someone close – will choose to describe you to others. For guys it's an instant evaluation of attractiveness and they will describe a new date to their mates as 'blonde' or 'brunette', a valuable form of cliché. To pander to this stereotype, girls will often dye their hair to exaggerate their identity through their locks. Men, though, tend to be au naturel, making this form of sexual identification less useful: 'He's got brownish hair' is barely worth saying. Why is women's hair colour so crucial? Because with the colour comes the character. Blondes, as we know, are supposed to 'have more fun'. Brunettes are more intelligent, while redheads will be fiery and troublesome. But is there any truth in these claims?

The Blonde

Socialite Paris Hilton once said: 'I think every decade has an iconic blonde, like Marilyn Monroe or Princess Diana and right now I'm that icon.' Blonde hair is often the colour of childhood hair and so adult blonde women can create the expectation of childish attributes like innocence, fun-loving and dumbness. Although the bleached blondes of the fifties like Marilyn Monroe and Jayne Mansfield negate the innocent air with unnatural tones and textures,

27

a natural-looking blonde will retain an air of childishness and adolescence. Blonde hair stands out as well, so a blonde will naturally be the first girl in a group that a guy tends to notice. Blonde hair at work can still retain an air of 'dumb blonde' stereotyping about it but as long as you can pack a good left hook you shouldn't have too many problems quashing that little myth.

The Brunette

Dark or black hair has a more adult look and dark hair in a male was once a sign of physical dominance. Brunettes are seen as more intelligent and assertive than blondes. Dark hair lacks the floating halo effect around the head and makes eye contact rather more likely.

In modern society there's considerable pressure on women to lighten their hair via highlights or bleach to be fashionable and stand out from the crowd. Therefore, the girl who stays resolutely brunette has a mind of her own and a high level of healthy self-esteem. You're not into compromise and you dislike being seen as a 'pleaser'. As a brunette, there's less likelihood you'll use baby talk to manipulate or get your own way than you would if you were blonde. You're probably quite grounded and focused.

Brunettes will also have grown up with hair colour stereotypes that are very persuasive. Blonde heroines tend to be ditsy, flirty and dumb while Brunettes are often sensual, serious and often more dangerous.

The Redhead

Red hair in a woman is connected to the image of fire, which in turn is connected to vitality and life. It's a colour that will naturally be seen running strongly through families and often undiluted, so it implies physical or 'gene' strength. Often it's the colour that many people see as being a breed apart. Whereas red-headed men suffer unspeakable amounts of loutish prejudice throughout their lives, red-haired women will often gain respect for what is perceived as their 'fiery' personality. Red hair in a woman often means long hair too, which is linked with sexuality in most men's minds. In stereotypical terms it's often portrayed as the colour of trouble.

The Ginger

Remember that song 'A Boy Named Sue' where Johnny Cash sang about being a boy given a name that turned him into a fighter at school and ensured that he toughened up to survive the ridicule? Well, ginger hair can be seen as nature's version of this idea. Gingers can expect a lifetime of prejudice about their colouring, turning them into either warriors or victims. How tragic that one of the most magnificent hair colours in the spectrum can be so unfairly treated and how sad to know that most people you meet will be instantly speculating on the colour of your pubic hair.

The Mouse

Although brown hair is natural, soft and flattering it's rarely, if ever, used to describe or define an attractive women ('She had lovely mousy hair' or 'Her mousy locks tumbled over her shoulders') so saying someone is mouse is the Bermuda Triangle of compliments. Which begs the question: 'Why?'

Why keep mousy when there's a whole raft of products on the market to enhance, lift and dramatise your hair colour? Why be mouse when you can be chestnut, bronze or flame? Either Mouse Woman has an innate desire to remain invisible, blending into the background while her blonde, redhead or brunette sisters take centre stage which prompts the question: 'Why is she trying to hide?' 'Does she have problems with guilt?' Is this mouse just a guise to mask terrifying levels of anger, hatred and murderous intent?

Or is Mouse Woman the ultimate in confident alpha qualities, so comfortable with her own natural beauty that she refuses to allow her hair colour to distract from or upstage her face? Does she know something we don't? Or is she that woman that all other women dread, the one who insists on staying 'natural'? The one who won't pluck her eyebrows or shave her legs and the one who prefers clear nail varnish and untinted lip salve to coloured lipgloss? For 'natural' read 'scary'.

Everyone prefers brunettes

A new study by Garnier found that blondes may not necessarily have more fun. Their survey showed that dark-haired women earn more than their blonde counterparts and that 71% of men would pick a dark-haired woman as an ideal partner.

WHAT YOUR HAIRSTYLE SAYS ABOUT YOU: WOMEN

Long Hair

Long hair is traditionally equated with virginity and even in modern life the pressure will be on for a woman beyond child-bearing years or even younger to have her long hair cut short. It is still seen as advertising availability, while short, neat hair suggests you're 'taken'.

Bobbed Hair

The bob is one of the most enduring classics, combining the 'adult' look of neatness and shorter length with the fringe and straightness of childhood. A woman with bobbed hair looks like someone who knows her own mind and will speak it quite happily, although the childlike aspect of this cut means your air of professionalism could be tainted by occasional bouts of tantrums, irrationality or tears.

Fringe/Bangs

A woman who sports a fringe is a woman who prefers to see life through a curtain. The fringe is a place of refuge for the shy or the sulky, a permanent 'cut-off' gesture that offers retreat and a hiding place, suggesting you are never quite as confident as you seem. Your fringe could give the appearance that you don't embrace the world, but rather that you peer at it from behind your safety-curtain and when you feel you can't cope your head will dip and you'll shut up shop.

There are also some women who suddenly adopt a full fringe in their thirties, a sure sign they're feeling their age and trying to look younger by covering forehead wrinkles and adding a more 'teen' look to their image.

Curls v Straight

In an age of hair-straighteners the curl is a near-extinct phenomenon but – as ironed hair shows a desire to be in control of life, love and everything else – curls register a sense of spontaneity and lack of control. The curl shows a woman who embraces all things natural and who is a genuine optimist who allows life to blow her along rather than fighting to steer or control. The more hair gets straightened the more of a control freak you look. Hair that has been battered into submission by straightening and flattening suggests a highly dominant character who will go to similar lengths to squash men.

Matching Your Haircut to Your Kids'

This might sound like an exclusive little category and in many ways any warning we offer might be too late as you're more likely to have found this happening subconsciously after you gave birth. Forget cute and winsome, this look merely tells those that meet you to run while it's not too late. There's no good in this trait, only bad. Get to the hairdresser ASAP.

WHAT YOUR HAIRSTYLE SAYS ABOUT YOU: MEN

Long gone are the days of a simple 'short back and sides'. Men's haircuts are now something of an art form involving more products than you can happily get into one environmentally friendly carrier bag. This craze for products may have changed the life of the average male in ways that he would never have thought possible. Once able to travel light and free like any good hunter, with only a small plastic comb in his pocket to ensure his sex appeal was in place, he now needs to spend his life within dash-distance of an entire chemist's shop of wax, gel and even spray.

Spiky Hair

When hair is gelled or moussed to stand upright it could be accused of mimicking one of three animal states: fear/surprise /shock, aggressive arousal or sexual arousal.

Anyone beyond the age of thirty who spikes their hair needs to know that they will probably fall into the first category. Although gelling your hair into middle age is a sign you wish to keep up there in the groove with the young 'uns the truth is the slightly careworn look of an older face means you'll more than likely look more like Ebenezer Scrooge when he first claps eyes on Marley's ghost.

Spiked hair in the workplace will tend to suggest aggressive arousal. This is the human equivalent of an animal puffing out its fur or feathers to look well hard in a fight. In many ways it's like armour for the head, meaning you see the challenge of work like some kind of battleground.

For all other occasions though it would be impossible to analyse the spiked hair without using the word 'erect'. Your head-erection is clearly intended to signal some kind of ever-ready virility. Another reason why the older guy sporting it will usually achieve sceptical looks from the girls.

The Hoxton Fin

This choppy cut, named after a trendy area of London, defies gravity as the hair stands upwards and into a tumbly-looking fin. There is nothing tactile about this hair and it is as rigid as hell. If you are Fin-man you will clearly enjoy having fully erect, stiff hair and those around you won't need to be a fan of Freud to get what this means. This look suggests you're ready for sex any time, any place: you are advertising the fact that you're a red-blooded male with a high sex drive. Although this is normal in your teens/early twenties, if you're an older guy trying to emulate this look by moving what remains of your hair into small stacks you will only ever look sad. Fin hair has to be thick. Anything else is a sham.

The 'I Ran Into a Wall' Hair

This 'Tin-Tin' style involves hair being combed forward and then up at the front. It's a cousin of the fin in sexual terms but this last minute rising up will set you out as a guy who will take what sex is on offer but only as an afterthought.

Long Hair

If it's long-ish, wavy and unstructured you are likely to appear uninhibited and come across as a bit of an animal in bed, despite being rather shy and quiet in social situations. The classic, historical look of this trend will imply you're there for the long-term though, or at least until the next morning (by which time fin man or wall man will have had to make their excuses and leave because their hair doesn't work in the cold light of day).

Ponytail

If you sport one of these you will signal you're well into your male andropause and fighting the onset of age every inch of the way, suggesting you're vain, tricky and paranoid with bouts of wild behaviour that involve lusting after Harley-Davidsons or pole-dancers. If you're younger you surely work in something like IT – but like to see yourself as an intellectual maverick. You'll look as though you hate your job and everyone you work with because you see yourself as deserving something grander than a guy who works in a service job.

Square Top

This is hair that implies you walked under a strimmer as the neighbour was cutting their hedge. The box shape implies a desire for power and leadership. By creating the impression of an android it also helps you to shuck off more natural emotions like empathy and become a tough-talking control-freak.

The Comb Forward

This quasi-mod, sixties look is back in fashion again, with hair all combed forward to provide a pretty long fringe around the entire face. This is a cute look, implying you're fully in touch with your feminine side but that you might easily go like a stoat in bed. The foppish look is often a sham, concealing a much stronger character than the look implies, allowing you to mingle in with the ladies while quietly picking them off one at a time.

The Comb Over Guy

This look suggests you're not only trying to hang onto your youth, you're also trying desperately to cling on to your sex life. For you, those few sorry strands that cross the top of your head show you're still in the arena, and still a contender in the bedroom department. They're symbolic and therefore you'd die to keep them to avoid falling into the world of the slaphead. You might look sad but you're a determined fighter and colleagues will know to cross you at their peril.

The Shaved Head

This look largely took over from the comb-over and thank God for that, as it meant slap-heads everywhere could crawl out of the closet during force 10 gales and wear their male pattern baldness with pride. It's the cut that returns control back to its wearer: why wait for nature to shed your hair like leaves in autumn when you can step up to the plate and shave it all off yourself? And of course there's always an air of mystery about the shaved head: did he fall or was he pushed? Did he shave off a head of thick flowing locks for the sake of fashion or did it bid adieu of its own accord? Only the dark re-growth shadow will provide clues as to the answer.

Once assessments have been made via your hair, bag and hot drink there comes the truly telling moment when every eye will slip down to that most basic of image-info providers – your feet. Footwear has long been considered the ultimate guide to personality, defining taste, class, employability and, of course, sexual tendencies . . .

WHAT YOUR FOOTWEAR
SAYS ABOUT YOU: WOMEN

What's so special about a pair of shoes you ask? If you do ask, it means that you are probably a man, because every woman is born understanding the mystical value of footwear just as much as blokes are born knowing exactly how to get more life out of the remote control long after the batteries have died. Women spend around five times more on shoes than guys. Yet for both sexes your feet are the powerhouse of your confidence and self-esteem. The way you stand has a lot to do with your ego and the way your feet make contact with the earth via your selection of footwear is a crucial factor in creating the legend that is 'You'. Little wonder that employers judge as much from the footwear of candidates as they do from the CV, or that much of our dating/mating selections will stand or fall from what your potential partner has encased his or her feet in.

The Soft, Suede, Sheepskin-lined Slipper Boot

Many years ago the wearing of slippers in the street was a sure-fire signal of the onset of senility but now, thanks to this nouveau-classic footwear (thank you, designers, thank you!) women the world over can make the transition from bedroom to boardroom without any risk of trauma to the tootsies with the wearing of the snuggle-fest for feet that is the suede slipperboot. Every season men hope and pray that the fashion for this classic will go away but each season it's back with a vengeance, so much so that, in an 'if you can't beat 'em join 'em' capitulation many men have even started wearing them.

Every woman can remember where she was when she saw her first pair of slipper-boots and for many it was Pamela Anderson wearing them with a skimpy bikini on a

Baywatch beach. If you're Slipper Boot Woman you are defiant about your desire for comfort, however you're still massively aspirational in terms of sex. By wearing a boot that is a turn-off for most men and a total antithesis to the brittle foot cramping that is the killer heel, you're asserting your right to have sex on your terms. Those heels are still in your wardrobe but you'll wear them as a treat, not a wholesale token of general man-pleasing. Slipper Boot Woman is a pack-mentality kind of girl, as this is the boot you either 'get' or you don't and all women who do will achieve a sense of bonding that transcends age or class. Slipper Boot Woman is also sassy as an unexpected by-product of the design is that – apart from the hugely elephantine – the width of the boot makes legs and even thighs look slimmer by comparison. You're also confident about change as these boots require a whole shift in deportment style to enable the wearer to become mobile.

Shoe's who

A thousand women were questioned for a survey by *Harper's Bazaar* magazine about their shoe habits and half admitted to owning in excess of 30 pairs. Eight per cent confessed to harbouring at least 100 pairs.

The Killer Heels

Pointy-toe stilettos – what Germaine Greer dubbed 'fuck me shoes' – have been a sexual cliché since the 1950s. The woman who wears them knows the four key signals these shoes send out:

1. By making her taller they increase her chances of attracting attention.
2. The angle of the heel makes the legs take on a rigidity, making them appear more toned.

3. Wearing them requires the pelvis to be pushed forward and gives a more sensual bum-movement when walking.
4. Walking is slower, meaning escape from a guy is difficult!

If you're Stiletto Woman you're a man-pleaser but in a pseudo-aggressive way, rather than being a push-over. Patent exaggerates all these sexual signals as it mimics the idea of wearing mirrors on your feet. Red patent is the ultimate sado-masochistic turn-on, which is probably why it gets used so often on book covers and in TV ads.

Heels with Platforms

These Jessica Rabbit-style shoes are a recent arrival on the scene but already a classic and a firm favourite of celebrities. The 8-inch heel plus platform combo defines the same attention-seeking tactics as the killer heel but the signals here are less about man-pleasing and more about status. These are Queen-bee shoes with a vengeance. Heels with Platforms Woman towers above her man and then, by wearing shoes that are as effectively disabling as having your feet bound, you ensure his buzzing assistance to teeter from house to car. These shoes say that you're a control-freak who doesn't do walking, thereby implying huge wealth that necessitates chauffeurs, plus you're happy to cripple yourself to bind your man to your side, forcing him to dance attendance on you like hired help.

Sensible Shoes

Every girl owns a pair of sensible shoes, just like every girl owns at least one pair of big pants. They are for those 'screen-saver' moments (those times when you tune out of your public performance mode and tune in to just being 'you'). If you're Sensible Shoe Woman you're announcing you're either off the radar as far as mating is concerned, or that you have caught a new man/house-husband, who has long since stopped noticing what you've got on your body. Sensible shoes mean longer paces and splaying behaviour (legs wider apart when standing), which are both signals of status and power. However, every woman knows in her soul that this logical-thinking method of power-broking is risky. In a boardroom battle the flatties lose out to the ruthlessness and determination of the super-aggro killer heels every time, as Stiletto Woman is announcing through her shoes that she's prepared to put up with pain to get to the top.

Strappies

Strappy sandals imply a softer sensuality with their semi-naked look that means the feet are open to more tactile elements like sun and fresh air. The blatant baring of the toes implies body-confidence and a pre-prepped approach to sex, especially if the toenails are well manicured. If you're Strappy Woman you are not assertive by nature, preferring to project a sense of easy-going charm. You're likely to be girlish and compliant and your core goal in life is to get married. Hence a tendency towards eternal hen-night social behaviours, where your tendency to herd with like-minded females on nights out can lead to binge-drinking habits that lead to staggering home barefoot, while the sassier Heels with Platforms Woman is being lifted into a 4x4 by her attendant and obedient male.

Ballet Pumps

How cute are these? Well, a whole load more cute than the girl that wears them usually, because the ballet pump often appears to be the shoe of choice for drunks, lushes, rowdies, yahoos and other non-clean-living female hell-raisers. The point with these shoes is that they are impractical, meaning you have a complete disregard of danger or discomfort. Or to put it another way, you're one hell of a tough cookie who is resilient enough to face dirt, cold and nails, stones or broken glass clad only in the very lightest of flat sliperettes.

WHAT YOUR FOOTWEAR SAYS ABOUT YOU: MEN

While men might not be quite as obsessed by their choice of footwear as girls, don't underestimate their power, even those guys who pretend to have loftier things on their mind than what's happening at the other end of their body. After all, documents show that evolution genius Charles Darwin spent more money on designer shoes while at college in Cambridge than on books.

Trainers

Trainer Man is in a state of eternal childhood because, no matter how many designer labels you hang on them, a plimsoll is still a plimsoll at the end of the day. Your rubbery footwear gives a rewarding and childlike bounce to your walk. You are primarily into conformity, meaning you'll go to great lengths to gain acceptance of whichever social pack you opt for. You're also a bit of a chameleon though, as you know these shoes will render you acceptable to other groups outside your own. The solid 2–3 inches of layered rubber that cushion Trainer Man from the ground suggest you have a rather practical or 'naughty' view of sex and that you're not keen to advertise more advanced skills of sensuality. There's a current 'everyman' aspect to the trainer. Having once been the 'youth shoe' its buyers have aged but refused to give it up, meaning currently guys up to ninety are clad in the things.

So it signals no huge desire to emphasise your youth and therefore your virility. There's a safety thing about Trainer Man (after all, you know you'll never be killed by electric shock) that can imply loyalty in a relationship, although this shouldn't be seen as a given. Like your trainers you might end up sticking with your woman for ever, but possibly only because you can't be bothered to go out looking for anyone else.

Brogues

If you're a Brogues Man you're either resolutely posh-aspirational or you're retro man, with a desire to appear eccentric and 'different'. Wearing such a classic design means that you stand out from the crowd and shows a strong sense of irony blended with some shots of vanity. If you're not just wearing them because your dad did then you're fussy, strategic and probably intellectual. You're a difficult date because your taste in women is as specific as your taste in shoes. You have a very inflated sense of your own purpose on this planet and may come across as arrogant and ruthless, albeit charming and possibly fascinating.

Converse

Sometimes smelly, goofy and often so determinedly flat and pancake-like that they are probably way more uncomfortable than the wearer would admit, Converse footwear are all about style over substance. Their history is so long that Moses probably owned a pair, but their key appeal is the kind of retro-American thing that places a guy in a style that makes him look like a walk-on from *Happy Days*. If you're Converse Guy then you're likely to be cheery, chippy and sexual in a casual 'I-might-not-be-very-good-at-it-but-we'll-have-a-laugh' way. You work in the media or want to look as though you do. You're happy to advertise your youth and your streak of innocence, and in many ways these are your Unique Selling Points. You like girls that will be your best friend prior to taking things onto a more sexual footing and you're happy (and more comfortable) allowing the girl to do most of the seducing.

Loafers

The word says it all, really. You're clearly too rich and/or lazy to bother with laces and happier padding around the workplace in something that is the second cousin once removed to the moccasin. You're laid-back and probably portly but you love to look successful in a golfing-at-weekends kind of way. Loafers are the shoe of choice of financial types who want to signal they own the firm rather than work for it. Your appeal is primarily Alpha in its purest simian form: you like space and sitting still, fart a lot and let others do your running around and fighting for you.

Builder's Boot

Fashionable they may be but the sand-coloured lace-up builder's boot will always have echoes of resolutely macho pursuits like lumberjacking, log-rolling, scaffold-construction and double-glazing, which is why the guy wearing them could either be more butch than Bluto or as camp as Christmas. These boots, which exaggerate the size of the foot and the sturdiness of the sole, negate any feeling of being at one or in touch with the ground beneath your feet. They lengthen the stride and make the wearer feel physically important and invincible. If you're Builder's Boot Man then you like to be grown-up, even if it is in a cartoon kind of way. You like to be taken seriously as a force to be reckoned with even though your weapon of choice for attack might be sarcasm or other forms of character assassination. There's an intrinsic insensitivity about you as these juggernauts of the shoe world can crush without even alerting the wearer.

Health Sandals

These sandals take the Jesus look to a new level of holiness, with footwear that looks hewn out of logs carrying the extra implication that you're into the new religious pursuits of recycling and environmental salvation. If you're Health Sandal Wearer you're stubbornly self-righteous, especially if you live in the city and wear them in the street. They come with other 'outdoor' garb like rucksacks and all-weather anoraks, all of which you'll insist are trendy making you look like Barbara Woodhouse. You have active values and campaigns, plus you use a 'friendly fire' volley of tutting if anyone uses their car for journeys of less than twelve miles. In sexual terms these shoe wearers are a void. You only mate with one another and when you do your offspring emerge pre-clad in baby sandals.

Cowboy Boots

These make the ultimate statement about their wearer because, of all the shoes, they are most like fancy dress that you've opted to wear for day-to-day life. Cowboys are long-lasting and rarely a one-off, there's likely to be more than one pair in your cupboard. They warn everyone that there is more to you than meets the eye. Forget the Next suit or fleecy gilet, you're clearly a dreamer and a fantasist, someone who grew up watching *Magnum* and listening to Status Quo and who lives in a permanent state of mid-life crisis. Being Cowboy Man means you are sexy, funny and a bit of a loner. Although you pride yourself on your ability to be cool you're also opinionated and will happily get into stand-offs and conflict.

Brown Suede Shoes

There's something of the gentleman about the brown suede wearer although, as gentlemen are largely a long extinct breed, your desire to cling to the genre suggests you have a little of the roué about you, too. This comfy option describes a man keen to show rebellion against the glossy black leather that is City life, suggesting creativity and a touch of the artistic temperament. Made famous by Tory MP Ken Clarke, his brown brogues were enough to set corporate jowls aquiver and were the visual proof of a liking for beer, whisky and jazz. Laid-back by nature and with a desire to steer clear of rules, systems and red tape, if you're Brown Suede Man you'll nevertheless often find yourself washed up on the shores of the teaching profession, about as regulated and rule-based a culture as you can get.

WHAT YOUR SLIPPERS SAY ABOUT YOU: WOMEN

Does anything define the real you more than the footwear you snuggle into once the working day is done? Day shoes are performance shoes and a symbol of our 'ideal social self'. They are the face we present to the rest of the world, but slippers are a guilty secret, the alter-ego that places emotion and comfort above ego and fashion and just 'tells it as it is' in image terms.

Retro Wedge Mules with Pom-poms or Fur

These are the Dita Von Teese of the slipper world, meaning you're a closet glamour puss who places glitz above comfort or practicality. You see your home as one great big boudoir and fill it with tokens of girlie glory like Marilyn Monroe posters and faux leopard skin cushions. These show that you've still got it, no matter that the dressing gown is now tartan thermal and that the cat's eaten at least one of the pom-poms. These references to feminine ideals pre-second-wave feminism are signs you are fully in touch with your superficial side no matter how hard-nosed and practical your daily life or job. It's your inner diva that makes you different and no one could ever call you dreary.

Fluffy Animal Slippers

Inside this girl is a cute little child who desires approval and unconditional affection and any man spotting these on a girl's feet should understand he's in for a rough ride with his sweet little cuddle-bunny. If you're a Fluffy Animal Slippers Girl then kittens, teddies and other accoutrements signal the fact you have never totally grown up. Sexy, confident and intellectual you may be, but you are also flagging up that you reserve the right to be irresponsible, petulant and a bit of a spoilt brat too, should the occasion demand.

Socks with Soles

Socks should have done it – in fact, if you're Socks with Soles Girl you probably began by wearing your boyfriend's socks around the house as a cute homage until you trod on a nail around the same time you discovered he had Athlete's Foot. The sensible option was these pretend socks with a sole-grip that means you can walk up walls like The Fly. But Socks with Soles Girl hates being seen as sensible so you bought a pair in a crazy design. You're a rebel without a cause, a woman who has fought against the dull safeness of the slipper but succumbed to something even more middle of the road. You pride yourself on your ability to challenge and be wise, although – in your bid to be reasonable – you can sadly come across as a ditherer.

Tartan Slippers

Why tartan? Who knows, but the traditional granny slipper has been tartan since before the Crimea and there's something endearingly unpretentious about someone who'll stick to your style guns for what must have been more than a handful of decades. People used to mock grans who refused to budge from this classic (Tartan with red pom-poms in summer and tartan zip-up bootees for winter) but now they've become admirable in their ability to make decisions and stick to them. No designer would dare take an ironic poke at this footwear because women who wear them can only be described as formidable.

WHAT YOUR SLIPPERS SAY ABOUT YOU: MEN

Sheepskin Slippers

These slippers reveal Sheepskin Slippers Man to have a dual personality: on the one side there is 'Comfort Man', a childlike lover of security and reassurance who loves the inner feel of snuggle on his feet. Then there is 'Roadkill Man', the guy who feels he has to pay for this comfort by an outer pretence of hunting and stalking his prey to obtain this inner sense of security, hence the outer display of animal hide and what is often a caveman-like sense of design and stitching. For you life is one huge quandary about 'New Man' versus 'Alpha Male'. You understand that you should be able to shop in Waitrose and leave the toilet seat down but there are times when you yearn for a Bullworker in the basement and ultimate power over the remote control. You're soft-hearted and funny but with a bit of a hard edge that normally only emerges over blatant acts of unfairness to others or when you're asked to explain why you read both the *Guardian* and *Nuts* magazine.

Moccasins

Moccasin Man is probably over forty and ashamed of the whole concept of slipper-wearing, so these quasi-shoes that trot happily from hearth to shed or front gate (and possibly even down to the newsagent's on a Sunday) are practical and also strangely pleasing. You groaned when you were given them as a present but the sight of them at the end of your legs provided a secret pleasure because they have subliminal connections with all those Apaches in the cowboy movies of your youth. To other people you look like an old git but in your mind you are Leaping Bull.

Big Foot Slippers

Most men get at least one pair of these huge, humorous slippers in their lives, usually as a gift at Christmas, and once they've waddled around the floor growling to scare the kids and woken all the elderly relatives up to make them laugh, the comedy element tends to run out about the same time as the health and safety aspect kicks in. Three accidents later, after you've slid down the stairs on your bum or pirouetted over next door's cat and most men have taken them off and hidden them in the recycling bin. The fact you're still wearing yours tells us only one thing: you value comic potential above your own life, and that in turn can mean that you have no real sense of humour. This is the man who wore comedy ties to work and even musical socks in a bid to raise a laugh. Well meaning but basically dull.

Novelty – Beer or Football Logo Slippers

These slippers are only ever trophy presents from relatives caught up in the panic of the Christmas shopping rush. By buying them they identify you as either an alcoholic or imply you're spending too much time on Sky Sports. Wearing them is a sign of an externally gregarious fun-loving male who masks his inner melancholy and bouts of depression. For you these slippers are a reminder that even the finest, bravest and most manly of life's rebellious, tribal pursuits can be demoted to a logo on a pair of big boy's indoor footwear. By wearing them you show loyalty for and love of your family who bought you these things, but by allowing yourself to be castrated in this way you may also be a seething cauldron of resentment and angst.

Of course, the examples in this chapter are just a small sample of the decisions about yourself and your image that you make every day. The list is endless. But with these decisions we tend to know we're making a choice. In fact, we'll often be aware of what another person might think because we'll be interacting with a hairdresser or shop keeper when we make the choice. We hear ourselves make the choice. But there are many decisions we make that are more instinctive – based on our behaviours. Here we often allow ourselves more free rein as, in a sense, we're not so aware of how they impinge on others, and how they might view them.

In the next chapter we'll uncover how these less 'advertised' choices reveal even more about us . . .

3

HIDDEN MESSAGES IN YOUR BEHAVIOURS AND CHOICES

Of course, not all of your communicated impact or image is created or defined by your consumer choices, like the coffee you drink or the pom-poms on your slippers. Some verbal or body language habits are more deeply entrenched and all the more telling because of that.

Although consumer choice can be based on a confusing underlying miasma of impulses and urges, many of those choices will tend to be quite recent, and therefore consciously based selections. When you grazed around the slipper department you were likely to be aware that your decision-taking processes were in place even though you might not have had a full grasp on their prompters. You chose, you bonded with and you bought those furry mules, but what about the behaviour 'choices' that were much more sinuous and subliminal?

Your body language is primarily a selection of learned behaviours, meaning that – apart from the odd physiological or spontaneous gesture or response – you copied, mirrored and aped the people around you, primarily your parents. Learned and absorbed actions are vital for our survival as, like any other animal, we pick up all we need to know about feeding, protecting and keeping ourselves safe and comfortable from them. But along with those survival skills, other less useful tendencies can slip quietly into our repertoire without us knowing.

These subliminal behaviours that become habits can remain invisible or hidden to us while annoying the hell out of other people. They're the body language or verbal oddities that can seem random, but which help to define us to others in a way that far outweighs their importance to us. We're talking about all those little gestures, fiddles, sounds and fillers that decorate our communications like chocolate sprinkles atop a mug of foamy coffee.

WHAT YOUR VERBAL FILLERS SAY ABOUT YOU

Verbal fillers or tics are the guilty pleasures of the communication world, all those useless, fatuous repetitive pieces of nonsense that we belch out the moment there is the slightest pause or hesitation in our stream of speech. Sometimes we start with them, often we end with them. Occasionally we use them instead of speech altogether, as in 'Right, okay, well, basically you know, I sort of actually, kind of – if you like . . . innit?'

These words come courtesy of your subconscious during micro-moments of panic and to fill gaps to show that you believe it's still your turn to talk, and it could be you sprinkle them throughout your conversations like confetti. Okay, so you mimic them from others but why did you choose the particular words you use so constantly? Think your choice was random? Think again . . .

'Right'

Often accompanied by a smacking and rubbing of hands, this is the ultimate clapper-board word, the one that announces you're about to start a new job or train of thought and it's performed as much for your own benefit as a signal to others that you're about to kick off. The question is, why the need to scoop up your thinking and self-motivate on such a regular basis? You're a positive person but the trouble is your thoughts tend to run out of control and you struggle keeping track at times. This leads to mild levels of stress and confusion leading to you becoming your own little police force, dragging the threads of your thinking together and galvanising your brain into action. Use this too much and you'll appear bumbling, chaotic and just a little bit of a control-freak. Those around you will soon answer your motivating 'right' with silence.

'. . . you know . . .'

These two words need to appear during, rather than at the start of a sentence, or in reply to a question, as in either:

'How did you feel when the rhino trampled you?'

'Well, you know . . .'

Or: 'I only had about three seconds to . . . you know . . . run away and I was . . . you know . . . very scared.'

Do we need to point out the obvious: you will only use these words when you patently don't know what you're talking about or what to say? The words 'you know' are the ultimate cry for help. When you use them you're asking 'Do *you* know? Can you help me out please?' and this plead for empathy suggests severe brain break-down, albeit temporary.

Watch a professional speaker like a politician during an interview and the moment he/she emerges with his/her first 'you know' you can tell they've lost the plot and are bluffing big time.

'Actually'

Why use a word to prove the truth of what you're saying unless you're lying in the first place? 'I was actually very upset' 'We could actually see that our plan was working' 'I was confused by that actually'. This is your personal attempt to underline what you are saying and it implies you're used to being doubted and feel you have to over-prove your point. 'Actually' is a weasel word, flung about with desperation in a flaccid attempt to provide validation that is clearly missing, actually.

'Literally'

Read all the above and add a drizzle of intellectual pretentiousness.

'Basically'

Only ever used by people who have relinquished all control over their ability to précis. 'Basically' signals a warning that the speaker is about to ramble on with a severe case of verbal diarrhoea. This is another self-policing word as you try to form structure and clarity to your points and therefore a clear sign that you have none. By using this word you also give false hope to your audience, demanding their attention by suggesting you will be good to listen to. The small break-down in trust once they realise you have more rabbit than Sainsbury's will become part of a general decline in your overall credibility.

'Innit?'

Why place the question mark at the end of this word when it is nothing other than a statement or rhetorical question at best? At least three centuries ago this was a cockney abbreviation of 'Isn't it?' and worthy of a reply, as in:

'It's raining out, innit?'

'Yes, I do believe you will need an umbrella if you are thinking of venturing outdoors.'

Now though it's become a meaningless full stop to any sentence, a kind of verbal bum-boil that makes all speech as unattractive as possible, as in: 'I'll call you tomorrow, innit?' Even the vaguest whiff of fashion has long since left this word, which means that by using it you show you're nothing short of a sad soul who believes wearing your hood up makes you look like a gangsta.

'Yamean'

This intense abbreviation of the words 'Do you know what I mean?' is like a verbal concertina that suggests a permanent state of acute cognitive confusion. By using this at the end of every statement you are elongating your speech to enquire after the understanding of your audience. By abbreviating to this one word you also imply that you are time-poor and need to get your messages across as quickly as possible, which begs the question: Why not use words that are easily understood in the first place, meaning you would have no need to enquire that everything you say is comprehended by your audience? This constant, unrelenting checking suggests weakness. You are part of a pack that will reject members at will, hence the need to keep confirming that everything you say is 'on message'. You are desperate to please and possibly a little paranoid to boot, yamean?

'Do you hear what I'm saying?'

See all of the above but add a massive pinch of egocentricity. You don't talk to other people, you preach. Most of what you say is incomprehensible gibberish but you demand an appreciative audience and by adding this phrase to the end of every statement you force listeners to nod sagely, as though pure verbal gold had just tumbled out of your mouth. You like to feel you are a guru in your own lifetime, although genuine gurus rarely use this verbal tic. Did Martin Luther King say 'I have a dream, DO YOU HEAR WHAT I'M SAYING?' No. He used eloquence and a microphone instead.

'Sort of /Kind of'

These words suggest you have a tippy-toes approach to life, qualifying everything in case someone accuses you of being bold. These phrases suggest life events are so baffling or astounding to you they make you run out of words. 'It was a sort of recession issue' or 'It was a kind of unhelpful thing to say' is like air-brushing your statements to avoid disagreement and portray you as a liberal thinker without opinions. You tend to dither big-time over most of your decisions, sticking a big toe into the pool of life rather than pulling on your cossie and diving in.

'If you like'

This oily, obsequious phrase is the Uriah Heep hand-wringer of the verbal filler world. 'It was an – if you like – unfortunate type of behaviour' or 'We have an – if you like – unhelpful situation here.' When you use this phrase you are like a creepy, deeply bowing, toupee-wearing waiter presenting a ghastly, over-inflated bill on a small silver platter. 'Do you like my choice of words? No? A little too radical or in your face? Please feel free to insert your own, we'd hate to cause offence.'

The problem with 'if you like' people is that their utter submissiveness masks an inner stubbornness and will of steel. Just as you know you're going to have to pay that dinner bill, so you know this 'if you like' user has no intention of changing their point of view. Passive-aggressive defines this person perfectly.

WHAT YOUR FIDGETING SAYS ABOUT YOU

The body is capable of a staggering 700,000 unique movements with 90% of the messages conveyed in a job interview, for instance, sent non verbally. This is in contrast to about 70,000 words typically used by someone with a very good vocabulary indeed. It stands to reason that fidgeting and fiddling are an important part of our secret, non-verbal language.

In psychological terms, fiddling tends to be classed as 'leakage' – it's your body leaking out all your genuine thoughts, feelings and emotions via small body language tics and rituals. While you can mask with your posture and facial expressions, the hands and feet tend to take on a life of their own, tapping, shuffling and otherwise self-heckling to let people know exactly what's going on in your mind.

Many of our fiddles come under the heading of self-comfort gestures: tiny rituals that remind us of being safe and secure as a child which is why so many are pseudo-suckling, like thumb/finger/pen sucking. Others can be caused by suppressed irritation though, meaning your polite smile while you deal with your boss or a customer could easily be undermined by your fist-clenching or lip-chewing signals of attack or even 'kill'.

The Leg Judder

This irritating habit has a tendency to make you look as though you have an urgent need . . . However, in reality, it is a sign that your engine (i.e. your body) is always ticking over and primed for action. Because you're juddering is rarely tuned in to the rate of the situation you're in it often means that you're more bored than excited. You're a thwarted fighter-pilot in an IT analyst's body.

Ring Fiddling

This is usually the wedding ring, in which case your fiddle is like a litmus test for the state of your marriage. If it's being turned around during a moment of pressure at work you see your family as your lifeline and means of back-up and protection. If it's going up and down your finger it's far more Freudian, suggesting a desire for sex but if it's coming off the finger and then back on again you're imagining life without your partner altogether and probably have your eye on the cutie in Accounts.

Necklace Fiddling

Fiddling with anything close to the neck is a signal that you feel under threat. The hand-to-neck gesture is self-protective and the items worn around the neck are often lucky charms, personal items of security like crosses, lockets, hearts and other trinkets. You're giving the person threatening you the evil eye.

Tie Fiddling

Okay, let's be honest, the tie is a long, arrow-shaped thing that points towards the penis. What do you think you're saying when you twiddle and dangle it in front of other people?

Doodling

Doodling is only performed when you're doing something else, otherwise it's called 'drawing'. As a subconscious gesture it spews out psychological information about your thinking and emotions at the time you're doodling. Circles are about contentment or sex, zigzags suggest suppressed aggression, boxes hint at a desire to create order out of chaos. If you're doodling in a meeting you will look bored and you will also forget to take your doodles with you, in which case your boss will be presented with visual proof of the inner workings of your mind.

Pen Chewing/Sucking

You were probably a thumb-sucker as a kid and this is your replacement object for something that was in the first place a replacement for the nipple and the comforts of being breast-fed. Oral comforters look cute but you might like to ask yourself whether looking like a suckling infant during board-meetings is going to get you places.

Pen Poking

As in poking your pen into the side of your cheek a la Simon Cowell or poking it about in mid-air as you speak. This is pseudo-weaponry and by waving or jabbing it at others you are miming the action of stabbing them. Jabbing it into your own cheek/leg/arm/hand might seem to imply you want to self-harm but in animal terms this is more about thwarted aggression aimed at others. When apes can't attack other apes they will often attack themselves in frustration.

Helicopter Pens

Whirling your pen around on your hand like the blades of a helicopter is a neat trick that needs many hours of practice. This suggests you are no stranger to boredom and that you are comfortable expressing that boredom, too. By creating a 'toy' from your pen you're making a pseudo-infantile statement that appears to rubbish the speaker.

Foot-tapping

This is a classic metronomic gesture – one that ticks over at what looks like the pace you would prefer the speaker to be speaking at: much quicker. It illustrates your thinking speed and suggests impatience bordering on irritation.

Nail Biting

Self-consumption in the form of nail, lip or even inside-of-cheek-chewing are prime examples of the self-attack gestures described above on pen-poking. These miserable-looking displays suggest frustrated aggression that you are too much of a wuss to display towards other people.

Hair Twiddling

When you were a baby your parents got you off to sleep at night by stroking the back of your head and it stays with you to this day as a self-comfort ritual. It makes you look sweet but you may find the opposite sex reads it as a self-grooming flirt signal. Dream on!

Origami

Paper-folding is an exaggerated form of 'box-doodling' – a desire to create order out of chaos. Its sense of creativity is even greater though, especially if you're making 'things' out of your origami. In this case it signals your mind is bigger than whatever's being discussed and this desire to build is a symbol of what your surplus cells are busy doing to keep themselves occupied.

Paper Ripping

Your desire for destruction is worrying. Paper ripping is one of the most destructive acts because what is written on paper represents thought so you are making very conclusive statements about either your own or some-one else's. If the paper is blank you are frankly a mindless vandal.

Glasses Cleaning

Repetitive rather than functional cleaning of glasses suggests you're constantly shocked, depressed or confused by the real world and hoping to make sense of it by polishing the windows you view it through.

Glasses Twirling/Waggling

Removing your glasses lets those around you know that you have finished listening to their ideas and views. By ceremoniously 'blinding' yourself like this (when we listen to someone we hear better if we can see their face and mouth as they talk) and waggling your specs, you threaten other people with complete cut-off unless your own views are heard and respected, making you look like an opinionated control-freak.

Cuff Fiddling

If you keep touching, pulling or adjusting your cuffs you have a deep desire to appear polite and pleasing, suppressing an even deeper desire to cut and run.

Pocket Patting

Patting and checking your pockets forms two services for you. Firstly it keeps anxieties at bay with a self-check ritual, suggesting you have previously emerged from your house without keys or a wallet, plus it provides the opportunity to give yourself a wake-up pat, spurring you on and helping with shyness, boredom or self-esteem problems.

Spot a good catch

Wealthy people fidget more. Researchers at the University of California in the US studied 50 video-taped conversations between strangers. They found that those from better off backgrounds displayed more fidget rituals such as playing with their hair and removing flecks of dust from their clothes.

So, as you retire anxious from analysing all your pet fiddles, words and shoes choices what better way to relax from the pressures of image management than to sink into a chair with a favourite book? But did you know that even your reading behaviour speaks volumes? Are you a peeker, a page folder, or even a crusher? And what do all these habits reveal about the dingy workings of your inner mind?

WHAT YOUR BOOK BEHAVIOUR SAYS ABOUT YOU

Your book behaviour says a lot about your approach to education, creativity and all things intellectual. A book is something that comes clad with an aura of authority and self-respect. The majority of book lovers seem to take themselves very seriously and many bookshops retain an air of mystique and gravity. Even the trendier ones with a buzz of magazine and games-buyers around the tills still manage to have the hush-and-tiptoe feel of a library once you get in among the high shelves at the back. The older you are the more respect you will feel for books and paper. On the whole, you believe that what's printed on those pages has been thought of and sanctioned by a higher authority. You may still find yourself treating your chick-lit with similar amounts of physical care as you would an antique first edition.

The Peeker

For the Peeker the book is God. You see yourself as a temporary recipient of the knowledge being passed on by the writer. You prise each page open carefully, peeking at its contents without once breaking the spine. A book read by the Peeker is a book that still looks pristine. Fan the pages gently and there's barely any sign that eyes and fingers have been devouring the contents.

Peekers are timid, polite and thoughtful of others. Your carbon footprint is probably the size of a kitten's paw and you tidy, clean and neaten your route through life. For you a book is an heirloom, something to be read and then passed on, stored or sold on eBay. In the Peeker's mind is an imaginary client who will tread the same path, nodding with approval that the book has been left in such a pristine state. Peekers do love approval, even if you have to imagine it in your own head. You still listen to imaginary compliments from long-dead school teachers whose rules you still adhere to with pride, and you try to encourage approval-worthy behaviour from those around you, never realising that your own rules and standards are woefully out of sync with the modern world. This might mean you suffer from stress (the suppressed kind, not the drama-queen kind) and suffer from anxiety at the thought that your own tight 'rules' might be pointless.

The Finger Licker

This reader likes to lick each finger before turning a page of the book and will often read with their chin held high, creating a rather superior and judgemental expression as they browse the contents. The Licker is almost literally devouring their book and their attitude to life and relationships can be the same. This gesture is controlling as the Lick means no pages will escape their grasp when turning, plus they leave their DNA over the pages like an animal spraying its territory. The combination of senses employed (oral and visual) means you like to double-bag your pleasures in life although this might only stretch to an ability to make love and think of the following day's dinner recipes at the same time. Lickers are controlled, controlling, vaguely superior and with a sense of steady pace as they make their way through life.

The Crusher

The Crusher trashes a book as they read it, using every which way to make their reading easy and comfortable. You break spines, bend corners and fold open because for you reading is all about intellectual messages, not tactile or artistic ones. You only have respect for the message itself, meaning you have a rebellious approach to authority or academics. You devour information quickly, have a very short attention-span and – if you don't enjoy what you're reading – will cut yourself off with a ruthlessness that can be scary. Spontaneous to the point of scatty, you can appear kindly and friendly but your overall approach to life is focused around your needs rather than the feelings of others. For you life is a tool to be used for your own benefit and with little in terms of long-term strategies or worry about consequences.

The Hopper

The Hopper has very little in the way of a linear approach to book-reading, preferring to hop and flick their way through a book, even sneaking a quick look at the last pages before starting at the beginning. You suffer from terminal distrust, often leading to a lack of adherence to life's rules. You play by your own rules and have your own version of logic that doesn't always agree with other people's. For you discovering how a book ends is necessary knowledge before donating the time and effort to read it, and the question 'Is this worth it?' tends to dominate the majority of your life. This negative approach to risk means you miss out on surprises and unexpected pleasures. Speed-dating might have been invented for you, allowing you to second-guess a relationship and the odds of it going well or ending badly from a few moments of chat.

The Scribbler

This ASBO book-reader likes to write, draw and even scribble all over their books, sometimes even adding margin notes of incredible arrogance like an unofficial editor. You are narcissistic to the point of scary, mentally imagining that every book that passes under your nose has been submitted for critical comment which will then be read and enjoyed by anyone else stupid enough to read the same book afterwards. You are a lover of the exclamation mark, which you use like a sceptical TV interviewer uses his eyebrows – as a method of implying ridicule and scorn. You might go through life looking normal and even polite but in reality you see yourself as Master of the Universe and this suppressed or thwarted sense of superiority might lead to bouts of anxiety, aggression or even bullying.

The Librarian

Each book a librarian picks up is like a life-long relationship opening up because you take your books seriously and will store them or display them after use, even the ones you didn't enjoy. You aren't a passive door-mat but you do feel that every experience in life offers learning potential and that even a crap book must have had something redeeming about it. You're all about the saving and cherishing of memories and like to mark your route through life with small 'trophies'. Clever, warm-hearted and fiercely loyal you will be quietly optimistic and full of encouragement of others.

The Curator

The Curator has similar habits to the Librarian in so far as you tend to hoard and display your books, but with one huge difference: the books you display are very unlikely to have been read by you, meaning you are a true trophy-hunter, but having put in the minimum effort possible. Displaying books that are unread means a superficial and rather lazy personality, someone who is happy to take short-cuts to achieve a desired effect. You're a bit of a cheat, a scamp and a sham, someone with clear goals in life but no real regard for how you achieve them.

The Passer-on

Although reading a book is a largely isolating and solitary pursuit the Passer-on likes to try to turn it into a team sport. By getting friends/relatives/neighbours to enjoy the same experiences you show that you are sociable, empathetic and a little bit bossy. Reading a book in a universally empathetic way ('I wonder what Amanda would make of this?' 'I bet Norman will chuckle at this bit!') amounts to almost a fear of 'solo' thinking and enjoyment and a love of shared ideas and gossip. You love book clubs too, meaning an aversion to risk-taking as approved books are normally safe and well-tested and if you don't like one it's probably your fault, not the book's. This means you are likely to be low-risk in terms of love and sex too, marrying someone in your own social circle and preferring sex that is wholesome rather than dark. Your 'nice' moral values can be evaluated at the moment you pass the book on. Do you blush and giggle as you apologise for the anal sex scene on page 309? Do you imply that you hope they won't think any the less of you because of it? Or do you snarl 'You'll love this – just your thing' and let them spend years puzzling why you made the connection between them and what they perceive as sordid sexual practices?

The Page Folder

Practical but timid, the Page Folder turns one very small corner back to keep his or her place before shutting the book. This tiny act of rebellion is driven by necessity because you love books so much you will carry one everywhere and be terrified of losing the plot (literally). You're also showing a liking for possession and ownership that suggests you're allergic to sharing. Once a page has been folded a book is rendered almost impossible to pass on, meaning this person will often take a similar stance on relationships, spraying his/her territory to stake their claim and having jealous or possessive tendencies.

Reading between the lies

A poll of British readers found that 65% admitted to having lied about reading a book in order to impress others. More than two fifths, for instance, had fibbed about reading George Orwell's *1984*. Eighty-five per cent of us admit that there are books we love to read, but wouldn't admit to owning. Stephen King novels and JK Rowling's Harry Potter top the list, according to a 2007 survey.

And if you thought book-reading was bad enough, what about your TV viewing habits? Your telly is more than just another tool for entertainment, in many ways it's also the cuckoo in the nest, an ever-present access to the outside world with only one small remote pad to control it.

WHAT YOUR TV VIEWING HABITS SAY ABOUT YOU

How do you see that box in the corner/hanging on the wall? Is it your friend, foe or sexual substitute? The way you watch your TV reveals much about how you treat your friends and family and reflects your overall approach to your social life. And don't underestimate its power. We watch TV for 25 hours a week, on average, with a fifth of us goggling a massive 36 hours. Once the TV was shoved away in a cabinet or awkwardly in the corner of a room. Today there's every chance that the TV will be above a fireplace, set into the wall proving that it's as almost embedded in our psyche. So what are your viewing habits saying?

Always Turned On

The Always Turned On Viewer sees their TV as a pseudo-friend and keeping it glowing means you never get lonely. In many ways it replaces the crackling fire, supplying a source of colour, movement, noise and life, and when it is turned off the ATO viewer feels a sense of loss and fear. You are warm, sociable and optimistic with low stress-levels and a high tolerance for waffle or trivia.

Highlight Programmes in the Weekly Planner

The Planner/Highlighter is a troubled perfectionist who has clearly taken forward-planning to a stage that could be labelled 'Sad'. You need your pleasure/relaxation fixes to be unspontaneous, often prompted by the fear that you might be missing something and unable to forgive yourself for it. Life for the Highlighter is one long struggle with time-management. When you were a child you were forced by your parents to keep your bowels as regular as clockwork.

The In Bed Viewer

The In Bed Viewer is so into comfort it hurts. Ostensibly a move that suggests 'sexy' ('Let's snuggle up and watch *Panorama* in the bedroom') the chances of real sex are rare – after ten minutes of viewing and snuggling, you're fast asleep snoring on his chest. There's still something splendidly sensual about you though because even though you're nesting like a bird in winter you're also sharing and touching. The time to realise that things have gone too far is when you start eating in bed, too. This is a slim whisker away from never getting up which is a serious matter, usually dealt with on TV programmes titled *Twelve Ton Man*.

The Gunslinger

You're a control-freak who sits watching TV like Wyatt Earp with at least two remotes lying by your side for sole use without consultation. You like power and will fight to the death if necessary if anyone else tries to touch your weapons. This control might seem selfish but it's also protective. Like all good Alpha males (for the gunslinger is surely only ever a man) you feel the need to protect your brood from attack from the outside and the TV is the nearest thing in your home to an outside invader.

TV jungle

It's what women have known for years. Researchers at Oregon State University found that men really do believe they should be in charge of the remote.

Double-bagger

You are incapable of doing one thing at a time and will only watch TV if you can also read a newspaper, make a phone call or de-flea the cat at the same time. You believe you are capable of following both trains of thought but all you end up doing is peering at the TV over the tops of your glasses like an elderly judge, or trying to share newspaper snippets in the middle of a whodunit. Anxious, distracted and impatient you find it hard to discover peace in life, even though you spend most of your time doing nothing of any meaning or consequence. You spread your time around so much that you end up focusing on nothing and therefore suffer either from bouts of depression or retaliation after you have annoyed people around you. You're forever catching up, needing simple facts or plans to be repeated at least five times before they sink in.

The Tutter

You treat your TV like the enemy, making every night's viewing one long litany of pain as you complain about programmes, tut through the adverts, moan about reality TV or quiz shows and constantly misplace the remote control. Despite this, you're always watching, proving that you receive some obscene form of enjoyment out of being unhappy. You're one of life's observers, constantly carping and criticising things but never taking action to try to improve your lot. You might sound angry and cynical but in fact you've got 'Wimp' written through you like a stick of rock as this impotent moaning masks an avoidance of genuine confrontation. The big problem with being a Tutter is that it makes your life's work to spoil other people's enjoyment too so in many ways your negativity is toxic. A 'professional' Tutter can merely walk into the room, stand by the door, watch the screen for two seconds then either tut or snort in derision to render any programme being enjoyed by the rest of the family worthless. If this technique doesn't work you will start to ask questions like: 'How come that one's married to a tranny then?' 'How old does that twerp think he is?' or 'What's the plot of this one then?'.

If book-grazing or channel-surfing aren't solitary enough, what about the hours you spend scouring the Internet on a voyage of discovery that would make the Starship Enterprise *look lightweight.*

WHAT YOUR NET HABITS SAY

eBayers

You're thrifty and competitive with a strong but thwarted entrepreneurial streak. And you're also obsessive as this behaviour really does take over your life. It marks a nostalgic return to exchanging small amounts of money for large amounts of effort. The innate pleasure of spending several hours selling some old piece of tat for a few pence is tragic at times. A closet Ebenezer Scrooge who thinks he or she is actually Sir Alan Sugar.

Facebookers

You're someone who uses your social life to endorse and stroke your ego because this site is all about numbers rather than quality of chat. 'I have three hundred friends' is the frequent boast of the Facebooker and the fact you have never met your 'friends' and that you could be conversing with a serial killer doesn't matter one jot. Trusting and boastful with a coating of superficiality and fun around a hard centre of low self-esteem.

Netting love

A survey by www.OnePoll.com revealed that one in four British people are dating – or used to date – someone they met through social networking websites like Facebook.

Twitterers

If you're a Twitterer there's a strong whiff of narcissism about you because you must live in the belief that the world is waiting to hear every beat of your heart or pick of your nose. Why stand idly in a queue in Waitrose when you can be announcing to the world the contents of your shopping trolley? You're the grandiose type who sends round robins at Christmas, not realising that no one is interested.

Friends Reunited Users

Life probably isn't exactly quite the bowl of cherries you were expecting, which is why you've scurried back to your past when ice-creams lasted a week and beer cost half a penny a pint. This makes you a 'grass is always greener' person, wanting one more bash at your life starting from all those guys/girls you lusted after but lost while you were in 5A. Time-warp thinking, a little like *The Likely Lads*, with some fear about moving into the unknown . . . or the future.

Second Lifers

You don't just fear real life you've abdicated from it as it's far easier to create yourself as a winged, size zero maiden of the night than it is to get down the gym, tone up and get a proper haircut. This really is like deleting your existing life and starting all over from scratch only this time you get to put in even less effort to be successful because nobody will ever know what you look like unless you decide to marry 'Son of Thor', in which case have some smelling salts ready as you wait for him to disembark at the airport.

You Tubers

You're the perennial student with the attention-span of a newt, finding other people's misfortune desperately funny. You have a healthy lack of respect for authority and for life in general and love nothing more than seeing the great and the mighty cut down to size. There's the notion of being part of a secret club about this site and – although you have absolutely minimal communication with the sharers – your life is shored up by the knowledge that 6 million people out there in the world also find the sight of a monkey picking its bum screamingly funny.

Bloggers

The Samuel Pepys of your time, you are clearly full to bursting with wonderful thoughts and takes on the world and as sure as eggs that there will be takers out there for all your wisdom. Bloggers can be neurotic extroverts: neurotic because diary-keeping is therapeutic and can offload all the stress of the day via a form of confessional, and extrovert because planting all that info on the web is a little like psyche-flashing. This person really does feel that he/she has fans out there waiting for the next public performance.

Of course some of our communication habits are more social and what better way to annoy people than standing in the middle of a crowded train discussing your day at work with your loved one via your mobile? Of course there is one way to annoy people even more and that's to allow your mobile to ring unanswered as you check your pockets and root around in the lower depths of your handbag or hunt through all those pockets of your briefcase while the ring tone drives everyone around you to go quietly nuts.

WHAT YOUR RING TONE SAYS ABOUT YOU

A recent survey of 18- to 34-year-olds showed that a massive 97% of those asked judged someone's personality from their ring tone. And with good reason. The ring tone is the ultimate attention-seeking show-off signal most people possess, attracting attention for all the wrong reasons and screaming out the inner workings of your psyche. It's the naughty brat of your image world, an opportunity for you to reveal your dark side in a way that you would never dare to do via clothing, speech or behaviour. This small siren is like a call to arms of your evil twin. Why else spend so much time selecting two tiny bars of tinnily played music or noise, trawling the Internet for something that resonates perfectly with the side of your character that you like to reveal to the rest of the world in a series of small peeks, like a diffident stripper, rather than unveiling totally?

The Original Ring Tone

This is the one you get if you're careless or carefree enough about your image to not bother to change the tone which should say nothing about you but which really speaks volumes. Why fail to make a selection unless you have no personality or preferences to connect it to? Did nothing tickle your fancy in terms of either style or irony? Why miss the perfect opportunity to add to your profile? This image black hole is worrying.

Comedy Voices

Oh how you laughed as you heard this one for the first time and downloaded it. That nagging old woman or giggling baby would show the world your talent as a wit and joke-meister extraordinaire. Except all it actually makes you sound is sad and annoying, especially as your slobby personality means you have to spend a full four minutes rooting for your phone at the bottom of your bag when it does go off in public.

Old-fashioned Ring Tone

You purchased something modern and possibly state-of-the-art and then decided to make it sound retro. Can you hear the confusion rattling around in your little head? Quality and age give you a reassuring feel of permanence and lack of change, meaning you have a capacity for worry and anxiety.

Trendy Music

You saw a chance to prove you're not the boring old fart you look like and grabbed it with both hands. No real fan of this music would ever demean it to ring-tone status because they'd know it would cheapen something they love. You have severe doubts about your own life and lifestyle but trying to re-balance with the aid of one tiny ring tone was never going to work, was it?

The *Jaws* Music

You just love to grab attention, which is probably a throwback to your status as second or third child in what might have been a very large family. Now you're an adult you see no reason why you should continue to be ignored but this ring tone is about the best you could do. You feel it will create an empathetic response in everyone who hears it, a gasp of recognition and a knowing nod and chuckle but in reality all you hear is a succession of tuts. You're a happy enough soul but probably very lonely.

Classics

Why not up your status and intellectual clout with a short burst of Vivaldi, showing although you pander to this annoying desire to be instantly accessible you are keen to prove the rest of your life is choc-full of quality and class.

Scottish Music

Only ever heard played by foreign mini-cab drivers with absolutely no links to anywhere north of the border apart from they once got asked to drive a punter to Glasgow and they charged them £300. You can catch their eye as the bagpipes break out, waiting for some hint they get the fact that this is an obscure choice but there's never a flicker of acknowledgement crossing their face, which can only mean one of three things: either the very macho sound of the pipes and drums hits a nerve; this is what is being sold as a download 'British sound' in whatever country they originate from; or that a lot of very drunken Scottish people hire cabs and then leave their phones behind on the seat.

Mood Music

Pan pipes, harps and cool sounds suggest you're prone to stress and liable to freak out on a regular basis. Your phone is just one more nail in your break-down coffin and by setting it to play calming music rather than that nasty ringy noise you hope to make it seem like less of an attack or invasion.

Novelty Ring Tones (like 'Crazy Frog')

You adore attracting attention and you are happy to annoy people to do so. In fact, you advertise your capacity for being an annoying human being as though it were a badge of honour. This means that you have no capacity for offering pleasure to others, other than offering them an excuse to enjoy punching you on the nose. You were the type of kid that is incessantly naughty in the belief that a shouted telling off (or a smack, depending on your age) was preferable to being ignored. And so now your whole life is one huge, unrewarding spiral of uninspired behaviour where you use techniques like teasing, winding people up and making crass, insulting comments in a bid to get a response. No other path has ever occurred to you because your entire persona has been trained like Pavlov's dog to find some kind of succour in misery.

Just Rings

It's quite hard to get normal ringing on your phone, meaning the 'Just Rings' is a little like a salmon swimming upstream in terms of trend and innovation. You bought something state of the art but then got scared of it and needed it to sound familiar just to make the fear go away. For you comfort is all about the familiar. Making something portable sound exactly like a land-line is a little perverse, even you have to admit.

Although your ring tone took moments to select and install but defines you for a whole lifetime as a nerd or an anal boffin with no mates, there are other choices in life that take longer to make but which become adopted as a life pattern, meaning the way we behaved when we were five years old becomes much the same as the way we behave as adults, especially when there is a cake and candles around to mark the occasion.

WHAT YOUR BIRTHDAY BEHAVIOUR SAYS ABOUT YOU

No matter which way you look at them, birthdays are like a marinade of self-esteem and the way you choose to mark your own lets everyone know exactly where you stand in terms of self-perception. In many ways a birthday is the closest you'll get to celebrity, with strangers being forced to wish you happy returns and pubs and clubs being expected to provide free drinks for the occasion.

The Liar

The Liar claims: 'I don't want any fuss, I just want to hide away until it's all over' or even 'Don't buy me anything, I don't like presents' etc. What you really mean is: 'Surprise me with something expensive and personal, plus a surprise party for all my friends'.

In many ways though, there's no pleasing a Birthday Liar and it is this state of cognitive dissonance (or god-awful confusion) that you seem to enjoy creating in your victim. Some Birthday Liars will go to great lengths to make their point, getting forceful and angry as you deny wanting anything to do with the day itself. Some are less strident, simply asking for a modest gift like flowers – or adopting a goat in a Third World country – but then, after being given exactly what you asked for, you begin to look about for the real gift. All the sweetness evaporates and, rest assured, your selfish, mean behaviour will use this as an excuse for starting an affair with your personal trainer. Lying like this is manipulative, and means you can be all about power and control and messing with other people's minds. Either way you tend to get what you want in life, often by playing dirty.

The Party Prince/Princess

A birthday can be 'all about me' and the Party Prince or Princess milks that notion for every single last drop. You never, ever grew up and will plan the biggest, most egocentric bash on the planet and woe betide anyone who dares to rain on your parade. You spend birthdays in a state that is a cross between Violet Elizabeth Bott, Norma Desmond and Scarlett O'Hara, expecting friends to act as courtiers and sycophants which they happily do because anything less will produce psychotic tantrums, sulks and even a quitting or closing down of all the festivities. Selfish, spoilt and narcissistic the Party Prince or Princess might seem like the life and soul of any gathering but only if you're getting your own way.

The Partyphobe

This modest character hosts something so small in the way of birthday bashes that it might even involve just you, a bottle of Blue Nun and a straw. If there are Twiglets and Hula Hoops involved though you might be looking at a small party. This is more of a wake than a celebration, a kind of 'beat me with birch twigs through my hair shirt' kind of affair where the theme is apologies, recriminations and tears of worthlessness and broken affairs.

Despite the sobbing into cartons of chocolate chip ice-cream though, the Partyphobe can be surprisingly good company long-term. Your ego is small but your sense of humour and of the ridiculous has potential and your parties can take off into rather jolly, reckless affairs once the photo of the ex has been ceremoniously burnt or used as a dartboard. Chaotic and a short-term planner but loyal and fun in short bursts.

The Hunter

The Hunter uses his or her birthday as an excuse to stalk and kill their prey in a way that they have been planning all year, meaning you're strategic and as focused as a hawk. You either host huge parties for everyone you have ever met in your life just so you have an excuse to invite the one from Friends Reunited that got away the first time, a smokescreen for seduction while everyone else riots and orgies, or you take a select tribe of closest mates and go grimly out on the prowl to stalk your prey in situ, catching the nubile young barman behind his own bar.

The Dinner Party Host

There's something hugely controlling about the Dinner Party Host as inviting people into your home to force them to sit in ways that you have chosen (even using name-cards) and to eat food that you have selected leaves very little scope for individual choice. The Dinner Party Host employs the air of a martyr ('I've been marinating these olives for nineteen years', 'This yoghurt has been made from my breast milk', 'The saline solution those rabbit testicles have been rubbed in came from my own tear ducts' etc) and although the guests arrive clutching token gifts of chocolates and flowers by way of compensation they know they can never match the near-fatal stress levels their host has suffered on their behalf, chasing that last bottle of quadruple-distilled-through-the-robes-of-Buddhist-monks balsamic vinegar around every supermarket in London.

You tend to call the shots throughout the evening, telling guests what to wear, when to arrive and even what cheese to try ('It's cat's cheese – do try it, you'll love it'), and you make sure guests realise you have slaved over a stove on your one special day of the year, making guilt-level reach an all-time high.

So where, you ask, does all this image-management end? At what point do you take off those fluffy slippers and stop worrying about the dinner party fondue and decide to embrace what you rashly describe as your 'true self'? Well, not during your time on this earth we're afraid because a huge cause for concern for modern man is ensuring his or her send-off doesn't undo all the hard impression work undertaken during their lifetime. Your funeral is your last big 'Hurrah', the way they'll remember you for the rest of their lives. Do you really want relatives and friends picking your flowers, hymns and prayers let alone your play-in and play-out music or that huge blow-up photo that stood alongside your coffin? Okay so you might be dead but would you really risk crysanths and Chris de Burgh and a blow-up of your passport photo? Or would you prefer something more like a Lloyd Webber production?

WHAT YOUR FUNERAL MUSIC SAYS ABOUT YOU

Even in death we are obsessed with how we come across. Admit it – even though you haven't planned your send-off down to the last detail you've probably thought about how you'd like your friends and family to see you off, just a little bit? While your birth was out of your control in terms of choreography, and your wedding meant some degree of limelight-sharing, your funeral really is the biggest 'all about me!' moment of all. In death you can quite simply scale heights of impact that you would never have been able to achieve during your life, and all to a captive audience. No wonder we spend secret moments planning how we want to be remembered by those who we leave behind. And it's your choice of funeral music that will remain with your nearest and dearest for ever! So beware the casual or random selection lest they are forced to wipe their eyes every time 'My Heart Will Go On' from *Titanic* comes on the radio.

Hymn and hers

A 2008 survey for Co-operative Funeralcare found that hymns are the most popular request at 35% of services, more contemporary songs for 58% and classical pieces making up just 7%.

Here are what some of the top songs reveal . . .

'My Way': Sinatra

The anthem for machismo and rebellion, ostensibly crafted to be sung by a genuine hell-raiser like Frank – successful, talented and rich beyond most people's wildest dreams – by using this song at your funeral you'll probably be guilty of power-by-proxy – that is, cashing in some of the great man's reputation to enhance your own. This is a wry poke-in-the-eye to life in general, suggesting you grabbed it by the gullet and wrung every last drop out of it. It's the middle finger to anyone who had to put up with you en route and it's to imply to all those left sitting smugly in the pews that the muesli-munching, gym-bunny, organic, 'my body is a temple' lifestyle is not the only fruit. Those health freaks might still be left standing in there when you have fallen but it's not all about quantity when it comes to life span.

In reality though, this is often the final song of a divorced man who drank, smoked and maybe ate more kebabs than the government medical guidelines but who is trying to recast themselves as a legend in their own death-time, through this vision of an alternative lifestyle, and hoping to beckon many others into the grave after them.

'Wind Beneath My Wings': Bette Midler

It might be wise to play part of this one only as the title will create a positive image of you soaring up to heaven but the 'plot' of the song could leave your audience confused. They'll know it from the movie *Beaches*, and read it as a friend letting her chum know how fab she is, and so could make you appear egotistical unless you get someone else like a best mate to pretend they chose it for you.

'Time To Say Goodbye': Sarah Brightman

If your audience weren't crying before this song started they will be once the chorus starts but only if you chose the English version, meaning they can hear you bid your final adieu.

This song starts gently but rises to a climax, suggesting a romantic or spiritual soul with a sense of occasion who obviously takes death seriously. Loving but lacking in self-pity, too. This is your rather grand way of saying: Bye bye, I'm off now!

'You Raise Me Up': Westlife

Unpretentious, fun-loving, popular and openly uncomplicated, your choice of this song pegs you as someone spontaneous who possibly shopped at Primark (in a good way). For you it's all about living life in the moment and sharing with friends. This is the type of song best sung with your mates after a couple of bevies, when that key change sounds like the most amazingly emotive thing ever. You're even sharing your funeral, too, because they'll be mouthing the words as you go down.

'Angels': Robbie Williams

Lovely though The Robster is, never forget you'll be vying with him in the self-pity stakes on the day of your own funeral if you choose this. Plus there's the connection with angels that will let everyone know you have career pretensions even in death, not to mention the fact that this is such a big stadium number that they'll all be wanting to hold their cigarette lighters aloft and sing the chorus. Pick this yourself and the chances are you're a bit of a drama queen who enjoyed being centre stage.

'Over The Rainbow': Judy Garland

Apart from the gay thing, this version of this song says more about your idealised thoughts on childhood, innocence and a desire to be seen as that lost little kid as you shuffle off this mortal coil. The voice is high and childlike, the words suggest life had you beat but that hopefully there's somewhere much nicer with bluebirds waiting for you. You're looking for pity here, suggesting you were way too precious to survive in the real world. Sad, and cute with a tinge of rebuke in your tone for those left behind. Did you not realise I was really a confused child? Shame on you!

'Hallelujah': Alexander Burke/Leonard Cohen

It's the choir-like side of this song that appeals to you as its soaring notes and spiritual chorus has a profoundly religious spin to it. This suggests you're someone who liked to hedge their bets in terms of heaven and hell, but also someone with a rather short attention-span because the words to this song aren't really religious fodder when you listen to them closely rather than just joining in with the odd snatches you remember. For you it's the thought that counts, though.

'Always Look On The Bright Side of Life': Monty Python

While few would risk the use of comedy in church during their lifetime, your lack of religious respect means you refuse to be denied your moment of irony in death. By choosing this you remind the congregation that you used to be very much alive and have no desire to be seen as precious or celestial. There's a hint of the control-freak about you too, as you know this song will bring a wry smile to your audience's faces and you like that idea of one last moment of power. Almost worth dying early just to be the first corpse to have gone to its grave on this one but now, sadly, a bit of a cliché.

Now we drag you back to the land of the living to turn our gun-turrets to the place you inhabit when you're not at work – that place you like to call home. Dinner parties and funerals are two of the ways we end up hosting family and friends and inevitably both end up with our homes being used as a social display-cabinet. Your home is your nest as well as your hosting area. So what are the meanings behind the way you have furnished, arranged and decorated that private place of retreat?

4

HIDDEN MESSAGES IN YOUR HOME

The idea that an Englishman's home is his castle is a relatively recent one, at least as far as the lower classes are concerned. Up until around the early 1800s the place you lived in was also likely to be your place of work, and therefore a steady stream of co-workers, suppliers, lodgers and even livestock would have been regularly traipsing through your home, making design details like shag-pile carpet and recliner loungers an impractical and inconceivable concept.

As 'going to work' became an off-shoot of the Industrial Revolution though, so battening down your home against the outside world became a popular trend. With names like 'Mon Repos' and 'Dun Roamin' being hung beside doorways and porches the house increasingly became somewhere to find rest, peace and a refuge from the outside world. Doors were fitted with locks and chains and outside visitors tended to be invited in for social 'set pieces' like that weekend fave of the seventies, the dinner party. Doors were thrown open to provide official house/flat tours around the stripped pine and velour interiors. Background music was chosen with care (usually something by Mike Oldfield), nibbles were laid out in Habitat bowls and a thousand cows and prawns were slaughtered per week to provide Piat d'Or slurping diners with their prawn cocktails and Beef Wellingtons.

Once the craze for home-ownership kicked in the property we lived in became our core investment and source of potential wealth. Property prices became the favourite subject-of-choice around the IKEA coffee table on which was placed the cafetière and the After Eights and it was little wonder when the nineties kicked in and our homes became temples of Hint of Puce paint and MDF-crafted radiator covers, closed to the public for on-going renovations during the week and open for tours Christmas and bank holidays only. DIY stores ousted church as the place to worship on a Sunday as we treated our properties like miniature stately homes, and as a result the effect on you and your self-analytical signals can only be described as profound.

Open the doors to your home and you fling open the portals to your dimmer switch, dado rail, mug-tree, toilet-roll holder and Monet print, providing unarguable clues to the code that is 'You'. Like the priest's entrails in *The Da Vinci Code* they are a vision of your inner workings that all point towards the truth, and here's the evidence. Read it and weep.

WHAT YOUR HALLWAY REVEALS

In Freudian terms this is your place of entry, a kind of public orifice that defines the level of acceptance you have to the outside world. It was the first feature you saw when you viewed the place to rent or buy, and its impact would have been a deciding factor on your decision to move in. How better to analyse your approach to life and sex than by the less-than-subliminal signals thrown up by the decisions you have taken to decorate and adorn this passageway to the inner secrets of your sexual soul?

The Hobbit Hallway

These are narrow, dingy and made even narrower by the hanging of redundant and un-owned coats on a series of pegs or hooks along the wall right behind the door. This means the door only partially opens and you are forced to offer an instant disclaimer to guests: 'Mind the coats' or even 'Sorry about the mess'. Bikes and other paraphernalia litter the rest of the domestic orifice, making entrance to your home a virtual assault course, prompting a volley of apologies and warnings throughout its entire length.

What it says: You barricade your life against forced or even unforced entry but you lack the balls to just lock yourself in and pour boiling oil from the top windows. Therefore you hint and imply rather than just announce you're a bit of a loner, suggesting you have assertiveness issues tinged with a slight whiff of self-loathing that causes you to suffer from bouts of resentment against the world. You're letting people know you don't like being invaded but your first words will include 'sorry' as you apologise for your own mess and chaos, suggesting you're the passive/aggressive type. You're a bit of a social enigma: grumpy, cynical but also sensitive and self-protective and in sexual terms you're all about putting up obstacles and barriers to deny access to what can possibly be your inner slut. Once you go, you go, but it's all or nothing with you and you've been hurt enough in the past to make you wary and guarded until you feel you can trust.

The Hessian Hallway

Your hallway is clean-limbed and practical with wheat-coloured walls and hessian carpet underfoot. You use plug-in air-fresheners in flavours like 'newly pressed linen' to ensure instant ambiance and hide the scent of nappies and – apart from the odd book or toy strewn by the kids, the only decoration are the framed prints along the walls.

What it says: We'll use the term 'practical idealist' here because your approach is all about serenity and the 'perfect' life that is underpinned by a much more sensible approach, hence the trend for all that is washable, wipe-clean and hard-wearing. Your sensible approach is firmly anti-sensual though, as a home owned by someone with a more tactile sense of well-being than you would never contemplate something akin to the kind of Desperate Dan's stubble effect that hessian has on the undersides of your feet. You are a keeper of order against an ever threatening tide of chaos, and 'stress' is a word that is firmly in your vocabulary, along with 'yoga retreat' and 'a large glass of chardonnay, please'. Superficially you're a bit of an approval-seeking 'pleaser', although your approach to sex and relationships can be moody and demanding once you get into a long-term relationship, mainly because you normally do what you feel you should be doing rather than what you want to do and once this façade slips your true nature asserts itself. You can be socially competitive and into quotas – like keeping the times you have sex per week up to the national average. Once your buttons are pressed you can go like the proverbial rocket and you're a fiercely loyal friend but anyone taking you for granted will get short shrift.

The Trophy Hallway

You use your hall to introduce 'You' by adorning it with items that act like a warm-up act to the star of the show. The walls are painted in a 'statement' colour and hung with photos and mementoes of your life, hobbies and interests. Your sense of humour, for instance, might be validated by cartoons while your job is defined by small samples of what you do for a living. This presents a living tribute titled 'this is who I am', forcing guests to dally in your hallway to discuss your favourite topic.

What it says: What you see as signs of an open and gregarious personality are seen by others as signs of vanity and self-obsession. The world revolves around you and boy do you feel you have a lot to offer it! If you're not sending round robins to people at Christmas you're telling your life story in diary style on your personal blog and counting the hits it gets. You're a larger-than-life figure who has to be the centre of attention, but only because you know that your jokes are funnier and your set-piece stories more interesting than anyone else's. Deep down you're insecure but we're talking neolithic layers here, meaning you keep it well hidden and the only clue to this lies in a tendency to suffer from verbal diarrhoea after a few drinks. You want everyone to enjoy life but you see yourself as the key catalyst to achieving that objective. Sometimes it's good to realise other people's fun doesn't depend on your own entertainment value.

The 'We Are Family' Hallway

Very similar to the above, except the entire flaming family has to be venerated in this mini-walk of life. Wellington boots are arranged in order of diminishing size von Trapp-style, there will be dog leads, framed kiddie drawings, pebbles in boxes, hats, scarves and at least one very silly thing like a giant china frog that you would never have tolerated prior to breeding but which you can use to show how tolerant and laid-back you have become since having a family. As you say, it 'puts things into context'.

What it says: Hopefully you do have a Waltons-sized family because if you live alone this hallway places you in the 'mad, bad and dangerous to know' category of pervert. If you have been breeding non-stop you protest so much – that is, you advertise and extol the unmitigated joys of family life to all and sundry, which in actual fact gives the impression that the only person you're trying to convince is yourself. You're secretly flummoxed by or struggling with the whole concept and have subliminal yearnings for those heady days of your virginity when you could sit on a settee without having to then prise a large and painful piece of Lego out of your backside. Your party piece is in acting empathetically bemused to friends in a similar boat, as in a 'how did this happen?' way, but you're privately riddled with the need to make singleton friends jealous by all this emphasis on the happy family unit. Why? Because if they show no flicker of envy you will be forced into an in-depth analysis of your own personal choices and you know it's too late to take the little angels back to God's returns department.

The No-hallway Hallway

There's no foreplay here: your front door opens straight into the front room, or what is possibly the only room in the home if money is tight, and the result is a kind of knock-through studio-type thing. This always shocks your guests who were expecting a bit of a pre-amble and time to rearrange their 'stressed from the journey when the sat-nav conked out' facial expression into something more sociable. Instead they have to feign pleasure and mask surprise as they discover your wife/husband stretched out on the recliner on the other side of the letterbox.

What it says: You're an upfront kind of a person who is happily instant-gratification when it comes to love, life and sex. With you, what you see is what you get, and anyone uncomfortable with that will struggle maintaining a relationship with you. You have a peculiar ability to be comfortable with change and a lack of privacy. Check out exactly how much of an emotional nudist you are by seeing whether you have applied your own barriers to the door in the manner of letter-box guards, covers or boxes, door-curtains or any attempt to create a virtual hall by placing furniture between door and lounge seating. If it's a straight, unfettered run-through you're happily at one with the other people you share the planet with. This means a lack of paranoia and a tendency to see the best in colleagues and friends until proved otherwise. There's nothing formal to you as greeting rituals are kept to a minimum with a space like this. Once you're in you're in.

The Aspirational Hallway

You saw *Gone With The Wind* and you drooled over *Sunset Boulevard*. If you're younger you watched *Cribs* and *Dynasty* and the definition of wealth and success became the huge hall with the winding staircase and possibly even a balcony. There is a BHS chandelier in residence and some nice studio pics of the wife and kids, all smiling through a fog of soft-focus.

What it says: There's nothing inconspicuous about your consumption, and you want to impress other people almost as much as you want to impress yourself. You're a great respecter of social class and success, even if that does over-stretch you at times. This means you very likely have metal gates that are, at least, three times larger than the home you live in, and that your magnificent staircase has meant space in the rest of the house has been whittled down to compensate. You have very focused views on who you want to be and where you want to get to and your 'flaunt it' behaviour would achieve praise from motivational gurus across the world. Your idealism is refreshing in its lack of irony, meaning you can happily enjoy gazing at those airbrushed family pictures on your return from work each day even though they bear no similarity to the less than perfect (but equally lovable) reality.

The Pseudo-Victorian Hallway

Your walls are like Neapolitan ice-cream with one flavour missing, that is, it's two-tone with a plain-ish top half and some stripy stuff underneath, segregated by a co-ordinating paper border or dado rail. Colours are red or maroon/ pink and the floor is either tiled or clad in a garish but practical swirling deep red carpet. Furniture includes a hat stand that you inherited from your gran although the brass-topped sticks were a touch you added yourself.

What it says: In the warfare that is modern life your own personal solution is to return to your roots, reconstructing the home life of your great-grandparents in a bid to create security through challenging change. Your antidote to stress lies with a sense of history that puts daily aggravations into context, thereby diminishing them. Alongside the adult who goes to work to perform tasks under pressure is that 'small child within' that psychologists are always banging on about and your home is all about re-creating that childlike state each time you come back from work and step inside your own home. By re-creating the solid values of history you make yourself feel satisfyingly younger, with the protection of invisible parental supervision. The richness of the red tones implies a warm personality and a desire to conform to please others. If your hall is ersatz-Victorian you can often feel that you're taking a stand against the lack of values of the rest of the world. If it's the B&Q version from the nineties you are a happy conformist, sociable and entrenched in family values.

But your hallway is only one portal into what you're likely to see as your castle, because what doesn't enter your house via the front door will often sneak in via your PC. And unlike the social, shared company of friends and relatives, your PC lets in a far more personal choice of companions, making it far more indicative of what psychologists refer to as your 'dark side'. So how do you host this smaller but often far more telling portal?

WHAT YOUR HOME COMPUTER WORKSTATION SAYS ABOUT YOU

They are the private portals to the outside world that reveal our inner selves. First it was the TV, although this was a relatively secure portal as it was about as interactive as the goldfish tank (although we had yet to discover the subliminal effects on our tastes, opinions and decision-taking capabilities as in 'You know I really like that *Eldorado*, I think it's quality drama', 'I'm up for a spot of queuing for ten weeks for the *X Factor* just to indulge in a little sado-masochistic banter with Simon Cowell' or 'I could just do with a Cheese String right now' etc). Hence the change of roll for the household telly from Dalek-sized room invader to something that now looks as if it's been flattened with a rolling pin before being hung up on the wall in the spot over the fireplace vacated by the mirror. The fact it's been swapped for a mirror should delight TV execs as proof that viewers now see most programmes as a direct reflection of their own lives and aspirations.

The real black hole of portals is the PC though. One small screen provides access to the entire planet and beyond and – having snuck into our homes as a purveyor of Game Boy and other innocuous pieces of fun – it took over as a new 'home-working opportunity', replacing looms and other weaving implements as the remote worker's weapon of choice. Your PC or laptop will have its own home and paraphernalia and the way you present it speaks volumes about your relationship with everything 'outside world'.

The Shrine

Your PC (rather than laptop – you'd rarely think of moving it) is placed slap-bang in the middle of its own desk in its own room. Surrounding it are all its paraphernalia, such as mouse mats, Post-its, a telephone and notebooks, and around it hang photos, cuttings and other obsessive-compulsive bits and bobs, although all placed in some strange type of order and although there are crumbs of toast to be found lurking in the gaps between the keys your screen has the mark of Mr Sheen upon it, even if the duster has created a subtle round hole in the static grime of the glass.

What it says: The prominence of your PC suggests you have an almost mystical view of it, suggesting a pseudo-infantile sense of awe and respect for all things technical, work related or even connected to the outside world. You accept authority readily, and even though you might moan about your boss you always do it when he or she is well out of earshot as – deep down – you don't like to make yourself unpopular. You have a tendency to over work, and will probably enter 'see who can send the most out-of-hours email' competitions with your colleagues, having boasted about replying to one from the boss sent at midnight on a Saturday within ten minutes of receipt. In many ways, this PC is your own little virtual boss in the home, taking priority over most of your other pursuits. You tut, you puff and you whinge about the hours it 'forces' you to put in but in reality it's you who is doing this prioritising as your PC can neither shout, stare or place its hands on its hips in order to boss you around. This machine is your power-base, as well as your escape from everyday life. Your business emails define your status and indispensability and the Internet is somewhere you can trade and graze as a true Master of the Universe.

The Temple of Geekery

Your PC is state-of-the-art but suitably distressed. Used more like a musical instrument than a processor it bears similar scars and signs of use to Keith Richard's guitar. It's probably in your bedroom and the desk it sits on is irrelevant, like your personal comfort when you use it. It's probably something your dad bought as a self-assembly unit from Argos for you to do your homework on when you were nine but it's since disappeared from view beneath mugs and pizza cartons, plus the odd dirty sock. Geekery portals are often housed in some sort of alcove, making hunching necessary but hunching is good as it adds to the Davros-style air.

What it says: Your PC isn't an escape from real life, it *is* your real life. You have a life, of course, but it's nothing to the limitless ocean of creative potential that is your life on the

World Wide Web. Your approach to life is pure fantasy. You see yourself as heroic, just like the World of Warcraft character you created, but the reality is that you're more like your average geek, complete with ear-studs and a ponytail.

The Family Member

Your PC/laptop was adopted by your family from day one and is often found in the heart of the house, lying on the kitchen table to be viewed and used by all. Its outer case is in a fun colour and bears crayon marks as well as the odd doggie tooth mark.

What it says: By ingratiating your laptop into family life you attempted to negate any threat from this portal to the world, meaning your thing is killing with kindness or asserting your power by nurture. Placing it on the kitchen table makes it part of the family and, for you, keeping a strong family unit together is the key priority. You derive strength from numbers and sprinkle reminders of your tribe around other areas, like in your workplace where photos of your kids are strewn around you. Trust is a huge issue for you and if that means pruning the power of the PC, so be it. You have every device in place to filter dodgy sites or lock the kids out without permission and although you look like a walking ad for unconditional love, your laptop – like everything else in your home – knows it is only accepted and nurtured as long as it plays by your rules. The threat of 'Turn it off, we're eating' followed by 'I'll throw the thing in the skip' regularly rings around your kitchen.

The Cuckoo

Your portal to the galaxy is forced to room-share, although its 'cuckoo-in-the-nest' take-over increases on a daily rate. The place it resides in is still known as the guest room although any guests would soon understand who's really in charge as, although lying in a strange bed (or inflatable bed) in an ice-cold room is bad enough, being stared at by the cuckoo with its unblinking but reproachful eye and knowing it clearly has another agenda is considerably worse. Having someone else's PC as a room-mate is a great leveller. You know it's waiting for you to sober up and go, and you guess your host is, too.

What it says: Your life is a constant struggle between your work and social life and in many ways your 'solution' is faint-hearted enough to mean that both suffer from neglect. By banishing your PC to the chilly, unwelcoming guest room you hope to stop it from dominating your life. However the message to your friends is equally aggressive, as your actions have the effect of making them feel as though they're sleeping in your office and time-sharing with a computer. You're announcing subliminally that neither can be allowed priority in your life and this emotional dithering suggests you're sitting on a whole barrel-load of suppressed stress. You worry that you're struggling to keep up with your workload but you also worry that you're losing touch with friends. You're a sitting-on-the-fence type of person, and if your loved-ones do get irritated with you, it's probably because you try to agree with each of them, meaning you often allow yourself to get dumped on from a great height. Your greatest goal is to write a novel but only once you've remembered to buy a halogen heater because that bedroom is currently sub-zero, meaning your fingers risk freezing to the keyboard. This also makes you a lightweight who fears failure and risk so much that you often avoid trying in the first place – to say you'd write your novel if only the room wasn't so cold means putting off your dream because never achieving it is more comfortable to you than putting in effort to risk watching it crash and burn.

PC or Mac?

It's the age-old question. Sure people are fiercely loyal to brands. But when it comes to the great computer divide there's a key difference in personality too. Analysis has suggested that Mac users are more open minded, but also less modest than PC users.

If your PC is your place of mental retreat (especially if you find yourself surfing the Net on Christmas Day in a bid to get some intellectual release from all your loved ones, then your bed is your place of physical refuge and the longer you spend in it alone the more 'refuge-ish' it becomes. Tracey Emin got it right when she placed her own bed on display as a revealing, autobiographical work of art.

WHAT YOUR BED SAYS ABOUT YOU

If you're an average human being you spend 25 years of your life in bed. Your bed is your place of vulnerability, the nest where you choose to be for the hours you spend unconscious and open to attack. It's the place in your world where you can hunker down, curl up beneath blankets and open your psyche to dreams, fears and worries. In many ways it is your ersatz womb and you may even still sleep in the foetal position. But your bed is also likely to be your place of sex, too, meaning infantile comfort turns to grown-up frenzy as and when your mood demands.

The Schizo Bed (tidy on top, chaotic below)

You have very strong ideas of how you would like to be perceived and how you would like life to be and this is reflected in the top half of your bed. There's a studied sense of calm, order and cleanliness to your duvet covers, pillowcases, throws and cushion that is reminiscent of a cheap hotel room once the chambermaid's given it the once over. However, all this tidiness is a sham because below the bed is the hidden kingdom of trolls, hobbits and Borrowers. You rarely look under your bed because it is like your secret psyche, a desolate and dangerous land-scape of ancient tissues, dust balls the size of small rats, odd slippers with no apparent provenance, and a grave-yard of books that have been read to a certain point and then abandoned, still open at the page on which you quit.

What it says: At worst you're optimistic and pretentious, showing your 'ideal' face to the world but masking something much more slutty and chaotic that lies beneath. At best you're nice, polite and well-behaved but with a naughty streak. Life is all about new starts and good intentions for you and many of your abandoned books will be self-help or highbrow literary novels. Your life is all about fire-fighting, that is, handling one emergency after another with little time for planning or reflection. You manage to hold things together and the top half of your bed reflects that but this pristine effect is only pulled off by turning a blind eye to what lies beneath. You probably drink too much, prepare ready meals for the kids (albeit organic) and mourn the fact that you never got around to doing that degree/writing that novel/cooking like Nigella Lawson.

The Show Bed

Your bed is decorated in a way that only looks 'right' when you're not in it, with a massive refurb being necessary before you can get into the part of the bed you've allowed yourself to sleep in. This bed is covered with plumped-up quilts, neatly folded throws, drapes, peplums and lots and lots of huge, coordinating cushions, all of which you have to remove every night in a kind of archaeological dig before you can get down and dirty or prepare for the business of sleep.

What it says: If we take the bed itself as a symbol of sex then your cover-ups are about as prudish as the Victorians placing covers over their piano legs. The amount of work involved in getting into your bed at night suggests you see sex as something a little base and grubby. This bed is all about delayed gratification and a smudge of compulsive orderliness too, that might be down to an anxious need to control the world you live in. This ritualistic undressing then re-dressing of the bed suggests you see sex and spontaneity as dangerous and scary and that by burying it beneath a mountain of huge cushions (each having its correct place in the formation) you feel control is somehow back in your hands.

The Fairytale Bed

We're talking posters, drapes, huge pillows, satin, bows, tie-backs, flounces and fancies. This bed is a performance in its own right, an important and possibly dominant member of the household with something quasi-magical about its construction and dress-sense. It's a reconstruction of all those beds of your childhood stories and by exaggerating its size with drapes and posts you're making yourself feel smaller and more childlike as you snooze in it.

What it says: You're clearly an egotist because this bed is like a stage that you perform on each night. It's an important bed, meaning you rate yourself as quasi-regal and see yourself as standing apart from the rest of the crowd through your individual sense of style that borders on the eccentric. And now to those four posts. Could they possibly not be symbolic of erections? We'd be letting down Freud if we implied anything else. This is a bed for mating then, but the bloke isn't going to get his own way. Those drapes lend a touch of female control to the proceedings suggesting that although sex might be a priority it's going to be hideously romantic too. Think thrusting young swains in a Barbara Cartland novel and you'll pretty much get the picture here.

The Playboy Bed

Hugh Hefner eat your heart out! This bed is made of leather (or at least hewn from MDF and then covered with something that looks like it) and is clad in satin sheets, preferably black although maybe deep maroon or grey. There are hidden spotlights and drawers and possibly a TV on the unit beside it.

What it says: You're a bit of a bloke, and a bloke who likes Jeremy Clarkson. You're someone who feels he's achieved something in life. This bed is your reward, a machismo indulgence and temple to the power of your sexuality. You might enjoy intellectualising this bed by pretending it's ironic and retro but in actuality you love what it says about you. Tasteless it may be but women get the message when they're invited back: this bed says everything about fun and three-times-a-night marathons but nothing about relationships or commitment. You pride yourself on your honesty in this respect. Humour is your thing and, although the thought of public displays of affection with anyone other than a goal-scoring footie mate makes you shudder, you have been known to buy a woman flowers, although it was probably your mum.

The Cot

Your bed is littered with cuddly toys, some refugees from your childhood but most are more recent gifts from friends, family and even the odd lover. When you show a man your bedroom your first act is to giggle in mock-embarrassment although secretly you're proudly displaying trophies of affection like golfers show off cups and shields. When you peel them off the bed prior to sex you even give some of the bigger ones a mock-cuddle or turn them to face the wall so they can't see what you're getting up to.

What it says: Pseudo-infantile? Yes. Desperate to register your adorability factor? Yes. Sad and scared? Possibly. This dumbing-down can serve several purposes, meaning that you're a lot more calculating, scheming and manipulative than these little stuffed toys might suggest. You're showing your new conquest that he will need to join the queue of adoring fans, plus the childlike nature of your trophies hints at what's known as pseudo-infantile re-motivational techniques, which describes the way that a smaller ape that is threatened by a larger ape will often perform baby ape body language in a bid to re-motivate or distract the larger ape, and manipulate it into doing something other than rip the baby ape's throat out. In human terms it means: you're playing the cute kid in a bid to be treated with kindness and not hurt. Ever. But this is because, when inevitably you the teddy child turn into you the Bride of Chucky and display your ruthless, egocentric side, you do the hurting and you dump the guy who added to your collection for new meat with an account at Clinton cards. You're often likely to talk in a baby voice and you can make an adorable, loyal mate. But you can also be thoughtless and selfish when it suits.

The Dog Basket

You share your bed with an assortment of animals: dogs, cats and possibly small children. It's communal sleep-in time at your house and the more the merrier, as long as there's room on the bed. You have a manky top blanket in a bid to pay some form of homage to hygiene but in reality the pets all know you're a sucker for a pair of doleful eyes and have dibs on all the hot spots under that duvet.

What it says: You're chaotic, friendly and ultimately a non-assertive push-over. Every week you vow to ban kids and pets from the bedroom so that you can finally have sex with your partner but in reality it never happens because until you place a lock on the door you know the critters will keep coming in for their sleep-overs. The point is you really love the communal sleep-thing. It's a throwback to prehistoric times, when animals and humans slept together for warmth and safety, and these are the core values for you. As much as you moan you adore all the snoring, shuffling about, smelliness and general body cosiness. You're a loving, caring and giving person and never in need of a lecture on the work–life balance because you already have things sorted.

The Futon

In many ways this bed is the antithesis of the Dog Basket bed. Futon beds are frugal, usually lonely and Trappist monk-like affairs and are the nearest thing to sleeping on the bare floor. They're the least grounded of beds, being easily moved, which defies even the act of tucking sheets or blankets in to create a semblance of permanency.

What it says: You have strong scruples, values and principles and adore the yoga/Zen life ethic. You're happy to suffer for your art and even find conspicuous comfort in something that triggers guilt. Why sleep on a bed when there are less fortunate people sleeping under cardboard on the streets? You like to create the idea that you have no ties and are a free spirit and this is true as very few people would be willing to share a bed like this unless they are either drunk or homeless. You are a good citizen even though you consider yourself a citizen of the planet rather than a particular postcode. You can come across as rather superior, especially when arguing that there should be the death penalty for all 4x4 owners.

In an era of central heating it should make sense that the fireplace vanish from the urban interiors landscape to be replaced with TVs or sound systems. But the mantelpiece is one dinosaur of décor that refuses to become extinct. Estate agents place 'original fireplace' top of the list of features that sell and home owners often uncover previously boarded-up fireplaces to return them to their role as the central feature of the room. And as old-fashioned as the word sounds, it's the mantelpiece that dominates once again.

WHAT YOUR MANTELPIECE SAYS ABOUT YOU

The mantelpiece first became a feature of homes in Europe around the twelfth century. Up until that point most homes had fires in the middle of the dwelling space. Today's 'self-shelf' where we display decorative items and mementoes from our lives came from the Renaissance as grand homes used chimneys to boast of their wealth through sculpture and design. The chimney – and the mantelpiece – became the focal point of the room and were a means of showing off. Today we have central heating to ensure we stay at an ideal temperature throughout the chillier months of the year. But the sale of fire surrounds is booming even in the most cutting edge of designer apartments. Why?

Well, the relationship between man and fire is part of our evolutionary programming: fire was vital for food preparation, for warmth and as a central meeting point for your tribe. Therefore a fire source, or even a virtual fire source, has been hard-wired into our make-up and we still have fire as central focus or even the 'heart' of every home. A mantelpiece even without the fire inside it, signals the place of congregation in a home. The TV might be where your brain rests but the fire is where you place your body and your soul. No wonder the newest spot for the plasma screen is hanging above the fireplace where the mantel mirror or flying ducks would once have held court – the requirements of brain and body have been fulfilled. Your mantelpiece is like your spiritual altar and what you chose to adorn it with reveals your self-regard and your perception of your standing and status, or what you would like it to be.

And for those of you who don't have a fireplace or mantelpiece, look for your pseudo one. Homes without a mantelpiece are often homes where people congregate around that other symbol of fire, the oven. Even in a modern house or flat it's unusual for some form of virtual fireplace to not have been created or built. The current trend is for oblong holes filled with large pebbles, concealing gas burners that simulate an open fire, albeit in a cold, ethereal way, or even some form of painting or print to be hanging there as a central focal point, often depicting flowers to bring a similar expression of nature into the home.

Photos

There's something very spiritual about placing ancestors and relatives around the fire. Fire keeps us alive, but it can also mean death as it's often the fire of a cremation that consumes our body at the end of our lives; the fireplace is therefore a constant reminder of both safety and danger. This shows you take family and relationships very seriously indeed and it also shows your key role models and intellectual and emotional coaches in life. This is the area your eyes turn to during meaningful moments and having an emphasis on blood relatives creates a feeling of genuine wholeness and ego. If your photos contain shots of dead relatives you like, your current lifestyle is tinged with reminders of more old-fashioned values and mortality. Although you will accept change in your life there is a constant and very strong thread of morality within you that you hope to pass on to your kids like a wooden wardrobe reeking of mothballs. If your pictures are all current then your desire to create strong family life means you've almost super-glued your kids and spouse to the sofa in a bid to create unity in the way you knew it as a kid. You constantly bemoan the fact that your children don't share their entertainments with you in the way you shared with your parents when you were a child but you forget that you grew up in a three-TV-channel society where watching brain-numbing programmes like *George and Mildred* was compulsory.

Keepsakes

If pebbles, sea-shells, grim-looking objets d'art cobbled together by the kids, dried flowers, old cards and ornaments litter your mantelpiece you're a sentimental soul who takes a very active approach towards creating happiness in your life. This should make you a dyed-in-the-wool sunny little optimist but sadly it can also mean you cherish these symbols of pleasure because most of your fun is in the past or – sadly – in your imagination. Genuine high-rollers in happiness terms are usually too busy enjoying themselves to hoard objects in this way, or they tend to have such a high expectation of on-going pleasure that they see no reason to collect today what will be plentiful enough tomorrow.

Travel Trophies

Your nan and granddad would have displayed these knick-knacks along their mantelpiece to show that their approach to life was cosmopolitan despite the fact they had lived in their home for a million years. Hence their china pots with Llandudno painted on the side, laughing cats from Chichester and spill-holders with leprechauns peeking around the side, all caringly brought back by either themselves or their neighbours as a gift from what used to be seen as the edge of the universe. You – of course – would never be so crass, which is why your precious ornaments and trinkets are even more hilarious. By placing your African tribal masks or wood carvings, Thai embroideries or Egyptian pottery on your mantelpiece you attempt to flesh yourself out into a rounded, urbane human being. With these trophies you aim to show – just like your gran did – that you are more than your boring appearance suggests. You have safaried, pyramided, camel-ridden and tent-resided but in your rush to boast to guests you have forgotten one thing. While your grandparents took trips to Devon with a sense of trepidation, you just hauled your bum into that economy air seat and complained that your complimentary diet cola had too much ice in it.

When it comes to 'the smallest room in the house' it's not so much the décor that reveals clues about your personality as the name you choose to call it. For many of us it's the embarrassment factor that leads to rubbish euphemisms but once selected they tend to stay with us throughout our lives, no matter how inappropriate or out of place they sound . . .

WHAT YOUR NAME FOR THE TOILET SAYS ABOUT YOU

If anything defines your class, age and attitude to life and sex better than the name you use for the toilet then we've yet to see it. This bodily function induces an air of enduring embarrassment that makes it the perfect breeding ground for inner-child 'leakage'. Potty etiquette is so diverse and cultures change from house to house, yet we still cling to terms we were taught to use as a child. Like sex, using the 'correct' word is often deemed ruder than stupid euphemisms. So what do you say when you want to pay a visit to the 'smallest room in the house'?

'The Bog'

Possibly too much information here as your term will induce thoughts of quagmires of effluent, suggesting you're about to void your bowels in spectacular style. Strangely though this word has a ring of poshness about it, suggesting a public-school education. However, the fact you're still using this schoolboy giggle-inducer suggests you're emotionally stunted. You adore sex because you still think it's very naughty and you probably have a job in the City or in law. Anything mucky makes you laugh and you still think farting is an awfully clever way to impress members of the opposite sex.

'The Lavatory'

Okay, so it's technically correct but it's still quite formal and rare. Even speaking the word makes your facial expression go a bit prim and that's exactly what you are: precise, logical and in many ways rather old-fashioned. You like to suppress your animal, primal side as much as possible and by doing so manage to give the impression of being anal and pompous.

'The Khazi'

You inherited this one from the armed forces, which means you've either been in service or have a military mind. You're loud, assertive to the point of aggressive and worry little about who you offend when you do open your mouth. You're probably quite old, too.

'The Loo'

This word manages to be a combination of naff and twee at the same time. You do mean well and try hard not to offend people and in doing so probably end up pissing quite a few people off, especially in the workplace where you try to avoid office politics to the point where, because you side with everyone in turn, you're seen as two-faced and bitchy. You'd describe yourself as sweet and honest or genuine and you probably use this word because you think it's the neatest, shortest euphemism that will cause minimum attention when you want to go and have a pee.

'The Ladies'

If you're a woman you're terminally polite and olde-worldy; if you're a man you're a sexist supremacist who feels a female's place is at home in front of the stove. This term should have died a natural death but it still endures. If you refer to a trip to the toilet as using the Ladies or the

Gents you're invoking parasols and twirly moustaches each time you need to urinate. As this is probably the least ladylike or gentlemanly part of your day you're not one to face life head-on or with total honesty. You prefer to ignore or sideline anything you don't like and hope it will go away. Your knack of giving ultra-polite names to very basic bodily functions probably extends to your sex life as well, which you may well refer to as 'playing ladies and gentlemen'.

'The Bathroom'

This term seems to have winged its way across the Atlantic, or should we say *crept* across, as it's one of the politer little euphemisms for the place that you want to go to pee or poo.

Calling it the bathroom makes the unsavoury sound clean and antiseptic, as though you're going to bypass all the nasty stuff and just get in there to have a good old hand wash or shower. This misleading terminology makes you a polite but easily shockable person who would rather find themselves being directed to the wrong room than ask for what you really want. You are a direct relative of the person who calls it 'The Cloakroom'. Good luck to you if you find yourself busting for a pee but standing facing a room full of coats.

'Spending a Penny'

The money you forked out on Botox was wasted because by using this term you let everyone know you pre-date decimal coinage. This term harks back to the days when toilet doors were fitted with a slot that took a penny for entry so by using this term you're clinging to the memory that bodily functions have to be paid for – and one can only assume what that says about your attitude to sex.

You're a fan of the public toilet too, but in many ways you come across socially as ultra-polite and inoffensive. This phrase is also used to reassure others that you're not off to do anything more serious or hard-core in the toilet, so you have a strong social identity and a hatred of doing anything inappropriate or offensive.

'The Toilet'

You're honest, open and a little bit bland. Your body is something to be obeyed rather than thwarted or repressed and you're confident enough to eat when you're hungry and sleep when you're tired. You have a healthy self-confidence and a dislike of people who waffle. There's a strong streak of sensibility to you but you can also be outrageous and fun-loving with the best of them. It's just that you know when to stop.

'The Smallest Room In The House'

You're polite to the point of neurosis. It suggests you have a contradictory personality as you use this phrase to be quaint and quasi-invisible as you trot off to the loo and yet it's one of the longest terms to use, so will attract the most attention. It's the mother of all euphemisms in many ways as it deflects attention to the size of the room rather than its usage.

'Tinkle House'

You see the whole of life through the eyes of a child, dangerously so in many ways. It's dangerous, but more to others than yourself as people within earshot are liable to suffer bouts of projectile vomit whenever you open your mouth. You like toilet roll holders made of lace and loo brushes shaped like puppies. To you there is nothing nasty in life that can't be sugar-coated with a few twee words or phrases. What this term really says about you though is that life scares you rigid and you spend much of your time in deep denial. Your escape route from everything nasty is via childhood memories. You have a dislike of confrontation and a fear of being disliked.

'The Crapper'

Your childhood was completely different from that of the 'Tinkle House' insofar as you emerged from it brash, offensive and insensitive of others' feelings and yet you're still a big kid at heart. You claim to excel at sex but that's only if it's basic: you go for stamina and quantity rather than quality and expertise. You have a tendency to be Alpha and dominate a group but you rule by physical strength and noise rather than job status or intellect.

'I Just Need a Wee . . .'

Saying exactly what you intend to do once you make it to the toilet is way too much information, but you clearly dread that anyone might think you're off for what you probably refer to as 'a poo' that for you declaring your intentions is both vital and preferable to any misunderstanding.

You need to ask yourself whether this poo-phobia is symptomatic of anything more troubling to do with sex? Do you ever find sex messy or distasteful? Ponder hard. It could mean you need therapy.

Of course, much of this chapter has been based around your social or home life, where friends might find it terminally adorable that you 'nip off for a tinkle' or store your family photos on the mantelpiece alongside the gas bill. If you're going to be yourself it will be at home where you do it, leaving visitors to your personal palace bewildered by those gnomes in the garden, that bed groaning with furry teddies or the hallway strewn with coats, shoes and hats. But what about the professional version of yourself? With the days of bowlers, buttonholes and rolled-up brollies well behind us, the workplace landscape and the image that goes with it has become much more open to individual interpretation, making your choices and selections far more revealing than they would have been decades ago, when a bright bow tie was enough to start something of a riot.

The next chapter helps you pick your way through the minefield that is the average office or workspace, letting you know exactly what that dying pot-plant on your desk or those vintage trainers lying beneath it are telling your colleagues and your boss about your talents, attitudes and capabilities.

5

HIDDEN MESSAGES IN YOUR WORK LIFE

The workplace is riddled with semi-mystical animal behaviours and subliminal communications that are much more important than the formal methods of contact like meetings and presentations. While your emails are largely unread, misunderstood or even mistranslated, your behavioural signals will ring out as clear as the office fire alarm on practice day. Your workspace, eating habits and dress accessories are all far more intense in terms of defining YOU than they would be outside work, where clothing is more informal and you spend less time vegetating or decorating your space with ancient Styrofoam cups or pot-plants that are well past their prime. We have fewer dimensions in business because we mask more and attempt to project a businesslike 'ideal'. Beware. Fewer dimensions means more radical judgements . . .

HOME FROM HOME: WHAT THE STATE OF YOUR DESK SAYS ABOUT YOU

Analysis of 'desk styles' and behaviours invariably brings about the shout 'It might look chaotic but I know where everything is', in which case we will happily call you a liar. Or it could be that you work for a company with a 'clean desk' policy, meaning the tidiness on display is the result of regulation rather than preference. Hot-desking was one of the most ghastly workplace inventions of the eighties that still currently has a hold on workplace culture, meaning you have no real home to call your own and risk finding someone else's gum stuck directly above where you put your knees. Like all good animals, though, you will leave your signature scent on any space you nest in, albeit for a few hours at a time. Serious nesters have the edge, however. Do you sit at your desk from 9 a.m. until 6 p.m. or beyond? Do you eat, work and even sleep there, spending far longer in harness than you do in your own home? Then your desk will hold secrets more profound and culturally defining than Tutankhamun's tomb.

Desk data

In a study for office supplies firm Avery one in ten people used the excuse that once the desk is tidied they can 'never find anything'.

The Concealed Chaos Desk

While the work surface of this desk looks relatively neat and orderly, suggesting a calm and logical approach to work, what lurks beneath is another matter. Glance into the hell that is your kneehole and there will be spare shoes or fitness gear, bags, food, rats (well, maybe not rats but they would feel at home if they did pitch up) and many things that you have long since forgotten existed.

What it says: Your life is a bit of a façade and you live under the constant fear that someone, sometime, is going to suss you out. You try hard to fit in with corporate ideals but your time-management techniques evaporate by the minute, meaning the odd moments you do have free are spent on dark wonderings about 'What am I really here for?' On the plus side you have a certain 'suppressed maniacal' charm, a bit like a pair of figure-controlling underpants that create a sleek silhouette but threaten to split at the seams if you try to do too much in them. You are professional and formal one minute but able to laugh at yourself the next. You adore your family but the most you tend to see of them is via that photo in your desk drawer.

The Trophy Hunter Desk

Everything about this desk says power and achievement, from the designer pen tub to the framed photos and awards. Your desk is more about display than work and you might even relegate your PC to a side desk rather than block the view between you and your visitors.

What it says: Your ego is clearly in constant need of stroking, however you come across to those you work with as bullishly confident, if not arrogant and highly competitive. Nobody at work really trusts you, although many admire you. Some feel uncomfortable around you because you dismiss the cliché of Britons' unassuming modesty, preferring to display your successes where all can see. You are determined and highly strategic and your persona can change to suit those strategies so some will see you as charming while others may consider you curt or even rude. You have a capacity for impatient outbursts and will even find yourself taking on too much work purely because you think no one else will handle it as well.

The Cuddly Desk

This desk might have one cuddly toy or it could house a whole tribe of them because when you start to display a liking for all things childish it's amazing how many turn up. You own glittery or tassled pens and you would happily have stickers around your screen too, except the boss banned them thanks to your habits.

What it says: You clearly feel a sense of threat about the work environment as a whole and this 'cuddle-bunny' guise is done to ward off attack as well as alerting the emergency services. Your vulnerable, unthreatening image is a ploy, of course. Deep down you are as tough as cow hide but this aura of cuteness is something you can hide behind when the going gets tough. In other words, you can give it but you can't take it.

The Family Space Desk

Your desk and the walls around it bear testament to your family life via a display of kiddie paintings, messages (I luv Mummie), photos of the dog and hand-made tokens of affection like satin hearts or plasticine cups.

What this says: You epitomise the working man/woman's vision of work–life balance, placing mementoes of your home life around your work area to both display to colleagues the fact you do have another life, and to signal to yourself that there is life and hope outside the office. If all this paraphernalia is current, chances are you work long hours and return home riddled with guilt, although the fact the au pair has been under strict instructions to film first steps, first words etc means you can catch up via laptop during your commute. If the photos are old, as in you still have nursery shots although your offspring is now on his/her gap year, you really have missed out on the 'life' side of the work–life thing and the word balance doesn't nearly apply. Soon you will be cutting your spouse's head out of all those photos with nail clippers as you divide up spoils for the divorce while wondering how that angelic little child on the baby bouncer turned into something more like a rehab-bound pop star on a bad day.

The Eccentric Desk

You work hard. You get results. You even seem sane and grounded. So why the assortment of show-stoppingly odd 'bits' on your desk, especially those you stuck around the frame of your computer screen? If you're an eccentric you love to mark your territory with an assortment of life's flotsam, including those things that have meaning for you but which serve to confuse everyone else. And this is your point, really. Those toys, slogans, stickers and pebbles are all trophies that you hoard for a reason. That teaspoon glued to your screen-surround and the pile of plastic paperclips that forms a pyramid on top of your printer are supposed to raise eyebrows and give out the idea that you're deeper than you appear on the surface.

What this says: All this stuff is very 'line of vision', meaning you have displayed it in places where it will ambush your subconscious and bombard it with corrective messages. If your company and job are so formal and dull that you are trying desperately to remind yourself that 'I am not a number, I am a free man!' the most simple solution is to hand in your notice. Why are you spending so many years of your life in a job that clearly has no outlet for your individuality? But if chucking in your job makes you anxious this suggests a form of emotional self-mutilation because when all is said and done you chose to be there. No matter how large the mortgage and kids' school fees finding a career that better suits your personality will be better for you than feeling unfulfilled in a job you hate. Staying put suggests you tend to take the soft, safer options in life but then spend a lot of time bemoaning the result. You probably have plans, like entering for *Big Brother* or *Britain's Got Talent* or even writing that best-selling novel but you also have a very long list of excuses about why you never got the entry form off in time or how you can only write when it's quiet/calm/sunny or there's an eclipse going on etc.

If you are in a job that offers a good outlet for your eccentricities, like an ad agency or PR company that encourages 'blue sky thinking' then it could be that you are using a very useful visual trigger for this part of your brain, although it might be fruitful to change the items or photos once the edges have started to curl or dust begun to settle.

The Nothing Functions, Hair Shirt Desk

From a distance your desk looks like a hive of industrial activity, cluttered with a useful arrangement of tools and paperwork. On closer inspection though it's obvious to everyone but you that nothing works, matters or is in the right place. Your telephone cable is so twisted you have to bend like Quasimodo to make a call, the phone itself is on the wrong side of the desk and not one of the pens in the pot works, apart from the yellow highlighter.

What it says: You're scatty enough to be a cheering presence in the workplace but there's some part of your soul that is into self-flagellation. Otherwise why would you allow your work station to be so inconvenient, uncomfortable and blisteringly un-functional as your one obviously is? Your day is reactive and nothing really goes to plan but you do manage to get things done, albeit not without a fair amount of discomfort and martyrdom. You bring jobs in right up to the deadline, although nobody can ever accuse you of letting them down. It's just that you could work more comfortably if you just spent an hour or so sorting those little inconveniences out in your life. The same applies to life outside the office, where you let things go for the sake of what you refer to as 'a quiet life', only it isn't, is it? It's a chaotic life that could be improved with some tweaking. Perhaps you need to ask yourself why you keep picking up that pen that doesn't work and then putting it back just so that you can repeat the whole unrewarding process just like *Groundhog Day*. You're virtually enjoying failure, suggesting that it holds some comfort for you. Fear of success usually means some form of low self-esteem. Get yourself some new pens, unravel that phone wire and maybe get a partner that isn't dysfunctional as well.

The OCD Desk

This is neat to the point of obsessive and you find yourself straightening pens and lining your mouse up with your keyboard on a regular basis.

What it says: Anal behaviours like this are all about control, meaning you feel you have none in your life. Your job and home life may be full of high achievements and your career may be impressive, but deep inside you feel the pressure of success keenly, to the point where keeping a lid on things has become essential. Tidiness is a way of coping with change so keep straightening things and measuring things but when it gets to the point that the meeting becomes unbearable because Nigel from Account's folder is unaligned with his name tag then it's time to seek professional help.

Perfection infection

If you really can't stop tidying your desk you might have what psychologists have dubbed 'perfection infection', a complaint caused by our need in an ultra-critical modern society to do everything perfectly.

The Health Hazard Desk

Your desk could win you the title of office slob of the year because you spend so much time living at it that it's covered with empty mugs, food crumbs, tissues, lip-balm tubes, half-eaten sushi boxes, hair-scrunchies, deodorant sticks and baby-wipes that it could sustain all remaining human life for at least one week in the event of a nuclear war.

What it says: You spend too long at your desk doing too little work. If they offered a commode version of your office chair you'd be ordering it on eBay because – once you're in harness in the morning – there's very little that will get you out of it before it's time to go home, apart from death. The Japanese have a word for dying from over-work, calling it *karoshi* and that will be your fate if you're not careful. Although it has to be said that although you spend long stretches in harness many minutes/hours go by spent gazing at your screensaver in a kind of prolonged daydream, rather than saving the universe with your intellectual skills. The worse thing about your desk is your claim that you 'know where everything is', yet when someone asks for the most basic document your search takes ages and involves rooting through the same wrong piles of rubbish every time.

The I Can't Believe It's A Desk Desk

This desk has a certain Hobbit-like quality to it, being covered with foliage or other decorative devices to the point where its basic function is in complete denial.

What it says: You spray your territory but not really in an assertive way. This is more like camouflage, suggesting a deep-rooted fear of work and the people you work with. Some decorations can appear inviting, like cut flowers, although the potential for accidentally overturning the vase and spilling water all over your work means any attraction qualities will be offset by the fact that nobody really wants to come near them. And this could define your general approach to life and relationships – you dress and act in a way to draw attention and attract others but that's undercut by brittleness or air of high maintenance that says hands off. Cut flowers are lovely but they can also symbolise castration! If your decorations are more dead-end – i.e. faded cards or postcards and the kind of dead-stick-in-a-foil-covered-pot pot-plant or cactus – you display a desire to appear caring and nurturing ('That plant's not dead, give it to me, I'll take care of it!') combined with the kind of interest Burke and Hare might have had for anything that is ailing. You are a moaner and a tutter and your dead conservatory desk is a form of reproach against hedonism, capitalism and all things to do with change and improvement. You probably wear cardigans with the sleeves pulled over your fingers, even in summer.

If you fit the profile of the average worker in the UK the odds are you eat your lunch at your desk, staring at your screen as you repel all approaches from colleagues by snarling 'I'm on my lunch break!' So a lot of people will see what you're eating – and judge you by it.

WHAT YOUR LUNCHTIME SANDWICH FILLING SAYS

How many food-related choices do you think we make each day? Most people think that it's around 15. However research shows that it's actually many more than that. In his study Brian Wansink, a professor of Marketing and Applied Economics, found that we actually make a staggering 200 food-related decisions a day, most of them subconsciously.

There are, of course, many competing reasons for the food you choose, including what you can afford, the influence of advertising, what you ate as a child and the limits of what's available.

But quite a lot of research has been done linking food choices directly to our personalities. Neurologist Alan Hirsch took a huge sample of 19,400 people and matched their snack food choices against two well-known personality tests.

His study revealed that there were clear links. Perfectionists, for example, liked to munch on tortilla chips while introverted types had a thing for cream crackers. His studies have even found a link to different choices of ice-cream flavour too. Chocolate chip ice cream lovers are competitive, ambitious and generous while strawberry lovers are logical decision makers.

The rise in eating out and eating on the move has brought our food choices under the critical eye of strangers. The average Briton, for example, spends around £229 annually eating on the go and a survey for officebroker.com recently found that 90% of us mostly eat lunch at our desks. But what are we eating during these public midday displays? Well, despite the rise in lunchtime food like sushi, more than half of us are still eating sandwiches. The lunch sandwich, therefore, has become a gastronomic personality badge advertising more than just our cravings.

The sandwich has a unique role in our lives as being the ultimate in food-to-go. The sandwich is all about what you want to eat (the filling) combined with an edible wrapper (the bread). This makes it part-civilised, part-debauched behaviour and little wonder it was invented as a way to feed while gambling – legend has it that it was the brainchild of the Earl of Sandwich in the eighteenth century as a quick meal, so that he could carry on playing cards.

The BLT

You're likely to be loud and lively. It's the American-style name of this sarnie that really turns you on. If someone offered you a bacon butty you'd think they'd lost their mind but slap some lettuce and tomato in with it and you believe what you're scoffing is the height of chic. You're a label freak, which means your self-esteem isn't quite as solid as you like to pretend, and by hiding behind designer labels you feel you've justified your place in the world. Money is important to you as you like to flash the cash. You're energetic to the point of fidgety but you play as hard as you work.

Cheese and Pickle

No one could accuse you of being pretentious; in fact you're well down the food chain as far as style is concerned. You avoid change, lack any sense of imagination and like to stick to what you know. When you go on holiday you either stay in the UK or visit a spot abroad that you know has a British pub where everyone speaks English. The same rule applies to your tastes in sex, marriage and love. If it ain't broke why fix it? The sad thing is you don't really know what you do like as you stopped experimenting at around the same time as you finished school.

It's an important point that the taste of the pickle drowns the taste of the cheese as it sums up your view on life. The whole point of your food choice, i.e. the cheese, is being lost in translation, which begs the question: Do you really like cheese or not? If you do, why drown its taste? If you don't, why continue to pick it? Confused? We thought so. It's probably how you spend a lot of your time. You're a bit grabby, a bit clumsy and you hate having to wait for anything you want.

Tuna Mayo

You're slick, ambitious and creative. Flirty and bright with a mid-range designer wardrobe and plans to buy a small place in France. You ooze confidence and aspire to the wealthy-but-understated look. You like to think you have a healthy lifestyle, although that gym membership did lapse before you made too many trips. You always intend to do the power-walking/circuit training thing but when it's a choice between the gym or the bar a nice glass of Chablis wins out every time.

Egg and Cress

You know you never grew up but you're happy enough living with your inner child. These sarnies smack of Enid Blyton and lashings of pop but who cares when they taste that good? You don't even mind the fact they smell the office out as you can sit and play computer games by yourself for the rest of the afternoon. You have an enviable habit of ignoring all the stressful things in life and living in the past. For you a disastrous day is finding a bit of egg-shell in your sandwich.

Roast Beef

You're so set in your ways you probably haven't even noticed that we're in a new century. You're principled and dogmatic and probably quite brave or strong. Roast beef sarnies can be a little tough so you also probably have all your own teeth, even though your hair's thinning on top. You're honest and decent and would like to see the return of conscription for anyone who isn't. Your main enemies are hoodies, ring tones and anyone who doesn't use wheelie-bin etiquette.

Prawn

The colour and look of the prawns describes you perfectly. You're pink and funny and a bit more plump than you'd like to be. You're a giggler and young at heart, although you're also quite bright. You like other people and tend to think the best of them until proved otherwise. Paranoia is not in your repertoire because you believe that life's too short. If you don't like something you'll just move around it. You like gossiping better than moaning or whingeing.

Chicken Tikka

Work for you is just something that comes up between TV, holidays and trips to the pub. You're a pack animal, socialising with the same group of friends and the highlight of your year is the trip abroad, usually in a gang and always to somewhere in Spain. You like karaoke and when one of your gang gets married the stag/hen nights are two-week safaris in Europe wearing matching T-shirts.

Healthy Options

You know that a low-fat sarnie has only got about half a calorie less than the bog standard type but it matters not because it makes you feel virtuous, almost to the point where you can chuck in a bar of chocolate and a packet of crisps for good measure. You're full of good intentions and good ideas but somehow you're always too busy to get around to them. You love to party but tend to feel guilty the next day when you remember everything you did. You've somehow managed to convince yourself that alcohol calories don't count.

The Jam Sandwich

If you made this yourself you're frugal and intensely old-fashioned, immune to the seductive charms of healthy options and protein injections. If you bought your jam-sarnie pre-packed you consider yourself cutting edge, ironic and a bit of a rebel. Eating a jam sandwich that did not come out of a Tupperware container is sure to elicit curious comments from colleagues, making you a bit of an attention-seeker who likes to stand out from the crowd. However, the fact that your point of rebellion is retro and childlike signals that you have no desire to court genuine controversy and wouldn't be caught dead wearing facial piercings or edible thongs. The clue that you are something of a sham is revealed in the fact that jam sandwiches only really work if made by the consumer. Allowing someone else to judge the amount, type and thickness of the jam-to-butter ratio and then trusting that it won't have been absorbed into the bread by the time you eat it is unnatural to the point of perverse.

If a life staple like food is linked to basic behaviours like sexual tastes and emotional/infantile motivators (like touch, hugs, food and warmth), it should make sense that there are other choices in your life that are more contemporary and therefore more intellectually revealing. Although your choice of computer was probably made on the basis of some logical decision processes – or was out of your hands, being the one chosen for you by work – the password you choose for it is most definitely not.

WHAT YOUR COMPUTER PASSWORD SAYS ABOUT YOU

Modern technology throws up a whole host of new choices for us. And it's not just the choice of which mobile brand or laptop we choose. Our personalities are revealed in even more basic techno choices like the typeface we choose on our computer, our email address, computer passwords and screensavers.

A survey by the organisers of Info-security Europe, found that the average number of passwords used at work is five per person and along with personal passwords, most people use about 12 passwords every day. It's almost impossible to use a different one for each place that we have to sign in so they often end up conforming to a pattern. A lot of subconscious thought goes into those six to eight characters you choose too. You might think you choose them instantly but the fact that you tend to go for the first thing that comes into your head means that they'll closely reflect what's important in your life. There is also a sense of ownership of them, so we choose something that is a window into what we hold dear.

Lovers

It's very sweet of course. And it shows that you're a loyal sort who is unlikely to stray. But isn't there something just a little bit clingy about this. Do they know? And if so would they think it was charming, obsessive or simply unimaginative? It might be time to put your relationship in perspective and stop letting it consume you.

Work Related

You're someone who simply needs to get out more. Either you're so dull that you can't think of anything more exciting or you're a career-obsessed workhorse who, given the lack of imagination you have shown in your choice of password, is, ironically, never going to reach the top of the corporate tree. In fact, the opposite may be true: you feel stuck in a rut but haven't the drive to get out of it. To you sex has its time and its place.

Numbers

Believe it or not one in ten people simply use numbers for their computer passwords. If you haven't met them then it may be just as well. If this is you then you should already be aware that you're someone who knows the price of everything and has a very regulated life in which all the Ts are crossed and the Is dotted. But you can be logical to the point of humourlessness. Life for you has, in many ways, become a boring balance sheet.

Your Name or Nickname

Confident, egotistical and driven. You want to get on in life. In fact, you're desperate to achieve, well, anything. But while you may have flair and a can-do attitude you can also turn into a selfish so-and-so under stress or when you feel cornered. While you pretend to be interested in others you know that self-obsession is consuming you.

Private Passions: The 'Fantasist' Category

If this is you, you're self-obsessed and you pick words like 'sexy', 'stud', 'goddess' and 'slapper'. This could refer to the person you're having an affair with or, at worst, a personal fetish. You're clearly someone who loves risk to the point of dangerousness. You probably like adventure on holiday rather than staying on a beach, and have wild sexual fantasies. But soon this carefree attitude is going to get you into trouble. And when you think about it, you probably want to get into trouble, either just for the thrill of it or so you can stop all this pretending.

Pet Names

A nostalgic type, you surround yourself with mementos of the past and probably spend time poking round car boot sales and markets hunting down retro goods. In fact you have been thinking about setting up a website dedicated to an obscure subject or hobby. Other people just don't understand you so you keep your sensitive side hidden, only revealing your innermost thoughts to the dog, cat . . . or chinchilla.

Favourite Band, Football Team, etc

You're a romantic. To you work and life is one long determined fight to stay happy and positive. Okay, so you're a bit too trusting in relationships but when you are let down you just pick yourself up again and carry on. There isn't really much of a problem with this as long as everyone likes your upbeat approach to life. The only downer is that those who don't like it think you're a gullible sucker.

The Cryptic

You go for words that mix lower- and upper-case letters with numbers and punctuation marks to create intricate, cryptic passwords. This air of intellectual mystery defines you as being pretentious, arrogant and more than a little paranoid; you'll have grandiose ideas about the value of what it is you're protecting. The deeply rich rarely bother taking huge precautions, tending to be frighteningly casual with a strong air of fatalism. It's the stingy paupers who tend to create the 'Temple of Doom' around their worldly goods.

And it's not just your password . . .

WHAT YOUR EMAILS SAY ABOUT YOU

Research at the University of Leipzig in Germany showed that email addresses can speak volumes. In the study a panel of 100 students were asked to guess the personalities of 600 young adults simply by looking at their email address. The panel's guesses matched up with a personality test the owners of the email addresses had completed. But what about the style of the content in our emails? This too is a rich feeding ground for analysis.

Shouty

The stress and pent-up anger fairly leaps off the page! You tend to write in capitals with virtually no punctuation at all. There are regular spelling mistakes and lots of abbreviations as you hammer your message home with as much emphasis as possible. Your emails are either sent on the crest of the angry wave because you find bashing away at the keys is a kind of therapy, or you send them off from home in the early evening after a tipple when you've started to get belligerent and resentful. You hate to be ignored and will do anything to make your point. You lose your temper easily but forgive and forget once you've blasted off. You're decisive and will speak your mind even if it hurts. Quiet people make you twitchy.

Long-winded

You write emails like other people write novels, page after page until your recipient gets RSI from pressing the scroll-down button. You're not a natural speaker and might even seem quite shy but when your audience is captive you suffer from verbal diarrhoea. You tend to over-think and over-analyse and have trouble getting to the point. You know you're boring people but you still can't stop until you've got it all off your chest. Emails are a kind of therapy for you. It doesn't matter whether they get read, it's more about opening up your soul and getting it up there on the screen.

Concise

You tend to send one-liners and are therefore decisive and driven. You're never in one place for long enough to think about writing more. Several of your emails have contained one word: Yes or No. This makes sense to you as you're time-managed and frugal with the hours. However you do tend to get puzzled when other people accuse you of being cold or rude. You don't suffer fools gladly and will get impatient with anyone who waffles or dithers. You can be bossy in your sex and social life and might even have been caught checking your watch over your partner's shoulder as you make love.

Exclamation Marks!

Your emails are expressive and lively and dotted with exclamation marks. You use these to diffuse any suggestion you're being bossy or overly professional. You like to be liked, and if this means people think you're a lightweight, so be it. You bound through life looking for positives like Pollyanna but you're also easily hurt when you get criticised or let down and this can emerge as sulking or other childlike displays.

Flirty

You're notorious for your email flirting, banging off sexy or saucy messages at the drop of a hat. This gives the impression that you're the office lothario but in fact nothing could be further from the truth. For you, emails are a virtual-reality thing. When you're tapping at your keyboard you're doing the equivalent of daydreaming. In reality, when you meet the object of your affection face-to-face you're a different proposition altogether. Shy and diffident you're no longer even sure you fancy them and so spend a lot of your time trying to get out of dates and commitments you make. You're a dreamer and a poet but you're mostly a figment of your own imagination. When life catches you up you run off in the opposite direction.

Jokey

On the surface you appear to be up-beat and vigorous, with humour being a sign of 'normality' in most people's books. However there is a clear difference between some-one who behaves in a humorous way and someone who sends joke emails, and most of this difference centres around the undeniable fact that the tone of any email is always dictated by the perception of the reader, meaning you are clearly aware that your comments could be judged to be either uplifting or deeply insulting, especially the ones you would mark out as sarcastic. It's likely then that you are a bit of a power-broker, using your 'humorous tone' as a whip that you crack above colleagues' heads, making comments and even insults that you can explain away as leg-pulling if needed.

Or maybe you're the kind of email joker who circulates recycled humour to everyone on your mailing list, meaning maiden aunts get copied in on the 'Two monkeys mating' gag along with your more risqué best friends. This is humour by proxy meaning you're using other people's jokes to enrich and bolster your own comic profile suggesting that – in reality – you don't have one.

Despite the fact that working from a PC has meant that working from home is now an option for a great many people, the seductive lure of the commute proves just too powerful for the majority of us. Commuting means crowds and crowds means danger in animal terms, which means that being crushed into a metal tube with a load of stranger animals should place us in a state of fear arousal. But evolution is a wonderful thing and we have acquired psychological coping mechanisms to prevent us all from getting the screaming ab-dabs en route. The trick is to switch off the conscious mind and find a diversion to help us ignore the potential dangers that surround us. Bring on the free newspaper or that dog-eared magazine . . .

WHAT YOUR COMMUTING HABITS SAY ABOUT YOU

Assuming you travel by public transport the chances are you spend your journey time in a state known as 'dog-facing'. This means you use visual and mental methods of coping with periods of your life that are not only in limbo but also in a state of preparation and survival. Underground habits are especially dominated by this suppression of your survival response as you sit or stand crushed into a metal tube way below the surface of the earth with complete strangers, most of whom you instantly distrust. Under these close quarters it would be virtually suicidal to employ eye contact or – heaven forbid – the normal human greeting and safety rituals like smiling or shaking hands. Which leaves you with no option but to pretend 'not to be there', lost in your own world with your eyes either fixed on to an advert, closed in mock sleep or reading a book or magazine.

Over-ground commuters are far more sociable although there are many war-like rituals concerning space and territory. They are more likely to perform workplace rituals to enforce spatial ownership, setting out their laptops and paperwork or doing deals on their mobile phones. This means they can retain the kind of status they enjoy at work, even exaggerating it by becoming 'space bandits', pushing legs, papers and other equipment into other commuters' territory and dominating the air space by speaking loudly on their phones.

Drivers already exist in their own space, being lords of everything they survey once they are behind the wheel. Unlike other commuters this means they adopt an unreal sense of omnipotence, treating their car as a personal chariot and seeing other drivers' behaviour as personally demeaning, leading to bouts of road rage. It is now illegal to do most things in the car apart from drive but public transport-users have virtually no restrictions, making your commuting habits especially revealing.

The Book Reader

Reading a book is the ultimate-but-one stage of removing yourself from the outside world. There is virtually no sharing with this method of time-spending, meaning you announce to those around you that you are completely closed to outside stimulus. Not only is your mind occupied but so is your imagination, while your eyes perform a long-term cut-off gesture but without the apparent rudeness of sitting with them closed or staring at the floor. A book has the capacity to make you look both normal and faintly intellectual, with an ability for long spans of rapt attention that a TV viewer or magazine-reader would not appear to have.

The News Reader

This is currently more like a team sport or flash-mob event, thanks to free papers that mean everyone tends to read the same things at roughly the same time. So even though you're lost in print your mind shows some enjoyment of team activity. You've all tutted at the same headlines and you've all read the same horoscopes. It's the broadsheet readers who are the commute-read rebels, insisting on retaining old standards while poking out eyes and issuing paper cuts to the faces of all the crushed-in travellers around them. Gruff, selfish and hugely opinionated.

The 'Real Life' Magazine Reader

There's a snobbishness that comes into play with commute-reading that doesn't really have a place in other locations. While a newspaper-reader appears tuned in and keen to update on his/her world and book-reader seems intellectual and remote, 'human-story' magazine-reader just sits looking rather dumb as he or she vacuums up the kind of 'My Rottweiler Ate My Kidney' features that all good life mags are full of these days. While fashion or gossip mag women manage to look elegant as they flick through fashion pages, commuting with a human story mag suggests you actually enjoy poring over stories of tumours the size of watermelons.

Eating

For many commuters the journey is all about grub, despite the fact that a less appetite-friendly environment has yet to be invented. Like sleeping as you travel, eating is a behaviour that is completely at odds with many of your survival instincts as it renders you both defenceless to and yet open to attack from other animals, most of whom fight to eat. This marks you out as a rebel with low levels of social empathy. Sitting in silence with strangers, before bringing out a Tupperware box and masticating your way through the contents is peculiar behaviour and should feel so. Your desire to scoff should be tempered by the social pressure to share, which of course you can't, without looking potty. The other animals around will still be angry at your act of non-share selfishness and be unable to allow you to eat without staring at each item of food as it goes into your mouth.

Listening to an iPod

This is the most 'non-present' way to commute, with your body being in the carriage or bus seat while your mind and ears are off with the latest band. Music gives a surreal feel to your travelling, making the commute seem like the soundtrack to some foreign language thriller. By deleting one of your key senses you show a wilful disregard of potential danger as you have effectively removed yourself from life and all its threats.

Instead of embracing life fully you like to keep your own space, thoughts and 'me' world. Music is great but this is like refusing to share biscuits you are enjoying, only worse. Hearing the vague tin-tin-tin of someone else's iPod can be dangerously like torture for many people close by. So you take steps to remove yourself from the society you live and travel in but instead of removing yourself completely you leave other travellers with the aural equivalent of a nasty taste or smell. Anti-social and vindictive?

So, you've discovered all about how the little things in your life will illuminate your personality. But once you've dashed off to change the pictures in your hallway and started searching for a new ring tone for your mobile your next step is to consider how you go about putting this kind of analysis to good use in other areas of your life. Part Two answers that question for you, by transforming The You Code into The *Them* Code.

PART TWO: READING OTHER PEOPLE

6

WORK, FAMILY AND FRIENDS

When you want to analyse behaviours of friends, family and work colleagues it's wise to take your comparisons from the animal kingdom. The workplace is especially rich in tribal rituals, with many zoologists putting this down to the fact that work is the new 'kill' – that is, by going into the business environment and working in teams to achieve blisteringly exciting, adrenalin-pumping goals you're sating your good old hunter–gatherer lusts.

Now there's an obvious flaw glaring out from this thesis in that a large swathe of business people would find it hard to make comparisons between blood-lust on the savannah and a day spent filling the stapler or staring at the screen-saver, but for those moments when you do happen to find yourself celebrating bringing in a new piece of business or not getting attacked by a client or member of the public then you can consider yourself fully in touch with your simian ancestry.

Which goes towards explaining why posters bearing myths like: 'There's no "I" in team!' could in psychological and evolutionary terms be considered to be having a bit of a larf. Your hunter–gatherer forebears formed teams at the same time they switched vegetarian diets for a lifetime of burgers and chicken nuggets, meaning that rather than going off alone to pick nuts they had to form teams to hunt down their meaty prey. Were these teams units of über-bonded loyalty? Probably not. They were individuals motivated by selfish values who realised working alone just wouldn't bring home the Sunday roast. And you can thank God for money, otherwise you'd have to be counting at least one farmer, slaughterhouse worker and super-market stacker in among your closest mates in order to survive.

So despite all those bonding water-cooler chats, generous leaving collections and cockle-warming team-building events where you build rafts, sing songs and play 'Who am I?' until the wee hours, it's vital to remember that your workplace 'team' only forms out of necessity and that necessity is survival.

Meat might have meant group performance and food sharing but it didn't mean friendship and loyalty. Hunting groups tend to be randomly cobbled together and the same is true of most work teams. Hunting groups would probably kill and eat one another if the food ran out and the same is true of most work teams. Start from the basic assumption that they all hate one another and work from that if you want to get an accurate psychological view of your colleagues.

And if you thought being a member of a team was hard try being team leader. A boss is normally someone whose promotion has far exceeded his/her level of competency, meaning they spend all day tucked up in meetings to avoid being sussed as a con.

HOW TO READ YOUR BOSS

The first premise about any boss is that he or she has absolutely no idea what leadership is all about. Any signs of genius or charisma you may have spotted are probably like a baby's first smile: it was just wind.

Smoke and mirrors, then. Disregard the trickery. They don't know how they got there. They don't know what they're doing and they're hoping you won't find out.

Animal bosses are called Alphas and they only get promotion via one route: they are the biggest and the toughest and they assert themselves physically.

Your boss is forbidden from punching, biting and wrestling his or her staff and so what should be a simple hierarchical procedure of thwack, gouge and kill has become a lot more complex. Alphas are so tough one glance will do it and their only fear is getting old or ill because that means physical weakness and defeat. Your boss has the age discrimination laws on his or her side and so can stay in harness until their dotage.

For your boss, then, it is a constant struggle to provide substitutes for brawn-power. Their status is anointed rather than earned and studying the alternative methods they use to assert themselves will give useful insights into the best ways of understanding and handling them . . .

Power by Proxy

This is the suck-up boss who attaches him- or herself to a sponsor, that is, someone higher up the food chain. This sponsor can be a lover, partner or golf-buddy but the threat hovers over the entire team: 'Dis me and I'll tell on you.'

Your proxy boss will spend much of his or her day locked in meetings with this sponsor and will be reluctant to brief the team on the content of those meetings, leading to what your boss sees as 'healthy' levels of paranoia. You will find your boss uses the term 'We' a lot and acquires a smug smile when talking about management issues.

How to Handle Them

Suck-ups have no personal power but adore office politics of the most complex kind. They are only concerned for themselves so gaining advantage means delivering ways to help them boost their profile and power-base. You'll need to appear totally in awe of the people they suck-up to but also to flatter them into believing they are better than these peers. This way you work on a divide and rule basis, getting to drive a subtle wedge between them and their object of suck-up desire. You'll need to become a suck-up's sucker-up to thrive here. Or maybe you should just leave and find a job with a real boss.

Power by Qualification

This boss gained all the right qualifications in management and HR, meaning theory is their only tool of power. Somehow they expected it to all click into place once they met and worked with humanoids for the first time but as most characters in the office failed to fit into their theoretical profiles they started to hammer them into shape instead.

This boss is little more than an over-grown school kid and they are very, very frightened. If you worked in a medical environment, it can be likened to the moment they first raised their nose out of the medical books and took part in their first real operation.

Qualification boss will scuttle back to his/her theories and training every time the complexities of real human life forms kicks in. They thrive on statistics and wield them whenever they can to prove what they are doing is right.

This boss is low-profile and low-charisma but just when you think they've gone away he or she will suddenly rear up with a complex and long-reaching programme of radical change that will be guaranteed to make your eyes water. Fight it and you'll be hacked to death by theory and stats.

How to Handle Them

You can do one of two things here. Look totally and utterly on board with their planned changes and even ask for a role in the new process. Be as flexible as Play-Doh and greet every idea with a whoop of excitement. Their biggest enemy is the Luddite, aka anyone with the experience and sense to spot the fact that what they are planning is dotty.

Or you could fight fire with fire. There's no point being reasonable with this boss. You need to roll up your sleeves and get into the same arena to fight them. Which means next time they quote Harvard business studies from 1999 as a means of endorsing their six-week residential face-painting course for managers you need to retaliate with stats that prove that company profits only rose because 90% of those managers committed suicide within the three-week period following their residential face-painting, therefore axing salaries from the profit-levels.

This boss is also terrified of tribunals, which are like a crucifix to a vampire. Throw the word into conversation as a last resort.

The Jargon Boss

This boss has no idea what he/she is supposed to do and so creates a whole new method of dialogue to pretend they do. This means you enter jargon city every time you have a meeting with them. Jargon is borrowed language and it is stale language, meaning they have no real thoughts of their own. Decades ago they would have been beefing up their presentations by quoting Churchill or Pliny but now they employ phrases like 'We're all singing off the same hymn sheet' or 'It's like nailing jelly to the wall' instead.

How to Handle Them

Remember that smug smile hides real, abject terror. This boss is scared but it's important you don't reveal that you see their fear. For them real reward comes when they realise their ruse has worked and that they have forged an entire universe in their own image, which means walking, moving, dressing and talking like your boss. When you have all cloned yourselves in his or her image their feeling of endorsement and affirmation will be complete. Once you've allowed yourself to be cloned you will find it easier to slip under the radar, using stealth techniques rather than direct challenge or conflict to get your points across. This is an easy boss to handle as long as you imply all new ideas were theirs in the first place. One tip though: remember to drop the ruse as soon as they've been ousted from power. Acting as their mouthpiece long after they've gone is an act that resembles stupidity rather than loyalty.

The Absentee Boss

This boss copies one trait of the Alpha male animal, which is to remove him/herself from the group to sit apart and ruminate. However the Alpha would always be a visible, brooding presence but this boss is just absent and inaccessible.

The first signs that your boss is an Absentee comes when you find all messages and communications come via the PA. Direct contact is no longer on the menu and – given time – this boss will begin to bolster up the chain of command, adding extra layers of management to ensure he or she has no contact whatsoever with the great unwashed that is the workforce. This boss lives and breathes email communication, sending messages to people who are sitting within physical reach. They are always 'in a meeting' and may even reach a level of incommunication which means when you say 'Good morning' to them in the lobby they no longer feel obliged to offer an answer.

How to Handle Them

This boss feels that the hands-off approach is appropriate but – given the fact that we all know a hands-on, involved boss gets the best results – there can only be one conclusion to draw: they are a sociopath, i.e. a boss with a fear or dislike of people. This is a medical condition and you should treat it as such. Never become attacking or sarcastic when he or she fails to respond to your cheery greetings and never try to inflict small talk on the Absentee Boss. Buddy up to the PA and make sure you're caught doing the right thing at the right time on those odd occasions your boss steps down from Mount Olympus to pay a visit. Acquire a boss radar that alerts you so you can be caught working and looking up-beat rather than snoozing at your desk or staring at your screensaver.

The Chummy Boss

This boss has an over-powering desire to be liked, which is always a huge disadvantage for anyone in the seat of power. The Chummy Boss tries to be everyone's friend, chatting, listening and acting in a generally nurturing manner. If this all seems like an employee's dream come true think again. At some stage in your boss relationship you will call upon him or her to take action or make some tough decisions and this boss just won't step up to the plate. Avoidance and prevarication are their middle names and they may even fight fire with fire by becoming a bigger victim that you, as in this scenario:

YOU: Those new sales targets are way too unrealistic. I'm not sleeping at night worrying about them and my job, and the doctor has diagnosed acute stress.

YOUR BOSS: Oh God, tell me about it, I'm under the cosh about performance levels myself. You don't want to have my stress levels!

This boss is impotent in the worst possible way and it's difficult to discuss the problem because they do nothing but agree with you, but then do nothing to fix it.

How to Handle Them

Offer to be their henchman. If they won't take action, use their dithering to your own advantage. Always take a solution along with any problems and ask if it's okay if you do it yourself. They'll agree to anything that means it doesn't have their name on it so take advantage shamelessly only don't expect endorsement or back-up if it all goes Pete Tong.

The Spatial Power-broking Boss

Size does matter when you want to look like a boss but it's the size of the space you inhabit that often seals the deal in modern business rather than body-bulk, however this boss uses space to create an illusion of physical power, spreading, splaying or even isolating themselves to make them look bigger and tougher than they actually are.

They sit with their legs splayed at meetings (aka 'Willy-waving'), they spread into the seats around them, they take the top seat at the board table and they have the biggest office chair and biggest desk.

How to Handle Them

You either need to appear big but on their side, or you need to appear physically diminished in their presence. A wise move would be to diminish short-term, keeping your head literally down until you have their approval and then re-inflating to full height once you have ingratiated your way into their closest team. Timing for re-inflation is vital though. Keep that thought in mind.

Leader of the pack

Hate your boss? In fact, it seems, many of us want to be exactly like them. An American survey found that a massive 49% of employees want to possess similar traits to their boss.

WHAT YOUR BUSINESS MEETINGS SAY

Business meetings are often the boils on the face of industry, expensive, manpower-wasting get-togethers that often achieve nothing apart from a general feeling that there is a problem and something ought to be done about it. In modern business the meeting disease grows by the minute. Now we have the meeting about a meeting, just like we have the phone call to set up a phone call or email to let you know you're going to be emailed.

You might like to think that your business meetings are very much like any other of its genre but each company tends to have its own style of meeting. Here's what yours says about you or your firm:

The Infinity Meeting

These are very like the infinity swimming pools in the US as they stretch out endlessly with no horizon visible. They're given what can be laughingly called a start time but after that it's just on into the afterlife, or however long the chair decides to let them run

Infinity meetings display a sense of waste that is almost criminal, meaning the company or individual who designs them is an egomaniac numbskull who will allow a business to go to hell in a handcart just as long as he or she can sit in a room with a long table, spouting jargon about 'blue sky thinking'.

The Brunch-bar Meeting

These are less meetings and more watering holes as participants either arrive clutching their brown bags of coffee and BLT sandwiches or they hunker in with the tray of coffee and biscuits in their sights. Eating and working is a novel idea but it's also a very bad idea. Food and drink are life's two greatest distractions, so why not scoff pre-meet and therefore focus on the job in hand instead?

Brunch-bar meetings are a sign of a company that might be high on altruistic thinking but low on working to their peak performance. The idea of food treats is hierarchical, going back to the days when bosses had their own dining rooms and special menus while the workers ate slops. Treats should come after the medicine so pander to your infantile tendencies by rewarding yourselves with biscuits once the meeting is over.

The Despot Meeting

These are the meetings that are all about Alpha leadership and political jostling for power. No one really knows what the point of the meeting is because they're all too busy sucking up to the boss. He or she sits in Sir Alan Sugar-esque splendour at the top of the table, using the meeting as a personal monologue with gaps in the middle for grunts of approval. People who get asked their opinion are torn between agreeing totally with whatever's been suggested and getting accused of brown-nosing, or speaking their mind and getting executed instead.

If you hold these meeting you probably consider yourself something of a brilliant entrepreneur when in reality you're just guilty of hiring donkeys so that there's no one in the firm to threaten your position of power. If you work for a company with meetings like this it might be wise to keep your employment options open. Meetings run with a rod of iron means business inflexibility and like trees in a strong wind, it's the supple ones that survive events like recessions.

The Creative Think-tank Meeting

God bless the boss who chooses to dip into the creative side of his or her management team's brains, especially those that stand eagerly in front of a flipchart, clutching a marker pen and asking you all to 'throw some ideas about, be as crazy as possible'. This is optimistic/desperate meeting techniques as everyone knows that whoever really gets in touch with their creative side risks ridicule at best or segregation at worst. The creative mind is a deep, dark dungeon and its use in your average office is questionable. Companies that hold 'creative think-tank' meetings are to be praised for their optimism but the best word to describe them – or you – is 'naïve'.

The Tag Meeting

This is the meeting where people arrive and go as and when they feel it's appropriate, a little like a tag team in wrestling. There's something worryingly vague but corporate about this, as though everyone who works for the firm is just part of one huge organic whole, rather than individuals. Grazed meetings suggest a bit of a hippy commune experience. These meeting are weird and unsatisfying, as well as being unproductive on the whole.

The Telephone Conference

Telephone conferences are so full of good intentions, saving time, effort and deodorant use as there's little if any face-to-face contact going on. Get rid of the echo-effect of the voices, make sure people are only recruited for variety of vocal tone so you can tell one speaker from another and make everyone laugh out loud at anything funny rather than going quiet and you could be onto a winner. Not for the paranoid who will believe in the presence of unseen others. Practical only when used by companies with no sense of humour or the ridiculous. The rest will just find them an endless source of merriment.

The Video Conference

So sensible it hurts in terms of environment and costs, this meeting format has hiccuped its way into usage, largely because it has a kind of JOE 90 surreal, science-fiction quality, and because they make you look and feel like a prize plum.

The problem with this format is it's very levelling in terms of status – that is, it makes everyone look stupid, which is probably why it tends to get neglected by bosses who cherish their sense of cool or power. Someone needs to invent a whole new system of power-projection via video. I suspect it might entail the wearing of crowns and ermine or something to go with the Logie-Baird era stiltedness of the whole genre.

FRIENDS AND FAMILY

But if you thought the corporate landscape was complex enough in terms of animal and evolutionary behaviours, what about that heady emotional brew of personalities known as your friends and family? While work colleagues can be dismissed as a random bunch of characters selected by someone in HR, and should therefore be allowed only limited disruption to your ego, emotions and quality of life, your friends are largely the result of your own selection process, meaning the buck stops firmly at your door.

By and large you get the friends you deserve, which can be a very sobering thought. Like mating and dating the recruitment process was all your own fault. You chose these people to be in your life

Your family is yet another cause for concern. Okay, so you didn't chose them and probably spent your entire adolescence reminding them of that fact, yelling 'I didn't ask to be born!' at regular intervals, but whether you like it or not their blood pumps in your veins and your DNA does whatever DNA does in your bodies (Dance? Swim? Ripple? Lie static? Whatever, it's there in abundance, even in your spit and leg-hair).

What this means is that any criticism you have of your friends and family is probably some form of self-criticism or diverted self-loathing. When you bitch about them you bitch about yourself. It's easier on the ego to find negative traits in friends and family and to criticise them than recognising and criticising those same traits in ourselves. Ego protection is a marvellous thing but it can lead to some vicious internecine battles.

One more thing about family behaviours. Keep in mind that it is always the most annoying habits and traits of your mother and father that you will be inheriting after they've gone. They live on through you like the alien lived on inside the body of John Hurt in the film of the same name. You think they won't burst out of you suddenly and surprisingly, but they will. Not only do we pass on genes, we also pass on that way of looking over the tops of our spectacles and that habit of groaning every time we lower ourselves onto the sofa. Your kids will be the ones who tell you that you're turning into your mum/dad, innocently oblivious to the fact that this birthright will be theirs one day. Birthrights are more about the way you say 'if you're having one' when asked if you want a cup of tea or starting to look for your door keys while you're still on the bus than they are about sprawling estates or inherited talent.

PARENTS

Forget all the psycho-babble about parenting skills, any mum or dad worth their salt will be easily unmasked in behavioural terms via one classic and telling scenario: The Untidy Bedroom. The child's room has long been the Marston Moor of the ongoing civil war that is family life, with parents falling on their own swords as they attempt to assert their power over what is a very trivial and illogical argument.

If you want to analyse your parents or your own parenting style look no further than the following options:

The Enforcer Parent

The order comes out of left field and an order it is: 'You *must* tidy your room, it's a disgrace.' This person believes in pecking order according to the basic queuing system: 'I got here first and you wait your turn until you are a parent before you can start getting some respect.'

There is no question in their mind that being born earlier makes you wiser and all the mistakes from their own youth only enforces their right to reign supreme.

Confrontational and with a direct line to God who tells them they are 'right', this parent will employ every piece of false logic in the book to prove this: 'Your room's a health hazard', 'The germs in there could kill you', 'You'll go blind', etc.

The Discussive Parent

This parent likes to believe they are logical and reasonable and will insist on having regular discussions with their kids, often in a very corporate format – for example, Friday nights around the kitchen table with agendas etc. They believe in rights for all, regardless of age and that everyone has a voice. They may even take votes.

The Discussive Parent can also be identified by their habit of cracking quickly though and this is often down to their high stress-levels caused by their habit of endless and pointless discussions in the workplace. This means discussions will end abruptly once they fail to persuade their kids to agree to their point of view. This leads to you being told to tidy your room 'Because I said so, okay?'

The Nuturing Parent

This parent usually had a tough childhood themselves and believes cosmic order will be restored if they can ensure their own offspring have an idyllic upbringing. This can make them both indulgent and annoying at the same time, often with tragic consequences. They are always identifiable by their battle-cry of: 'But I only want you to be happy', followed by a guilt-inducing reminder of how they were forced to beg for bread-crusts when they worked in a tanning factory. (And that's tanning as in animal hides, not spray-tan).

The Nurturing Parent will ask for the room to be tidied but then set about tidying it themselves once the child is out of the house. This act of 'kindness' is of course a symptom of their passive–aggressive 'victim' personality and everyone but them would see this is asking for trouble. First there is the invasion of the child's space and territory, which is about as great an attack as any parent can launch, then there is the compromising material that the Nurturing Parent will undoubtedly find hidden in the room, like dirty mags and tissues or a diary containing details (often made up) of underage sex parties and accounts of hideous behaviours like drug-taking and self-harm. These discoveries will 'force their hand' meaning that rather than putting everything back where it was and just quietly keeping an eye out they go for the full avenging angel bit, standing in the hallway to terrify the kid on his or her return from school, waving the offending item aloft with a face like Chucky the psychotic doll.

The Child Parent

This parent is too busy working his or her way through their own delayed adolescence to even notice the fact that their kid's bedroom is an unholy tip. The fact is their own living quarters make the kid's room look like The Ideal Home Exhibition. Selfish, egotistical, the only advantage for this parent is that the kid will probably grow up keeping a very neat ship indeed, not only tidying their own room but cleaning up after the parent as well.

You don't grow out of it . . .

Scientists have discovered that it's not only children who row with their parents. We're just as likely to have a set-to with our mum and dad when we're grown up too, according to a study by Michigan University which found that rows don't stop, the subjects of them merely change.

To test the mettle of your friend/family relationships you should start by examining the two extremes of emotion: how and when you argue and how you profess your love, also known as Flashpoints and Affection. Unlike sexual relationships that start from zero and grow and mature through several well-trod stages (Meeting, mating, marrying, divorcing etc) the friends/family scenario tends to be relatively static. Displays of affection and aggravation can be performed one after the other, with classic set-pieces occurring over the same stimulus, creating patterns of behaviour that can remain unchanged or unchallenged for decades. The wonderful thing about these dramas is that they provide rich pickings for analysis, giving strong clues about the overall state of your relationships.

WHAT YOUR ROWS SAY ABOUT YOU

The Time-bomb

These are the rows that start over nothing (Who fed the goldfish, who paid for the last round, etc) but escalate into dramatic set-pieces that rate on the Richter scale. One minute you're discussing shoe size and the next you're telling friends and family that you hate the lot of them and always have done, ever since they refused to pay for your ballet lessons or stole your best pencil in playschool.

These rows define the typical passive–aggressive relationship where you sit on petty angers, resentment and aggressions for so long they fester and grow like bacteria before exploding out to wreak maximum destruction as soon as the lid comes off the 'happy family' box. Ignore the trigger subject as it's not important. What is interesting is why you all prefer to suppress your problems in the first place rather than discussing them reasonably and calmly at source. Ask yourself:

Do I like the feeling of power that saving all this stuff gives me, knowing I am a better person than my friends and/or family? Or:

Do I secretly enjoy being the long-suffering victim? Does sitting on all my grief give me pleasure? Do I tell myself it's a case of 'anything for a quiet life'? And if so, why do I insist on dragging all these old carcasses out at the drop of a hat? Can having huge set-piece rows really be defined as 'a quiet life?'

This is a hooked-on-drama relationship and its participants are addicted to emotional big-stuff, preferring to save up petty problems until they have matured into something far more exciting.

The Rumbling Rumble

Some families exist in a state of constant fight, playing, disagreeing and even wrestling one another on a regular basis. This is usually big-family behaviour and it is often a survival-of-the-fittest culture with kids joining in the play-fights as soon as they're out of the pram. For some families and friendships there is almost no point of agreement and they'll row about everything from J.K. Rowling's middle name to the colour of Eamonn Holmes's hair. In many ways this behaviour fits the animal profile, where survival skills are uppermost and the family learn these skills by mock-fighting with each other.

One aspect of the Rumbling group is that they're famous for their ability to unite to ward off external predators, meaning you'll form a super-strong unit if anyone else attacks you or is rude to you.

The Festive Rumble

Some family groups or friends prefer to make their arguments diary-efficient, meaning they're pencilled in for high days and holidays, especially events like Christmas and weddings.

There's usually a brief 'arming-up' period prior to the event ('If your father gets me another ladyshave again this year there's going to be trouble') and then everyone sits around and waits for the touch-paper to be lit.

Unlike the Time Bomb, this form of arguing needs the pressure of high expectations to be added to the brew, and the consumption of alcohol ensures the mix is lethal. On the surface you want the day to be perfect but your underlying sense of pessimism means you cut through all the idealism and get down to telling it like it is.

If you're a fan of the Festive Rumble take an analytical look at your closest relationships and your life in general. People who indulge in Festive Rumbles are usually unhappy or dissatisfied with their own lives and are taking it out on their families. Attack his mother and you're actually attacking him. Scuffle with an auntie or friend over the wedding buffet and it's very likely you think your job is rubbish and your life is sad.

The Long Silence

You fall out with your best mate or family member and then you don't speak, sometimes for years. Of all the rows between friends and family this is the most painful and often the most stressful because it means you're attacking yourself as much as the other person.

Ignoring someone who has such a central role in your life is a form of self-denial that mimics physical self-attack. In animal terms, an animal that is ignored is then left to fend for itself and therefore probably killed by predators and so what you're doing is a voluntary version of survival of the fittest.

It's also possible that you fear the closeness of the relationship and are hoping to protect yourself by separating from the friend or family member, thus creating a false sense of loss to protect you from the possibility of the real thing.

Sadly many of these 'ignores' still involve massive amounts of love with stubbornness the only factor in keeping the ignore going.

This is dangerous brinkmanship, status-posturing and game-playing, suggesting you struggle to be honest to yourself. If these people were really 'nothing' in your life you'd ring them for a chat now and again or at least be polite.

Which brings us to the reverse side of the coin . . .

PUBLIC DISPLAYS OF AFFECTION

The British have been wrongly diagnosed as suffering from a syndrome known as the 'Stiff Upper Lip', meaning that we are supposed to eschew all forms of friend/family affection displays in public or private.

However this syndrome has evaporated to some extent, thanks to US influence, leaving the younger generation happily yelling 'Love you!' down the phone to friends and family alike. Whereas previous generations would have been hung, drawn and quartered in the playground for even mentioning the fact they have a mother, let alone referring to her with anything other than irritation, today's yoof generation can go misty-eyed over their nan in public and even kiss parents and best mates without risking being tarred and feathered and left to hang in the town square.

Telephone Hugging

Do you find yourself trilling 'Love Yoooou' at the end of every call to friends and family? This display of fondness might seem like a sign of genuine bonding and affection but in many ways it's become a mindless sign-off that demotes real-deal love to a rather phoney place.

If you perform it in a high-pitched, childlike, sing-song voice you're telling people more about your fears than your affections. This is passive, pseudo-infantile stuff meaning you want the whole world to like you so that you have less to fear and worry about.

Real Hugs

Do your friend/family greeting rituals involve full-on and prolonged bouts of hugging? Do you greet one another like survivors of a disaster, even when you've only been parted for a few hours? This is affection that's tinged by relief, suggesting you have an over-hyped sense of danger and disaster and see one another as a source of protection and safety.

Text Love

Sending fond messages to friends and family throughout the day via text isn't lacking in genuine affection but it could mean you struggle to replicate the real thing when you finally get face to face.

By texting your love you avoid all the potential disappointments of the response, meaning you get to imagine the look on their face when they read it, thus choosing their response. It could also mean you're time-poor and are using this quick way of registering affection as it fits into your day without too much disruption, in which case it might be time to get yourself a proper life.

Card Love

Some friends and family tend to either find it easier to express their affection at the bottom of a birthday card or they find it is the only way they can express it, employing pet names and lines of kisses that belie the fact that they're much less emotionally expressive in real life. If this is you then you could be a romantic at heart, as cards like this tend to live on well after the sender, meaning your written affection will be the heritage you leave behind once you're gone.

Parental values, strategies and behaviours can be variable as they struggle to come to terms with the ever-changing landscape that is their offspring's terror tactics in terms of negotiating, persuading and influencing. Kids make the best negotiators, having the skills of determination, grit and focus plus a complete lack of any sense of playing fair or by the rules. But there are some rituals or family values that often do remain unchallenged or unchanged and the most potent of these involve the consumption of food . . .

FAMILY FEASTING BEHAVIOURS

If ever there was a statement of family values and hierarchical structure it's the way that family goes about the most basic of survival functions: eating. For all animals the hunter–gatherer instincts dominate even when hunting involves a metal shopping trolley or a take-away menu.

All families have their favourite feasting rituals and just as those rituals reveal all about status and pecking-orders in the animal kingdom, so the way you gather to eat will tell all about the type of family unit you are.

The Kitchen Table

For your family the act of dining is a ritual, something regular, important and non-negotiable, making the act of gathering to eat more important than the food or the consumers. This is idealised behaviour that is often prompted by false memory syndrome, meaning either you or your partner has invented nostalgia for the trend, even though as a child you were very likely to have eaten TV dinners off your lap. Growing up watching programmes like *The Waltons* has scored the idea of table-dining rituals into your consciousness and even though the reality requires a three-line whip to get the entire family assembled on time and meals are eaten in a riot of argument or silence of sulk, the fantasy image of a smiling family unit indulging in quality conversations as they pass the gravy and biscuits still endures.

Your world crumbles every time you spot a BlackBerry or Game Boy being brought to table and your heart breaks when you see the kids wolfing down their food so they can clear off to play with their Wii. They don't get it that you've been slaving over your Nigella all day just to provide something that takes three minutes to consume. On the other hand, you don't get those *Groundhog Day*-style conversations along the lines of:

'So what did you do at school today?'

'Nothing.'

'Nothing? You must have done something!'

are not really the bait that will lure your children into your idealised world of chatter and bonding.

In hierarchical terms this set-up is often all about traditional pack values of dominant Alpha male and compliant Alpha female. The man is often at the top of the table being cajoled into carving and rationing out food while the woman brings it to the table. Portion control for the kids is governed by the parent/leaders, driving them to realise that success is all about the power and status that comes with age.

Take-away Feasting

This is low-hierarchical eating as the entire family, regardless of status, shares brought-in junk and rubbish 'treat' food that is often eaten with the fingers in an act of unilateral naughtiness that relegates everyone to the level of the adolescent. The instant-gratification style of the grub implies you are a family of smash-and-grab merchants, lurching from one indulgence to another with little in the way of long-term strategic planning. In many ways your love of paying others to prepare and deliver your food which you then eat in a semi-prone position in front of the TV suggests delusions of grandeur that implies you may have had servants in some past life.

For the kitchen cook, love is shown via home baking but for the take-away parent love is shown by allowing kids to enjoy artery-clogging, waist-fattening treats that will earn you praise at the risk of their long-term health. What does this say about your family/parenting style? Go figure.

Solo-scoffing

As a family you tend to graze on an individual basis, each family member eating as, when and what they like. This is closest to the earliest days of human existence when we were primarily vegetarians and therefore happy to forage for our own food which we were not expected to share.

This behaviour would be seen as tolerant and anarchic but only by a meat-eating society. The eating of meat meant the hunting and killing of prey by teams and the sharing of food in the manner of a feast. So the sitting around a kitchen table-style eating really only apes the rituals of carnivores. This grazing behaviour identifies the family as a collection of individuals rather than defining them as a vacuum-sealed pack, sharing food-tastes like you share DNA.

Creative but possibly emotionally tepid bordering on cold, your lack of ritualistic behaviour will probably lead to your kids nailing their own kids' bums on to chairs around a pine cottage table in a bid to revive the traditional ideals they missed from their own youth.

The BBQ

Never has a ritual so closely reflected the meat-eating feasting of an Alpha-male-dominated animal group as the ritual of the summer BBQ.

With very few exceptions this is all about the male chef, wielding tools (and often even wearing a pretend chef's hat to emphasise the dominant role) and standing by the fire-altar of his own making as the rest of the tribe queue submissively in line to have food allotted in a strongly hierarchical manner.

Even the eating of the food is animal, either involving the use of bare hands and fingers or paper plates and dodgy cutlery that makes diners look and feel even more compliant as they struggle to tackle hunks of semi-raw meat with a bendy plastic fork.

This ritual is all about male domination with surplus food being cooked and offered on a reciprocal basis, meaning it's offered as a trade-off for future favours. When your neighbour tucks into his chewy and charred burger he knows you'll be round for his hover-mower (or even his wife) within the next few days, because that's the way it works in all good Alpha-male colonies.

The Meal Out

If your family's idea of a favourite feast is to dine out in a restaurant you'll be less about bonding and more about performance and rewarded success. There'll be a strong whiff of status and show-off hierarchy about your group, as dining out is often about dressing up and paying up, suggesting power in your family is aligned to money and workplace success.

There was a film called *Festen* about a family disintegrating around a dinner table and the point is that the basic layout and 'who's paying for what?' nature of the average family restaurant feast can lead to formal rows that divide clans for years. Taking the oldies for a treat will emphasise the fact Grandad is no longer able to call himself head of the family all the time his son or daughter is the one throwing down the credit card at the end of the meal. And the foodie fashion trends mean at least half the table will be there under duress with either the younger element suffering through plates of half-price rubbery Sunday roasts or the oldies picking their way through snail porridge and tea-infused squid.

Whereas you can't choose your family, you can choose your friends. Proximity is often the key factor in your friendship selection processes, plus the fact that they accepted you, which may mean your choices were more limited than you realise . . .

TYPES OF FRIEND

Of course there is only one type of friend and that is the loyal life-companion who is there to accompany you through the fun times and to supply a shoulder to cry on when things go wrong. This friend is someone you love and trust in equal measures and someone who you know will always be there for you because friendship is thicker than either blood or sexual attraction . . . right?

Well, in reality it's more than likely to be wrong, very wrong. If this idealised view of friendship doesn't seem like a perfect description of the people you share your life with, it's worth spending some moments analysing exactly what type of friendship and what type of friend you really have got. While families should be there to supply emotional support and unconditional love and partners are there to take care of all things sexual, the role of our friends can be ambiguous and sometimes downright contrary to expectations. Do you have friends you're constantly at war with? Or friends you can trust only to drop you in it on numerous occasions? And if so, what exactly does that tell you about the deeper and darker sides of your psyche?

Fan Friendships

These are friends who are in your life purely to have you bolster, stroke and buff their ego, meaning they tend to ring you rather than meet up in the flesh and when you do meet it tends to be arranged around the fact they've just decorated the kitchen or lost some weight and are in need of more on-the-spot flattery than usual. These friends tend to drift out of your life when things are going well for them and only drift back when they're looking for succour or a reminder that they are always right and forever attractive. In many ways you play the same role as the Wicked Queen's mirror in *Snow White* and if you doubt this is true then just try disagreeing with them for once in the relationship. They will head for the hills faster than a speeding locomotive.

Fan Friends are only really useful if the service supplied is mutual, therefore if your relationship is vastly one-way it might be worth salvaging just to get an even share of the bargain. Once you've supplied your clichéd patter about their bum not looking too big in that dress or the fact that their boss only criticises their work because they feel threatened by them, do provide them with similar problems in your own life and lie back to await the same honey-drip of flattery to issue from their lips. If not, call time on the whole relationship.

Toxic Friends

These are the friends that pollute out lives, either by being a very very bad role-model and urging us into a life of tattoos, drugs, alcohol and general debauchery or by lying to lure us away from any moments of good in our lives: 'You don't need to go on a diet, you look too gaunt as it is. Eat this slab of chocolate cake' or 'Who's faithful to their partner these days? No one expects it, look at all those celebs. Your partner will be screwing around whether you do or not so you might as well get stuck in!' etc.

Toxic friends are your enemy but they are also your alter-ego, so blaming them for your bad choices is pathetic and self-deceptive. If you didn't want to stray off the path you'd ditch them as your friend, meaning all they're really doing is making you feel less guilty by being the scapegoat for your bad decisions. You choose to have them as your friend, therefore you choose all their life choices too. Time to take responsibility rather than saying 'they made me do it!'

Frenemies

These are friends so competitive that your lives appear locked in some gruesome fight to the death over career success, partners, offspring envy and even wardrobe warfare. The words jealousy, envy and resentment define this relationship and people close to you get both exhausted and puzzled as they take your side in yet another internecine battle. You have rifts that last decades but underneath it all lie strong bonds. With this 'friend' and your mutual envy and hatred being the focal point of your life you have found the ultimate tool to motivate you to career and partnership success ('I just have to go one better than that witch') and you know if the relationship folded you would never find the same anger-fuelled energy to do well. By competing with one person your entire life you also avoid all the stress involved in competing and vying against the rest of the world.

Shag Buddies

This friend sees you as having a sexual role in his or her life, either in buddying up to double his or her chances of pulling, meaning you add to his or her attractiveness profile and have been selected as a friend based on looks rather than personality, or you have been selected as a life-time fall-back: the one he or she can have sex with during a drought or procreate with if no 'proper' mate is forth-coming (bring on the turkey baster!) or even end up married to when the old folks' home looms.

There is little proper conversation with this friend, just a series of invitations out, usually last-minute when they've been dumped or stood up, or when some kind of hunting action is planned and they know two blondes tend to pull better than one. Any chat from this friend will tend to be focused around what you're going to wear and how all other men/women are unreliable bastards.

Dumper Friends

This friend uses you to off-load on, meaning their only form of conversation with you is 'having a good old moan'. They ring late at night or just as you are having dinner and they talk for hours but rarely, if ever, listen. They love you for being there but fail to see the truth of the phrase that the carer ends up becoming the victim, meaning that by the time they have off-loaded all their worries and whinge you are left two-thirds into a nervous break-down.

Narcissistic Friends

Your other acquaintances always take you for brothers or sisters, meaning you look alike and tend to dress alike, even acting as a bit of a mirror for one another when you're out buying clothes. Pseudo-cloning like this – picking a friend who is as close to yourself as possible – is a sign of exaggerated self-love or self-regard, meaning you make one another happy by being representative of your selves.

Proxy Pals

Your friend is a suck-up merchant who is only your friend because of your profile, your success or the power that you wield. They are often impotent or even timid types but they obtain their own little power-base by being seen around with you. This might sound like a one-way gain but selfish though they may seem, at least Proxy Pals know what they get from the friendship and will stay fiercely loyal to protect these benefits, often far more loyal than someone who is only friends out of love or genuine affection

---

Who loves ya?

The average Brit only has three real friends according to a 2009 survey. Though many of us make more friends during our lifetime, One Poll found that most of us admit to losing touch with an average of 36 people during our lives.

And speaking of affection, what do your friends' friends tell you about your friends? Or to distil things further, what about their very best friend in the whole world (apart, possibly, from you): their choice of pet?

WHAT YOUR FRIENDS' PETS TELL YOU

Psychological rich-pickings don't come much richer or pickable than they do with your best mate's other best friend: their pet. That animal might look relatively uncomplicated but the emotions of the person purchasing it would have been anything but. This is the animal they have chosen to spend part of their life with. If you thought the bonds between you and your friend were close just imagine how much closer they'd need to be for her or him to be happy following you around with a poop-scoop and a plastic bag. That creature with a collar around its neck is more than just your friend's chosen companion, it's likely to be their mini-me too, a miniature version of their heart, soul and personality all wrapped up in one furry little bundle.

Cats

Okay, so we all know about cat-women and the way older women suddenly acquire a passion for cats in multiple numbers but what about the average girl who numbers at least one moggie as her very best friend?

The moggie-lover was brilliantly defined by the character Holly Golightly from *Breakfast at Tiffany's*: beautiful, sexy but with the same ability to be loyal and dependable as your average alley-cat.

Cat-lovers love cats because they are proud, haughty and yet low maintenance, purring all over your legs one minute and sadistically playing a mouse to death the next. Your friend is fun and loving but rarely loyal. Someone to go to for a good time but not always the ideal shoulder to cry on in times of trouble or need.

Breed-cat-owners are the same times ten. Siamese cats are noisy, elegant and attention-seeking but rarely return like-for-like in terms of loyalty and affection. You can look and admire but there's something lethal about their overall appearance, as though they'd chew your toes off in the night if they had a mind to. Your friend is showy, stylish but hugely superficial. Avoid confrontation too, those claws can kill!

Rabbits

If your friend has a rabbit and she's over twelve years old she's making a declaration of bonkers-ness that you ignore at your peril, especially if the rabbit lives indoors. Rabbits are the ultimate signal of a kind, warm and possibly broken-hearted owner who makes severely bad relationship choices based on superficial appearances. She's just dying to be loved and cuddled but she's also low on strategic thinking. Most guys copping the sight of a rabbit on a first date will run a mile over broken glass to make their getaway. Okay, so it's not a boiled bunny, but it's a bunny nonetheless . . .

Dogs

All dog-owners will have a sense of practicality and responsibility as dogs are often more high maintenance than kids. However the dog-owner could also be a bit of a control-freak as they didn't just get a furry pet, they got the role of Alpha-wolf that goes along with owning one too.

Dog-owning friends are people that have bought unconditional love, so think how far up the control-freak Richter scale that puts them. For a dog-owner it's all about the way their dog will greet them with undisguised ecstasy, even when they've just popped out to buy a newspaper. These animals are ego-boosters extraordinaire, a sign your friend might need constant reassurances from any relationship, especially yours.

Then there are the types of dogs . . .

Small Dogs

These mini-pooches worn tucked into bags or under one arm a la fashionista are a sign your friend is selfish, attention-seeking and borderline sadistic, as these dogs are often just a fashion item worn to get attention and approval and to double her own cute factor. She's impractical but fun and will take your man off your hands before you can even say Pedigree Chum.

Bigger Dogs
These are serious pooches that require serious handling, suggesting your friend is loyal and trustworthy and someone who will go out of their way to help in an emergency.

Birds

Sadistic doesn't even begin to describe the bird-owner as not only do they hold beautiful flying things captive in a cage with only a mirror for company, but they also let them out when you're round for a visit just so they can crap on your head in a concerted bombing raid the Dambusters would have been proud of. Your friend has a severe lack of empathetic qualities. If she did have an ounce of empathy she'd realise how mean she was being keeping birds under house-arrest.

Snakes and Reptiles

Turning something that is clearly not a pet into a pet by giving it a name and a pretend personality should tell you something about your friend. Creatures like these just lie around scaring people, giving power-by-proxy to their owner as they hang them around your neck or make you touch them to 'see how warm they feel'. If we wanted to feel something warm a hot water bottle would do the trick, thank you, with no side-effects like being bitten, eaten whole or squeezed to death. Your friend is scary and that's official. You might not see them feeding their pet live mice but keep in mind that's exactly what they'll do once you've gone home.

Horses

Not a pet – or is it? Horses are probably the most romantic and pseudo-sexual of all the pets/animals and for most little girls they come in the stage of growing up that goes between hamsters and men. That your friend has a insatiable sexual appetite should be a given although horses are hard-core when it comes to maintenance so this could be one (chaste) relationship that takes top billing over the sexual kind. Breezy, confident and strong, your friend will be the most amazing of chums but only if you muck in (or muck out!) and help with the horse yourself. If not you'll be way down the pecking order of priorities after the horse and sex.

But even though friends and family (or, more specifically, your mum and your dad) can, as the poet Philip Larkin famously said: 'fuck you up' with respect to your head there are some characters in our lives that get to do so literally as well. Unlike F & F though, you do get to interview and assess them before you allow them into your life and your bed. Think you're good at sussing out a date? Well, you're going to get better with the next section : *The You Code* guide to dating and mating . . .

7

DATING AND MATING

Okay, so we scrutinise our work colleagues, interviewees, neighbours, friends and business partners to try and find out what they are really like. But in no realm of our interaction with others is there so much analysis as when we try to judge a potential partner.

We all spend a lot of time wondering what a potential other half thinks of us. And we spend hours concentrating on composing flirty emails or making sure that we look good for dates. Research for the dating website Parship shows that we actually spend a massive total of 20 hours and 9 minutes on each first date alone, including 5 hours 36 minutes on the 'set-up', 2 hours 'pre-date' preparation and 3 hours 30 minutes on post-date analysis. So it's interesting that we don't necessarily think about all the aspects of the mating game that might be giving our potential soul mate a clue to our personality – the love choices that send out important messages about what we're like: the style of a Valentine's card, even the underwear we choose to wear.

So how can you make sure that you're dating the right person? Our step by step guide, following the stages of the dating and relationship process, will help you find out.

Read my lips

The way you turn your head to kiss someone when you meet them shows how emotional you are. In a study, about 80% of men and women turned their heads to the right which researchers say shows genuine feeling. The rest, who lean to the left are using less emotional parts of their brain.

Jobs come via interviews, sex comes via the date. (Perhaps not if you're into one-night stands, or, if you're angling for something long-term, possibly more than one.) Dates can be just as hideous as the average job interview because the point is to make the best impression in a relatively short space of time with a relative stranger, except the pay-off is sex and marriage rather than a job.

Alcohol often helps, but as it relaxes you and makes your date less picky it can also take you to a point where your intention to be seen as 'normal' flies out the window and you're telling them all about your 20 rescue cats and the fact you were still breast-fed at the age of nine.

Recovering from all this grave embarrassment though, you do need to remember that, like any self-respecting job interview, you should be taking in as much information as you are giving out. Because dating is not, and should not be, all about being assessed. You need to be listening with both your eyes and your ears. Your ability to read your date is often way more important than his or her ability to read and assess you . . .

WHAT THEIR SENSE OF HUMOUR SAYS ABOUT THEM

In today's society, humour is seen as a way of proof that a person is 'normal' or even trustworthy, meaning everyone who speaks in public will feel the pressure to be funny – apart, perhaps, from the Queen.

Although jokers in history were called fools and the term 'clown' is still used as a put-down, the ability to recount events, information and experiences in an amusing way can, in modern society, create the impression of status and power. A comedian will often be afforded high status because the ability to launch verbal attacks can be as potent as physical ones in our 'aggression-free' society. It also displays potent sexuality (this power created Alpha status as well) and intellectual superiority (Oscar Wilde excelled in one-liners that proved his quick wit). Speedy thinking can appear clever but having a quick wit that you can convert into humour marks your brain power high up on the food chain.

Joke is on you

Research shows that 83% of people say that humour impresses them on a first date. No pressure then.

Psychologically, jokes are a rich form of communication. There will be elements of pseudo attack/aggression and suppressed warrior tendencies often comes out in humour – it's not surprising, then, that jokes often show our capacity for cruelty. The performance itself is equally revealing. Do you take centre stage and let rip or do you scupper your own punch lines with bouts of dithering, mock-forgetfulness or repeated apology?

The Sarcastic Joker

The Sarcastic Joker is all about power, status and control. Their withering put-downs aren't a full-frontal assault but these complex side-swipes can be every bit as deadly.

Sarcastic Jokers are cowards because they employ their humour to say things they would never dare say outright and they are devious because their attacks are elastic, i.e. their 'hits' will be snapped back if they appear to make their mark too effectively: 'I was only joking' is a phrase they overuse. Sarcastic jokers like to think themselves superior to others because the ambiguous nature of their comments causes confusion in their victims, meaning only the joker is 'clever' enough to know what was intended. They are not known for being empathetic or trustworthy as they sacrificed the values of trust and empathy on the altar of comedy many years ago.

The Shaggy Dog Joker

The long-winded joker enjoys telling jokes that take up to an hour to relate, often in large groups and usually over pints of beer. They will often be known in their pack for being the relater of long-winded tales and this probably means they have taken the role of old-fashioned story-teller, except a story that begins 'There were these three blokes . . .' will tend to receive a better audience than one that begins 'Once upon a time . . .' This is the only concept that might explain their survival because everyone knows (including the joker) that no one likes these jokes, and part of the humour lies in the groans and glassy-eyed stares that accompany them. It is part of the ritual that the joker must battle their way through a brief bout of heckling, therefore proving their warrior potential while also coming across as a berk. The Shaggy Dog Joker is the ultimate performer because these jokes involve timing, persistence, a complete lack of self-consciousness and an ability to overact. The punchline, even the rituals of rejection and mock-aggression from the audience followed by forced acceptance and unity when the Shaggy Dog Joker gets to the end of the story, are less important than the performance. In many ways this comic enjoys the insults and rejection as much as the ultimate acceptance. They were probably hugely unpopular at school and seek to re-create this social pattern throughout their life.

The Sick Humourist

Whole books can be written about the psychology of sick humour as everyone goes through at least one phase of sick gags in their evolution, usually in junior school. Sick humour relies on the 'forbidden' factor, taking swipes at subjects that should normally create a response of pity or horror. Tragic events often attract jokes of this nature and should be seen as a coping mechanism. When an event is too huge, too terrifying or too tragic, making jokes helps create a survival barrier and diminish the fear. People who work in jobs that involve regular exposure to tragedy or horror, like the emergency services, will often employ sick humour to prevent identifying with or becoming too emotionally involved with the victims.

No event or tragedy is too 'big' for the sick humorist, although 9/11 and the death of Princess Diana caused two of the biggest time lapses between event and jokes. Thanks to the Internet, sick humour is alive and thriving and has gone global.

Sick humour relies on the joker's desire to shock, meaning they will often employ an expression of guilt and whispered confidence, sometimes almost mock-cowering and face-covering as they tell their joke. These signals suggest the joker likes to challenge others' perception of him- or herself by shocking while still retaining the right to deny their utter horribleness by teasing their audience beforehand 'I can't tell you this joke I heard . . . no, it's really sick . . .' to somehow make it not their fault. Or they might tell the joke with bravado, meaning they're using the sick humour to make themselves look tougher and more dangerous than their audience.

The Self-deprecating Humorist

When someone aims all their gags at themselves they are employing a very basic technique of ingratiation. Self-attacks usually have the desire to prompt compliments from the audience or at least inspire warmth and empathy, leading to likeability. Often the joker suffers genuinely low self-esteem, meaning they perceive their self-attacks as being pre-emptory. They're saying what others are thinking before they get a chance to say it themselves. In some cases they are the opposite. People with high levels of confidence or self-esteem often feel comfortable using the odd self-deprecating comment because they know it will sound ironic and therefore highlight their fabulous attribute.

Clowns

These are the Mr Beans of the comedy world, using physicality to create laughs from their audience. In many ways these people are likely to be the nicest and most generous characters because they are using a lack of vanity to amuse, as well as indulging in a technique that a parent will often employ to make a small child chuckle. It's often the earliest type of humour we are exposed to in the form of pulling faces and 'peek-a-boo' games. There's a lurking undercurrent of fear involved because the faces and body-shapes pulled often mimic ugliness or 'monster' faces, and the laughter will often relate to that in the way that we laugh when we encounter safe fear, like a fairground ride or a ghost train. So in many ways the Clown distorts their normal image to induce mild fear before reverting back again, which their audience feels as relief. The Clown will even perform slapstick, like pretending to fall or be hurt, to evoke the same response.

The One-liner

Brief, funny comments used with perfect timing will often be used by someone hoping to lighten moods or pressure, often in the workplace. This person has a very strong defence mechanism but can also be charming and charismatic because their delivery and timing will display confidence and good self-esteem. The jokes keep them at arm's length from the rest of the pack by creating a sense of original thinking, yet these people will also have pack-acceptance because their wit makes them respected.

The Double-entendre Merchant

Although the double entendre achieved status as an ironic statement of cool in the seventies and eighties thanks to the likes of *Viz*, *Are You Being Served?* and *Monty Python*, it has since sunk to its historical place as one of the lowest forms of wit, suggesting a seaside-postcard sense of humour that is based largely on an infantile perception of sex being naughty or even 'dirty'. The Double-Entendre Merchant rarely uses strategy or performance in their jokes, and their usual routine consists simply of smirking, sniggering or saying 'Ooh, Matron' or 'Boom-boom!' after someone mentions words like 'bush', 'pussy' or 'coming' in an entirely innocuous way. Unsophisticated and juvenile, this person lacks cunning, wit or intellect although, like all kids being naughty, they can also have the capacity to charm.

The Practical Joker

This is the most strategic of all humour and possibly the most aggressive. Good practical jokes take planning or even props and are usually aimed at ridiculing the victim.

The practical joker is the true hunter–killer of the comedy pack, someone who selects and stalks his or her prey before humiliating them, often in public. There is often more laughter during the planning process than there is at the actual exposé, meaning the Practical Joker is likely to be selfish in their comedy, with the core aim of tickling their own ribs. Wanting to see other people in a state ranging from mild confusion to utter degradation has to be hugely revealing. Although laughing at someone slipping on a banana-skin might be excusable, being the person who placed that skin there makes you cunning, rather than an opportunist. Practical jokers are the true bad boys of the humour world, Machiavellian, devious and often vengeful, they use their humour for power and control. They are all about anticipation – watching the victim go about their normal business unaware they are about to sit on a whoopee cushion or wash with black soap is an important part of the ritual – and they enjoy creating chaos from everyday actions, which is a trait they will show through other aspects of their life.

Funny fact

Being funny doesn't always equal social confidence. Professional comedians are actually shyer than most other people according to a study by Gil Greengross an anthropologist at the University of New Mexico in Albuquerque.

If humour is bonding and ultimately revealing, what about the things that tell us all about your date's physicality and body-confidence? 'Clothing maketh the man' is a phrase that still resonates and nothing maketh the leg and crotch area as much as a nice pair of denim jeans . . .

WHAT THEIR JEANS SAY ABOUT THEM

Jeans are the modern social uniform, worn across almost every inch of our planet by every class, sex and age-group. Denim originated in the town of Nîmes in France and, via sailors, came to the US where, thanks to Levi Strauss, they became the mega commercial phenomenon we know today. It's reckoned that 2.5 billion pairs of jeans are now sold around the world each year.

As jeans are so ubiquitous you would think that they would say very little about the person they clad, but in fact the shape and cut of the jeans provide key clues to the character of the wearer. Once a point of fashion (in the sixties it would have been unthinkable to be seen sporting anything other than a flare) there is much more variety when it comes to choosing the style, meaning more personality clues are displayed by what the wearer chooses out of a huge range of options.

Drainpipes

These straight and extremely tight jeans are the choice of the fop and the dandy, someone who is not afraid to take risks when it comes to making as statement and defining their shape. Comfort is sacrificed for fashion, and the drainpipe wearer flirts with danger as these jeans look as if they can cause blood supplies to be cut off. Drainpipe wearers will risk all to show they are cutting-edge, so expect them to be more superficial than a dolly mixture. By diminishing their leg width and accentuating their leg length they suggest a spider-like approach to relationships – silent and creepy but also attacking and potentially deadly. By minimising their legs (and, for male drainpipe wearers, exaggerating their crotch area) they imply they are lovers not fighters but they will be very handy with the verbal put-down if not with their fists.

Flares

There is still a hippy-like sense of calm irresponsibility about the flare wearer, especially those new-to-flares because this time around they aren't paired with platform shoes and are therefore trailed in dirt, mud and puddles and are likely to be threadbare around the hemline within hours of setting out onto the streets. The flare wearer is happily grubby then and likes to adopt an air of manufactured whimsy. By emphasising the foot area they minimise the width of the thigh, meaning they are likely to be reckless lovers with a hint of stubborn rebellion if you try to tie them down.

Wide-leg Jeans

The wide-leg jeans wearer is unpretentious and their lives are unstructured. Often as wide as their jeans, they will eat, drink and talk without any form of strategy or awareness. Their total lack of regard for anything sexual in the lower half of their bodies suggests a rangy and random sex drive with very little in the way of effort being made to seduce or even get off the blocks.

Classic Straight-leg Jeans

This is someone reliable who will enter relationships for the long-term, despite having sufficient assertive skills to quit if it's not working out. Practical and usually responsible, they tend to be finishers as well as starters, with a strong dislike of superficial or fly-by-night types. They can be creatures of habit with strong family ties and values. Good with their hands, they like to get stuck in rather than intellectualising.

Shapeless Jeans

This is likely to be an older wearer who enjoys the kudos of denim-clad legs and bum but who has long gone past the stage of being able to put up with the discomfort of tighter, trendier cuts. Their kids laugh at the saggy-bum look but the shapeless jeans wearer is just happy to still be in the frame in terms of 'youthful' dress. As long as the likes of Clint Eastwood and Twiggy still appear clad in their Levi 501s then the M&S versions will still be a viable option.

Denim Shorts

When guys see a girl in denim shorts they think 'Daisy Duke', when in fact what they're looking at is a statement that mirrors something a little less wholesome. This is not intentionally sexy, just indicative of a wild-child sense of chaos, hence the teaming with opaque tights (rather thin on the ground among the Beverly Hillbilly set) and the wearing of pockets that hang below the hemline. This is a signal of cool and status from girls to other girls, and very little to do with 'come and get it' for guys.

If the wrong sort of jeans aren't the deal-breaker then move on to some basic everyday functions that should tell you all about his/her approach to even more basic functions like sex. Although Freud probably had little in the way of opinions about jeans we're sure he must have had a field day over the way we consume our food . . .

WHAT THE WAY HE EATS SAYS ABOUT HIM

It's impossible not to connect the sensual pleasures of eating food with sex, and equally impossible to not make this male behaviour related as it involves stuffing things into an orifice. For women the analysis is quite simple: if she eats readily and with open enjoyment she's likely to be enthusiastic in bed but if she's picky or finicky she's unlikely to go like a rabbit. If she eats right through to the dessert and beyond she's got no intention of having sex, because sex on a full stomach only happens with a woman once she's been married for over a year.

For blokes (and in a lesser way for girls) then, food and sex are two very basic, evolutionary urges that combine necessity with pleasure and how he blends gratification with technique is very indicative of what he'll be like in the bedroom. Is it surprising then that first dates often involve dining at an intimate spot where a small table for two means you sit face-to-face, monitoring each and every mouthful as it goes down? This is the modern way of judging sexual compatibility. Some of us pounce on the best bits of food first and others leave them until last. Some people throw their food down their throats and others tease themselves by toying with it like a cat with a mouse.

If you've ever wondered why you've been turned off by the fact that he scoffs in a way that suggests he needs a bib, or turned on by the way he handles his fresh oysters, here's why . . .

The Instant Gratification Eater

Instant gratification eaters are greedy and lacking in technique and they'll apply the same set of rules to their sex life. They attack their food, eating quickly and without any apparent strategy. What they see they want and while they're eating they're looking to see what to order next or what you might be leaving on your own plate.

This person will be happily into quickie sex, although you might get seconds if you're lucky. They go for quantity rather than quality and their idea of technique is turning the light out first. They can be noisy in their appreciation and easily pleased in terms of your own techniques or flair. They have a tendency to be opportunistic, although their loyalty as a lover is made more likely by the fact that other women tend to reject them on a regular basis. The more animal the eating the more animal he'll be in bed: direct, quick and thoughtless.

The Picker

If he picks his way through his food and complains about it we're talking picky lover with a low sex drive. If he's turned off by over-cooked veg he'll be turned off by spots, smells and body hair so expect to put in a lot of body maintenance for very little in the way of return.

The Allergy Freak

If he starts spouting lists of food intolerances then you can take The Picker and quadruple his lack of interest in or enthusiasm for sex. His hypochondria will extend to the bedroom, as will his self-absorption. He'll probably have issues with emotional commitment or uninhibited behaviour, meaning a well-choreographed technique with no surprises or fireworks.

The Noisy Eater

He butters and eats his bread roll before the first course has arrived and is asking for more before the second. He picks expensive foods like steak or fish but accompanies with goodies like chips rather than a side salad. Noisy eaters are the ultimate in uninhibited sexual partners. They go for it hammer and tongs, leaving broken beds and trashed hotel rooms in their wake. They enjoy food just like they enjoy life and sex. Expect energetic and noisy rather than sophisticated seduction.

The Foodie

This guy knows his way around a menu and is happy to teach you about food. His style of eating is careful and expert, planned to intensify enjoyment of each and every mouthful.

Foodie man makes the most seductive and experienced lover, going through every experience and technique in the book plus some that you'd never heard of before. He will be charming and thoughtful – if a little mature – and you will need to expect a long list of previous and possibly current lovers in his life.

The Planner

He tends to eat in a rather careful and choreographed order, making little mess and finishing everything that is put before him. He will tend to organise his food, moving it into little piles or segments before eating it. Planner man is a very strategic and methodical thinker who always finishes what he's started even if his enthusiasm dips in the middle. If you're looking for a long-term relationship then the Planner is a reasonably good bet. He can be a control-freak though, as he likes things to be 'right' – that is, right for him. If the straightening of cutlery and tidying and stacking of food is too ritualised he could also be obsessive-compulsive, meaning he'd probably be a good bet when it comes to cleaning and tidying your home too. What's not to like?

The Performer

This guy likes to play with his food and even show-off about eating, juggling cutlery, spinning glasses, shaking champagne bottles and flipping beer mats. He'll toss peanuts into his mouth, flick bread pellets and use his napkin for origami. Performer man is full of anxieties but loves to be centre of attention. He feels an intense amount of pressure to come up with the goods and this can make him impressive in bed, if a little anxious at times. His food-playing is part Alpha posturing and part a childlike desire to please.

The Sharer

This guy loves to share his food, ordering plates for two or dessert with two forks and offering chips, meat and sea-food across the table for you to taste or consume. This is family guy with a big heart and capacity for generosity. He's the traditional hunter, sourcing food that the whole pack can share and enjoy and for him the act of sharing reinforces his status. He also gets to seduce with food because holding out a chip with your fingers or lump of steak out on your fork for your mate to nibble is one of the more Freudian of dinner-table behaviours. Expect a meeting of minds as well as bodies in the bedroom.

The Calorie Counter

He'll be avoiding carbs and asking for low-fat spread, plus checking to see if the cranberry in his vodka cocktail can be counted as one of his 'five a day'. Although it's good for a man to eat healthily and watch his weight, men who discuss it rarely make good lovers because if you're afraid of food you're afraid of sex. Your only hope of any good bedroom action will come after you've told him how many calories get burnt off during orgasm. Dull and narcissistic.

Restaurant meal behaviour centres around certain rituals involving lingering consumption combined with tradi-tional utensils but we live in an era that also happily accommodates the finger-eater who prefers more animalistic methods of devouring their kill. Food 'to go'

*bears much more resemblance to the hunter–killer psyche,
meaning ripping that pizza apart with their bare hands and
revisiting the left-overs in the fridge the next morning will
say even more about him or her in terms of basic
evolutionary instincts.*

WHAT THEIR FAVOURITE FAST FOOD SAYS ABOUT THEM

Well let's begin with the premise that all regular fast-food
eaters are into instant gratification, especially if they're the
type that stand over the microwave, praying for the bell to
ping. However not all 'fast' food is really that speedy.
Some might even imply they're a good bet for a long,
rewarding relationship, especially if you fancy the delivery
guy . . .

The Pizza Lover

All yellow, round and greasy with flecks of red or pink,
what the pizza most closely resembles is a cartoon of a
spotty adolescent face, and this favourite food does let you
know that the eater is well in touch with his or her inner
student psyche.

There's a faint whiff of power about the Pizza Lover,
hence the preference for getting the item delivered, plus the
strong draconian rules about delivery that he or she
relishes as much as the food ('You're three and a half
seconds late, that means I get a free pizza. I don't care if
you fell off your scooter and broke your collarbone.')

Then there's the size of the pizza, suggesting further
signals of power, competitiveness and supremacy (look at
the titles of the things too, how much more Alpha could
they be?). It's no coincidence that it arrives in a box that
must be carried aloft like a royal platter.

There's a hint of sharing and sociability about the Pizza Lover but it's mainly a sham because, despite all the ads suggesting you work on a 'one slice each' process, what Pizza Lover loves most is to scoff it all him- or herself, having even acquired a taste for cold leftovers to ensure (in true pack-animal style) that there's no wastage the next day. This eater will represent good solid family values, but beware the streak of self-interest that lurks beneath. Ask to taste a bit of his or her pizza and watch the body language. They might pretend to enjoy sharing but the leakage signals will suggest suppressed anger or resentment.

The Burger Lover

This fast-food choice shows someone with water-hole tendencies – that is, they like to do their own thing with their own pack but will be quite happy to integrate with the larger population when it comes to eating out. This person is not into physical comfort (burger bars are notoriously uncomfortable) but emphatically into emotional comfort eating, as they will often order the same thing from what is a largely standardised menu, which in turn helps them with their issues of lack of confidence and low self-esteem. In relationship terms they're cheerful enough on the surface but in reality they hate change and are totally lacking in romance, creativity or even game-playing or strategy. What you see is what you get so don't spend too long plumbing for hidden depths.

The Kebab Eater

We all know the formula with kebabs: you go out, get drunk, get hungry, eat a kebab, throw it up on the pavement. The regular Kebab Eater is someone who relishes the rituals in life, even though they are of no direct benefit. They know where the evening is heading and they also know the risks of their behaviour but the brain circuitry that is to do with habit change is somehow disconnected. Their whole life is spent lurching from one basic need or desire to another with no real planning or long-term goals. Their favourite line is 'It's what you do.' Dating him or her requires you to put up and shut up. If you don't find botulism fun you should move away quickly.

The Curry Consumer

This is someone for whom there are moments in life when only the best will do and for them 'the best' involves extremes. What they lack in technique in the bedroom they will make up for in enthusiasm and energy as once they see what they want they will climb over almost every obstacle to get to it. Their only problem can be boredom. Once they've got what they wanted they will often regret their choice the next day.

The Chinese/Thai Eater

The subtler flavours of this food, as well as the use of chopsticks to eat it, suggests someone with a taste for classier living and a delayed gratification approach to sex. They like to savour enjoyment rather than necking it back quickly and they love planning and attention to detail. They're risk-takers (some dishes have hidden chilli) and can be devious or manipulative at times.

The Tex/Mex Diner

This food comes with shared rituals like loud music, bright colours and the downing of tequila slammers, meaning this is a sociable, fun person who might work hard but will also play hard too. They're confident and extrovert and a bit of a performer.

Fish Supper

Fish and chips are the ultimate 'queue at the counter, eat in the street' food, but without the 'hurl it back up' quality of the kebab. This food tends to stay put in the stomach and therefore implies a warm family type with no air of snobbery or class pretensions and a strong streak of loyalty when it comes to relationships. This is traditional food, but with some of the nutritional values that other fast foods might lack. This person might seem all about laughter and showing off but, just as all that pure white, healthy fish lies beneath that crispy, greasy batter, this person might hold strong and quite old-fashioned values beneath a more crumpled and random exterior.

Main-course food is all about hunger but dessert, pudding or 'afters' come once proper hunger has been sated, making it more of an indulgence. If he or she starts eyeing up the sweet trolley then, start taking notes . . .

WHAT THEIR FAVOURITE DESSERT SAYS ABOUT THEM

Your meal is over, you're full but the waiter brings a much smaller menu and places it just under your nose. This is the dessert selection and the confection you pick tells far more about you than your starter or main choice selections. This is the moment you indulge rather than eat out of need. It's your secret pleasure with echoes of childhood. There's something hugely sexual about a dessert, too. Notice the dialogues and the body language rituals that are an essential part of the process. First there's the surreptitious signals and quasi-demonic expression of temptation from the waiter as he hands you the sweet menu. You need to let him know that you're an adult and that you are replete, so 'thanks but no thanks' to the cherry cheesecake, and it is then his job to coax you into indulging in a sweet. If you push the menu away they will push it back or say something like 'I'll just leave it here in case you change your mind'. By this time your expression begins to wear signals of possible submission. You groan, you grimace but you finger the menu and glance through, just in case. By the time the waiter has returned, beaming coyly, their flirt signals will be mirrored by your own. You look up shyly, purse your lips and flutter your lashes. In effect, you have squashed your previously adult decision of saying no to the dessert and, just like a child, handed over the responsibility of eating naughty food to someone else. You order a dessert and the waiter brings two spoons and before you know it you're in some stage of sweet-induced orgasm, shoving mouthfuls of chocolate mousse down your throat while sounding like Meg Ryan in *When Harry Met Sally*.

The Trifle Eater

This smacks of childhood comforts as trifle was the glamour dish of your youth and you still see it as a precious form or reward in adulthood. It was a treat from your mother to you so therefore hints at a need for maternal approval, plus it was the first dessert that proved adults could be as fond of glace cherries and hundreds-and-thousands as a kid. Trifle-lovers are also delayed-gratification fans in the bedroom. Beneath all that cream and custard lies sherry sponge so they'll be happy to dig deep to get the real reward out of a relationship.

The Cheesecake Consumer

This is a slightly sour sweet dessert, implying a more sophisticated and un-showy personality but also indicates a high-achiever whose cool exterior hides a strong streak of competitiveness. This is an un-gooey confection as well, meaning they like structure and a sense of order in their lives.

The Ice-cream/Sorbet Lover

By freezing their mouth at the end of a meal this person shows they have a quasi-disgust for 'dirty' sex, possibly happily taking part in but needing to clean up straight away after. If it's sorbet (especially lemon) or vanilla ice-cream this person feels strong amounts of guilt about 'letting go' and having a good amount of fun. If it's flavoured ice-cream they might be less full of inhibitions.

The Fresh-fruit Eater

This is the goody-two-shoes of the dessert eaters, a pious health nut who likes to make their fellow diners, as they stick their snouts into piles of cream and meringue, feel guilty while they pick at a piece of watermelon. This is more about control than actual hunger. They use their ability to say 'no' as a signal of self-control and therefore status.

The Cheese-board Lover

Ordering from the cheese board is a little like starting a new meal again as the cheeses on offer in most restaurants are as complex and as deserving of the same amounts of expertise and decision-taking as the main courses. While most people are happy to relax mentally and physically and be seduced by their gooey dessert, the cheese-eater is still firmly in control of his or her destiny, questioning the waiter about sources, ages and countries of origin and pulling faces over the choices of biscuit. This is someone on a permanent state of alert who will never really let go and who has aims of taking over the world. And if you want to know their attitude to sex just watch the way they waggle that length of wilting celery about before crunching it between their molars.

The Chocolate-mousse Lover

Choccy-lovers will fight for each and every atom of high-octane pleasure life throws out. While other diners like the babyish delights of a mouthful of plain cream, the chocolate dessert-eater requires cream, sugar, cocoa, fat, caffeine-bursts and all the endorphin boost that good chocolate offers, and they don't care who sees them indulge. A person who chooses this dessert is likely to have an addictive personality and someone who will take their pleasure if, when and how it is offered to them with very little in the way of worrying about long-term consequences. Happy? You bet, but only if they imbibe with friends. Lone choccy-eaters are another matter. If they sit in their bedsit wolfing down chocolate desserts with the aid of a ladle you can guarantee they are manic depressives who still mourn about having been dumped by text in 2001.

One of the initial dating game plans is to use the shared eating process to seduce each other. But once the 'would you like to come up for coffee' phase is over we quickly move on to other traits in our bid to analyse a partner as we weigh up how worthy they are of our long-term affection.

WHAT THEIR iPOD PLAYLIST SAYS ABOUT THEM

Comparing music collections can be an intense bonding ritual, especially at the beginning of a relationship. If you like what they like then there's a good chance you'll get on.

But can you determine more than that? Is there a way of seeing into their inner soul through whether they are a James Brown fan or a Heavy Metal devotee?

If you want to get a nuanced take on someone's personality, however, take a peek at their mp3 player. For the modern music delivery device (even the Pope now has one) is a window into our souls.

In many ways, the iPod is in reality an 'I' pod. Yes, it really does deserve a capital I. By using an iPod or mp3 player you are entering a little world of your own. An iPod allows you to stand back from a world where there are a million muddled messages being directed towards you. It enables you to build your own perfect retreat. With an iPod you don't have to interact with the world if you don't want to. This means that, unlike choosing to go to see a band or listening to CDs at home with friends or a lover, an iPod playlist reveals a lot about a person's inner self.

So what does the type of music that predominates on their iPod playlist say about them?

Pop

Happy, unpretentious and fun, this person will happily sing along to the current No. 1 hit with no worries about being clichéd or corny. Honest but not intellectual (unless they're claiming they like Take That in an ironic way, that is).

Classical

Someone whose strong feelings of self-worth can border on the suprior or smug side. Classical music lovers either already have a calm lifestyle or invoke classical music to achieve those levels of calm in the midst of chaos. Even stirring classics like Wagner will only introduce a measured form of arousal, unlike the more agitating rhythms of more modern musical forms that tend to be written to get people to dance or jiggle.

Most classical music is well-established meaning that this person has a dislike of change and a desire to feel that through their intellectual curiosity, they can quickly understand and 'conquer' a piece, with few irritatingly new pieces to work out. This means they like to be in control and be lord of all they survey. No shocks or surprises for this person, they relish the value of the familiar.

Indie

There's something rewardingly 'opt-out' for the Indie lover even though the music sells in its zillions and the concerts get mass attendances. Being an individual within the comfort of a large group is important to the Indie lover, which makes them rebel lite. They hate being taken for granted or being pushed into commitment although their huge, puppy-like desire to please and be liked means they'll always come round in the end, their little knitted hat in their hands.

Rock 'n' Roll

Rock 'n' Roll lovers come with a backwash of historical rebellion. As their music hasn't really touched the main-stream since the fifties, this means they're loyal but often stubborn types with an overwhelming desire to prove themselves right about everything. If they toyed with punk en route they might have a genuinely aggressive streak but the purists shouldn't frighten the horses and will often keep themselves to themselves, usually during group bookings to Butlins.

Heavy Metal

The Heavy-metal lover is often a Second Life enthusiast, often in a dull or boring job and uses this alter-ego rock rebel image to gain relief from all the tedium. Machismo-R-Us whether it's male or female, although the gruff exterior will often mask a sensitive inner soul who can be brought to his or her knees by teasing or criticism.

Rap

There's an exhibitionist in here trying to get out although all the groundwork put into achieving that attention can be negated by a desire to dress and look like everyone else in the pack, which indicates that group identity and approval can be more important than solo achievement for the Rap lover. The fact that few rappers actually sing means this person has pretensions to fame, knowing that as long as there is a mike to stick close to your gob and a few hours put into practising your beat-box routine the sky's the limit, even if you can't hold a note.

Dance

Sexy, indulgent, but potentially fiery, this is an instant-gratification type who puts quantity over quality every time. This person probably has a bit of a disposable life-style with holidays rating top of their list of priorities.

Jazz

This person resides in Smugsville USA and is elitist and super-smart – they can spot a tune in a pile of musical spaghetti. The Jazz-lover is a true delayed-gratification type who will suffer for his or her art. This music is an acquired taste and their superiority comes from the fact they've either bothered to acquire it or are a good actor and are pretending. Oh, and they're probably also old.

Soul

Mellow and friendly with a tiny depressive streak, this person goes for quality and class above trends and hits. They're clubby and sociable, preferring to go out and even date in groups than hunting alone.

Opera

The one thing you can guarantee with the opera lover is that they have an ability to look beyond the ridiculous and not suffer fits of the giggles when a 38-stone woman sings that she is starving for her lover in some garret. These people are kooky and hard-core, seeking out the heights of bizarre creativity and posturing to get their hits. They are probably also rich because opera seats tend to be very expensive.

Show Music

Romantic, baroque, flamboyant and a thwarted performer. These people like their sexual hits to be frequent, intense and imaginative.

So you've secretly perused the music on their iPod while they made the coffee and decided to stay put on the sofa despite the definitive 'Sounds of the Pan-pipes' triple boxed set. So next it's off to the toilet for a little snooping through the most revealing spot in the entire place . . .

WHAT THEIR BATHROOM CABINET REVEALS

Many years ago Dame Edna Everage did a very funny stand-up sketch about nosing through the contents of someone's bathroom cabinet. She claimed it was the best way to find out all about a person, and she's right. The bathroom cabinet has two key pluses when it comes to divining the psyche of your new date: firstly it's about the most intimate piece of probing you can do to obtain a full character reference and health screening and secondly it's lodged inside the bathroom, meaning you get to pry with the door locked. It's also something that they tend not to clean away. Figures back this up: 42% of Americans don't clean theirs as the seasons change. Remember, though, that cabinet scrutiny can take time so avoid excusing yourself to go to the loo or your date may have an idea of what you're up to after the first five minutes have passed. Explain your absence in advance by saying you're off to refresh your make-up (guys never know what this entails) or that you need to check your contact lens (if you're caught rooting you can claim you were searching for solution or eye drops).

The Holistic Junkie

This one looks like something you'd see in a Chinese herbal shop or at least like the contents of the hypochondriac's corner at the health food shop. There are herbal potions, massage oils, healing balms and packets, plus tools and implements that you rarely see outside a farrier's yard.

What it says: Expect a calm and grounded person underpinned by the finest vein of hysterical hypochondria and egomania. This person is full of values and principles but they lack trust and have struggles with authority. Their obvious study of health matters may border on obsession, suggesting their search for 'cures' for life's woes and evils could be down to narcissism at worst or at best an unhealthy concern with their own well-being. And yes, there is a whiff of witchcraft here so do search the place for crystals and books on Feng Shui if spiritual matters are a turn-off.

The Health Freak

All the state-of-the art snake oil is here, including expensive vitamin tablets, spray-tans and teeth-whitening kits. Everything is very current and expensive.

What it says: This is a fashion health-fiend, meaning they'll combine expensive de-tox programmes with a twelve-a-day fag habit or fitness regimes with binge-drinking. This person is all about style rather than substance, meaning they'll be a cheerful blend of contradictions and shakily held beliefs. This is someone for superficial fun but also someone unlikely to be faithful or unduly loyal in a relationship. They're hugely into image and you'll need to impress their friends if you want to stand a chance of a second date.

The Medicine Hoarder

There are pills, potions and lotions in here that Florence Nightingale would have been on nodding terms with as the hoarder throws nothing out, especially stale prescription drugs and other medical paraphernalia. Along with the bee sting creams, inhalers and tubs of Germolene are ancient bandages, finger stools and sticking plasters.

What it says: The Medicine Hoarder is guarded, cautious and intensely pessimistic. All that has been bad in their life has been packed into their emotional baggage and dragged along as a type of warning system. If they dated a love-rat in 1996 they'll be looking for the flimsiest of warning signs that you might do the same to them again. Their hoarding helps ward off stress by providing a sense of continuity to shore up against relentless change. This person is likely to believe in fate and luck rather than action and control. They know that the moment they throw away that ancient inhaler they'll go and have an asthma attack.

The Sex Hoarder

He or she will have a respectable amount of self-owned medical and grooming products but lurking in amongst the moisturisers, deodorants and tweezing implements will be items that could only be owned by the opposite sex.

What it says: Check out the positioning of these items and estimate their age. If they're reasonably current, partially used and hidden away guiltily behind the products owned by your date then assume he or she is already spoken for and possibly even married (wondering why a married person would risk inviting you back to their home? Look for products like sun-tan cream or basics like moisturiser or deodorant. If they're missing the spouse is probably on a business trip). If the products look unappetising and ancient this is someone who has been dumped big time and is keeping this rather gross collection as trophies. This means he or she may fall in love with a vengeance but then be unable to cope once it's over. They're unlikely to move on and you will find yourself inheriting more ghosts that the second Mrs de Winter moving into Mandalay and finding traces of Rebecca. If you're looking at a random range of new-ish products that are mainly for grooming then you're looking at a serial cheat. If the products are still in their packaging and hugely comprehensive – beware. Who would buy a date their own range of overnight products 'just in case'? Think bunny-boiler and never allow your date between you and the exit.

The Opportunist

This medical cabinet has a heavy leaning towards all things sexual: KY Jelly, condoms, vibrators, etc, all piled high and with a look of heavy duty use about them.

What it says: This person clearly sees sex as a massive priority but do they really enjoy it? This cabinet suggests the bedroom is a bit of a war zone too. They take their sex seriously but not their emotions. Are they looking for a relationship? Their only desire for continuity is sexual. Once they've gone through all the positions with you and seen if you can add to their repertoire you could be out on your ear. A lover and a romantic would have hidden all this weaponry.

The Sexual Pessimist

This cabinet contains a worrying hard-core stock of pseudo sexual accoutrements like jumbo crates of tampons, haemorrhoid creams, thrush potions and pregnancy testing kits, plus grooming products like leg-waxing kits, bikini-line bleach, foot creams and fungal sprays.

What it says: Do all these signs of damage and what can only be described as genuine bad luck suggest a gung-ho approach to relationships or a sensitivity or timidity? This woman is so over-focused on her war-wounds and scars that she could have a sense of stoicism tinged with pessimism so expect nights of love and passion to be followed with the downing of litres of cranberry juice and an appointment booked with the GP 'just in case'. She's brave but realistic and sees sex as primarily for breeding rather than fun.

The Naturalist

This is the most stomach-churning cabinet, with lids left off products and items displayed. There is the tin of Vaseline with hairs stuck in it, spot creams oozing from tubes, toothpaste squidges and smudges all over the flossing box, gargles and mouthwashes with crystallised product around the lid, and empty deodorant roll-ons that have been balanced upside-down to eke out the last few drops.

What it says: This is an instant-gratification type with no real connection between behaviour and consequences or long-term life strategy. Their time and energy focus could be their career or even their love life but you need to be warned that they might have none at all. Slobbish behaviours can be a form of Venus Fly Trap, suckering nurturing types in by manipulating them into a desire to step into this alternative life and clean it up or sort it out. If make-overs appeal to you then go ahead with the relationship but remember you may never succeed.

The Label Lover

This is the *Hello!* magazine of bathroom cabinets, full of expensive perfumes and designer cosmetics/products, mostly matching and all displayed facing front.

What it says: This anal perfectionist has high standards and possibly matching stress levels. They are life's pleasers, doing anything to gain approval, although this desire to conform does not make them a push-over. Although they seek approval from others, they're not so keen on giving it out and can be complicated and difficult with impossibly high standards.

The Flood Barrier

This cabinet is full of products concerned with holding back the natural forces of nature: heavy-duty hair-removal products, grey-away hair dyes, coloured contact lenses, nasal-hair trimmers, diet products of any kind, panty-liners, and all-over body sprays.

What it says: This person suffers from low self-esteem, with all these products being purchased to prevent them from looking like themselves. Although some image alteration is natural, the semi-display nature of these products suggest someone who assumes they are unacceptable in their natural state and keen to avoid ever 'being themselves'. Life is a performance for them, but a masked and timid one rather than a display of extrovert behaviour. Encourage, flatter, coax and reassure and you could have a loyal partner for life. One implied criticism though and they'll be back in their shell of angst in a flash.

The Thrifty Miser

The cabinet is chock-full of free samples, including airline grooming kits, hotel soaps, shampoos and bubble bath and those sachets of moisturiser you rip out of glossy magazines.

What it says: Mean.

Although the bathroom cabinet is like his or her sexual underlay the contents of his/her wardrobe and the way they are presented are more like the shag-pile, i.e. the top, window-dressed layer that says more about the manner in which he or she would like to be judged by society . . .

WHAT HIS OR HER WARDROBE BEHAVIOUR SAYS

The wardrobe is a huge symbol of self-perception and even a quick glance through his or her clothing habits can be more than revealing on a first or second date. Our clothes show tribal and status tendencies and the way we choose to hang and display them shows us in our true colours in terms of 'ideal' or intentional image, personality and self-esteem. How we treat our clothing is how we secretly treat ourselves. The way those jackets, suits and shoes are hung, packed and stacked will also give you clues about his or her approach to relationships.

The Military Wardrobe Man/Woman

There's a slide-rule look to this wardrobe, with what appears to be strict laws about space and positioning. Hangers have been hung with equal-size gaps between them, sweaters and T-shirts are folded and stacked to look identical and shoes are polished and placed in pairs

What it says: Gazing at this sort of wardrobe arrangement can bring on a frisson of fear that may not be altogether misplaced. Military Wardrobe Man/Woman is likely to be a driven obsessive with perfectionist tendencies that may emerge as job-stress or someone who has worked in Benetton or Gap and can't drop the tidying habit, or a serial killer. The thing you can assume about Military Wardrobe Man/Woman is that they tread a very fine wire through life, creating this kind of order with their clothing to ensure the chaos and train-wreck that their life could so easily be never ever occurs. If a shirtsleeve falls out of line then the entire sandcastle of perceived perfection and control will crumble. Never try pulling a few bits of his or her clothing around and making a mess in a bid to attract attention or have a bit of a flirty laugh. Fun will never ensue, we can assure you. A frenzied, face-ripping-with-teeth attack, maybe. Your liver sautéed with sprouts and a nice Chianti, possibly. Laughter, no.

The Seasonal Wardrobe Freak

Although not obsessive-compulsive the Seasonal Wardrobe Freak likes to do regular bouts of spring/autumn cleaning that involves transferring lighter, summery garments from their wardrobe to black plastic bags and laying out the wintry gear or vice versa so that their eye never alights on the wrong clothes during the wrong season.

What it says: There's a good sense of logic to Seasonal Wardrobe Freak, although you might wonder what's so wrong with cross-over or blends. Could a thermal cardi not live side-by-side with a pair of linen trousers? The point about Seasonal Wardrobe Freak is their tendency to categorise. They will have work and they will have play and they will have marriage and they will have naughty sex partners on the side and all tucked into separate little mental boxes. They are also a bit of an optimist. By packing the old season away and dragging out the new they have high expectations of an improved future.

Piles of Stuff on the Bed Man/Woman

There possibly is a wardrobe in this person's home but when there's a bed around to fling clothes on then why why bother with the fuss of hangers?

What it says: To say this person is chaotic, messy and spontaneous would be stating the obvious but the hub of their personality lies in the way that they suffer total cognitive confusion about who they are and how they want to be seen by others. Piles on Bed Man/Woman is not just lazy, he or she is also unable to commit to any one statement or decision about themselves. They are an avid reader of horoscopes because it gives them guidance regarding who they are and how they will behave during each day. You'll love them for their scattiness and their fun streak (life's too short to use shoe-trees) or you might even relish the chance to move in and show them what tidiness and a laundry basket are all about, but eventually they will wear you down with their inability to make decisions, their lack of any forward planning in life and their way of manipulating you by turning on their cute, helpless child routine. On a Freudian note, did you ever stop to wonder why they have this habit of bed-littering? Bed = sex; bed + piles of clothes lying on top = no sex, or at least a very low sex-drive. Frisky, coltish but hard to pin down if it's a woman and vain but sexually dull if it's a guy.

The Labeller

Yes there are people who label their clothes and possibly more than you might think.

What it says: There's a maternal, stubbornly practical streak to the Labeller and if it's a woman she likely has kids. What works in the cloakroom at school has practical value in the wardrobe at home for this woman and never mind that guests reel back in revulsion when they see how sad she truly can be. This woman is a trier – someone who never gives up, the backbone of the British Isles in a wartime-effort way and someone who probably grows her own veg even though she has sufficient income to shop regularly at Waitrose. The Labeller makes a terrific sexual partner as long as you like lots of effort and a Julie Andrews wholesome sexuality.

If the Labeller is male he could be early onset Alzheimer's or someone who needs to keep himself constantly reined in because he has a tendency to fall off the wagon in either alcohol, drugs, sexual or just plain slobbish behaviour.

Warning: In the next section of the book we pander to sexual stereotypes – so apologies in advance. It may be that there are guys out there who stockpile shoes as though expecting the second coming of the cast of Riverdance *and if there are they should happily throw themselves in with all the upcoming analysis. We do feel that there is something primarily female about the habit of buying more shoes than you could ever hope to wear in your lifetime even if you believe in reincarnation, and we also believe there is a strong evolutionary reason for this and that somewhere is a pre-historic wall-painting waiting to be uncovered which features large caves piled to the roof with footwear hewn out of mammoth-skins. Until those paintings are found we tend to believe that shoes are either a substitute for children or sex or that (more sensibly) sex and children are merely a substitute for shoes in a woman's life.*

The Shoe Woman

When you examine a woman's wardrobe it can be telling to evaluate her shoes to clothes ratio. Shoe Woman rates footwear higher than bodywear and will spend and display accordingly. If she's a real shoe freak she might even have the things displayed around the home like ornaments, rather than tucked away in boxes. (By the way, boxes will be a big theme in the world of Shoe Woman and she has competitive traits regarding the storing of her shoes.) The shoe is more than just footwear, it's a symbol of status and success so the correct storing of them is essential. A lightweight might have them on existing racks or lined on the floor in pairs but a hard-core Shoe Woman will have gone through plastic hanging holders and graduated to boxes that have a Polaroid of the shoe on the outside, like mini shoe-coffins.

Messy Shoes Woman

If her shoes look scruffy and are stacked in mountains in no particular order and with no apparent pairing going on you're looking at a bit of a sleaze-bag with no real self-value or self-respect. You might find her lack of order enchanting as it echoes your own system of wardrobe untidiness but keep in mind that this is a woman who, every day of her life, maybe even twice a day, will be forced to get down on her knees and root like a rabid dog through heaps of dirty shoes just to find two that look alike. This does not make her spontaneous, it makes her worrying. It implies a desire to endure long-term pain and angst for a lack of forward planning. And this might one day be the mother of your children. Shame on you for even considering it.

Regimental Shoes Woman

This woman has her shoes lined up like little soldiers, each pair ready to do its duty beneath the matching outfit of choice. The shoes are polished and in good condition although there may also be a darker side to her life, like a bin-bag hidden away somewhere that contains shoes that are out of season.

Regimental Shoes Woman has a practical but also artistic approach to life and is big about interior design and matching valances on the bed. Her day is planned but not in a compulsive way, She's one of life's copers and a good ally during any form of emergency. If she has the alternative bin-bag there's even more good news: women who are too soft to throw away shoes are often too soppy to bin their men. If you've ever fancied being the type of guy who marries the ideal woman then slopes off to have affairs then this is the woman for you. The worst you'll get is a few suits slashed in revenge but she'll take you back if you apologise nicely enough just so she can get her life back to being tidy.

Imelda Marcos Woman

Imelda Marcos once claimed that she hadn't owned 3,000 shoes – it was only 1,060! Like her, Imelda Marcos Woman stores shoes in rooms, rather than wardrobes, and your first inclination will be to faint when you see the amount of footwear on display no matter how much prior warning you were given. A woman saying she owns 200 pairs of shoes is never lying or exaggerating and you should always realise that claims like this are not a form of code for 'I have around half a dozen pairs'. Women are very precise in their shoe-audits and they never exaggerate or joke. For them it's like penis size: lying is pointless because you'll get caught out at the end of the day. These shoes are like the mounted-head trophies that hunters collect and each pair has its own history of the kill. Never feign interest unless you're happy to spend a very long half an hour listening to stalk-and-strike raids in the Prada sale.

Imelda Marcos Woman has a powerful killer instinct and what she wants she will get. Strong, ruthless, focused and determined she'll bag you for her bed but God help you if your performance is less than stellar. She's probably quite large – bigger women who struggle to get into designer size zeros tend to re-align their wardrobe focus down to their feet – and every bit as strong as she looks so no arm-wrestling unless you like sitting in casualty on a Saturday night.

Hanging Bag Woman

Her shoes live in one of those wardrobe bags that hang from a hanger with plastic compartments that the shoes either lie in or hang out of. Hanging bags are often bought by women with a sense of relief that they finally have a genuine shoe tidy, meaning they are likely to have a practical approach to life. Be warned though because any suggestions that they buy these because they have so many pairs of shoes that they're struggling to find floor space is sure to be a sham. Hanging Bag Woman might seem a shoe obsessive but in fact it's very likely that what you're looking at in that sad hanging sack is all the shoes they own in the entire world. Now, before you go away celebrating her low-maintenance attributes do keep in mind that normal women – that is, the sort that have sex and get drunk now and again – own lots of shoes, so what you're looking at here is a freak.

Shoe Box Woman

When you open the wardrobe you won't see any shoes, just rows of white boxes that stretch out for miles and remind you of lines of small white beds in a Romanian orphanage: clean, practical and sterile. This woman has a very strong bond with her shoes but the bond is mystical rather than trophy hunting. The very lack of display (apart from the shoe snapshots) should tell you that this woman is competitive, high-achieving and frequently feral but she hates to share or boast so the only person she's trying to impress is herself. She's also a bit of a neatness nutter who feels stress and pressure when there's mess about. If you're allowed to peek inside these Holy Arks of the Covenant (the shoe boxes), you should react as though being shown a swaddled orphaned baby. Whisper, smile, compliment but never try to touch. Many of these shoes will be unworn, most with price tags still attached but if you joke about this, ask why they're never worn or imply money has been wasted you will never again be given entry into her mind or her life.

Shoes have a mystical link for women that the majority of blokes will never quite understand. Although many men like shoes and even enjoy buying them, few will manage to get the same complex blend of exhilaration mixed with depression when it comes to buying or owning shoes. One recent, high-profile celebrity court case in the US hinged around the prosecution's theory that the victim had to have been murdered, rather than taking her own life as the defence team suggested, because she'd just bought a new pair of shoes, which was not the act of a suicidal woman. Hopefully the verdict rested on more than this one point because we buy shoes to cheer us up but get even more depressed when it doesn't work.

Cars are also hugely unisex but we've focused on the chaps with the following analysis of car colour. Men still tend to see their car as a bigger status symbol and the colour of their car is always amusingly revealing as they tend to deny its importance in the buying-process. (The last woman we can think of who was connected with a status symbol car was Lady Penelope in Thunderbirds.)

WHAT HIS CAR COLOUR SAYS

A car is not only a personal chariot it is also one of the greatest statements of self-expression many people get to make. Interior design tends to be a family decision but car colour is often down to the car owner and therefore speaks volumes about their 'ideal' social image: the face they like to show to the world in terms of status, presence and personality.

Ever noticed how the average male driver is prone to drive casually with one hand while a woman tends to drive with both hands on the wheel? Psychologists believe men see a car as an extension of their own body, while women see it as a separate entity. A study called 'The secret life of cars and what they reveal about us' also suggests that men talk about their cars so much as a vehicle for expressing their own feelings. Therefore analysing men through their cars is much easier than women, who tend to think about them less.

Red

Red tends to be chosen by someone wanting to portray themselves as confident, extrovert, sexy and a risk-taker which probably means they are none of the above. Having a red car is a little like saying you have a blonde girlfriend. It's a clichéd attempt to prove how daring and successful you are. A red car owner is someone who feels they have something to prove, which could mean a tendency for bouts of anxiety and self-doubt. They will often sound controversial, although they hate being argued with or criticised as they're sensitive souls at heart and turn feral if they feel they're being ridiculed.

Green

When it comes to cars green is the colour of safety and cautiousness. The word itself connotes an interest in saving the planet and green car driver will certainly pay at least lip service to environmental concerns. The green car driver is methodical and thoughtful with an aversion to risk-taking. This driver has no desire to be flash but a possible liking for status and respect that could lead to odd moments of bullish or stubborn driving that can irritate other drivers, even though he will normally be well inside the law.

White

There should be something quasi-virginal and innocent about White Car Man but, since the advent of White Van Man, the image of the white car driver has taken a dent and it's now likely to be the colour of choice of the rebel and devil-may-care motorist. It's either bought by a guy who is genuinely pristine and who relished the challenge of constant cleaning and polishing, or it's bought by the guy who doesn't give a toss and is happy to encourage passers-by to write messages about his wife with their fingers in the filth of the back of the boot.

Silver

Once the colour of whizzy execs, silver is now so popular with travelling salesmen and other coves of the road that it says less about class and more about elderly-ish middle managers with unachievable targets. Silver car man is probably a failed wannabe who can appear laid-back if slightly pompous but who will become irritable when people mistake him for a minicab driver. He's invariably married but might claim not to be, and if he's a younger guy it's likely he's borderline dull, boring dinner party guests with his tales of spreadsheets and team-building days. This image is reflected in the fact that statistics from the University of Auckland show silver car drivers are also the safest on the roads.

Yellow

Optimist or idiot, yellow car driver is the ultimate attention-seeker but with a low regard for status or power. This person wants to be seen as happy-go-lucky and a creative thinker rather than a sex god or control-freak. They love to be seen as innovative and young and will describe themselves as 'a bit mad!' They love exclamation marks and smiley faces and tend to shout a lot when they talk.

Blue

These cars tend to be chosen by either serene drivers or manic depressives. Dark blue is probably the gloomiest colour on the road and can signal someone who has lost all sense of self-belief or self-worth. If it's clean and blue then this person could be careful and frugal having chosen a safe colour with a view to selling it on, rather like people who paint their living rooms Magnolia in case they ever want to sell.

Steel Grey

There's something a bit foxy about grey car-driver, they enjoy looking mainstream but secretly they're as sharp as a tack and a bit of a maverick in the workplace. They tend to be popular but also feared and respected because just when you think you know them they'll do something surprising, reckless or even devious that forces you to reassess their personality.

Black

Black car drivers are controversial but cool, people who will put a mountain of effort into making things look easy. They'll have been told that black is a high-maintenance colour as it shows up the dirt but they still opted for it, meaning they could well have the same attitude to potential partners. Status symbols and trophy-acquiring behaviour is their thing but they're subtle with it. Not a team-player but personally competitive. The sort of person who would own a swimming pool but never mention it in the office.

Cars get changed, swapped, stolen or sold, meaning there's a certain transience to the scope they provide for fluctuations in taste and style, but there are some person-ality-trait statements that are, or should be, like that dog you buy for Christmas: with you for ever. And using your body as a sandwich board by tattooing it with words and designs has to come under that category . . .

WHAT HIS TATTOOS SAY ABOUT HIM

Bringing a new dimension to the term body language, a tattoo is a way to turn your body into an advertising placard, with the underlying desire being to get people to believe what they read there, rather than what your other non-verbal signals appear to be hinting. In reality, this process appears to fool no one apart from the tattooed person themselves, so you can chalk the word 'self-delusional' down first on the long list of qualities your man will be revealing if he has taken his body off for some indelible etching.

The second overall message is that this is a guy who is spontaneous and high-risk in terms of long-term commitment and trust. For him all time is now. He lives in the moment and uses very little in the way of long-term thinking because if he had he would have thought ahead to how ridiculous that huge bird of paradise is going to look when his body is wizened in old age.

Facial Tattoos

The first thing to consider is that this is a guy who is going to be out of work on a regular basis. Men who want jobs keep their body art below tie-level so that their declarations of oedipal emotions can be concealed beneath their interview suit.

Hand Tattoos

As above, for all the same reasons. If he has 'LOVE' on the fingers of one hand and 'HATE' on the other he has been in prison or wants you to believe that he has been in prison, which could easily be worse.

'I Love Mum' Tattoo

You'll laugh about this one and think he's being ironic but keep in mind that he either does love his mum, perhaps in ways that could be described as obsessive, or that he has murdered her and dressed her and kept her in the attic like the guy from *Psycho*.

Small, Traditional Tattoos

He's an off-the-peg kind of guy but in relationship terms this could be a blessing as men who plot and design their own are clearly sauntering down Vanity Alley. This is not a daring guy as such, but a guy who likes to think he's daring now and again, so expect timid and dull sex and romance, interspersed with some moments of drama when he remembers – or when you remind him.

Big Block Foreign Symbols

This is the ultimate in body art, being visible from space like the Wall of China but only when the guy is stripped off, which he clearly intends to do on a regular basis otherwise all his investment down the old tattoo parlour will be wasted. Two things stand out about this guy: firstly he craves attention and secondly he considers himself deep and misunderstood. Far from being mere shapes, the use of words in some foreign scrawl, that even he is a stranger to, suggests that he has some deeper message to impart. He thinks this makes him look clever, which shows you exactly how shallow and stupid he really is.

Your Name

Oh lordy lordy, it must be love because he's gone and got your name etched on his chest. But keep in mind that you're looking at a guy for whom doing something stupid that involves pain is a more attractive form of commitment than, say, getting a mortgage, proposing marriage or even wearing a condom. He probably did it when he was drunk, which is why it's spelled wrong (he can't really sue the tattooist because that's how he wrote it down himself) and this should make you wonder what other acts of excess he's capable of when he's three sheets to the wind. You could also ask him if he knows the name of a clinic that does laser removal and see how quickly he answers. If it's less than 30 seconds he's had half the women in the UK tattooed across his buttocks at some time or other. And by the way, nicknames don't count. He could call them all Sweet Buns.

His Kids' Names

How sweet and what a good father! But before you go off thinking he's a combination of every quality of perfect paternalism take a long hard look at what he really might be saying here. Firstly, why should he need body art to explain what a good dad he is and how much he loves his kids? Surely it's natural for dads to love their kids, isn't it? It's what they do so why is he making himself exceptional? Secondly, why advertise something that everyone, including the kids, should be able to tell from his actions? There's a suspicion here that those who 'tell' like this don't always bother to 'show'. It could be that he's like your boss, sending you an email to say how valued you are rather than telling you face to face or giving you a pay rise. This could be the sort of dad who just taps his tattoos to illustrate to his kids the kind of sacrifice he was prepared to make for them. Also – is this the kind of guy who hates to be upstaged? Do you really want to go through all the agony of giving birth only to listen to him drone on to all your friends about how much tattoos really hurt? Think about it: this guy could be more self-centred than he looks.

WHAT HER TATTOOS SAY ABOUT HER

Mongrel Tattoos

Her body contains an eclectic assortment of tattoos, put together with no apparent rhyme, reason or sense of overall planning. If you're looking for a steady and reliable girlfriend with the capacity for settling down or at least staying around until morning then it might be wise to pass by this shambolic piece of womanhood. She clearly changes her mind with the wind and is a highly spontaneous type, but in an annoying rather than an appealing way. Having anything permanent done to your own body without really thinking it through first is worrying. Once, maybe, but any more should say terminally scatty to the point of toxic.

Tramp Stamps

Once upon a time it was enough to merely hike your thong above belt level and thereby get grown men fainting and old women tutting at your sexual derring-do, but now it's the turn of the tramp stamp to create a more hard-core effect and this has subsequently become the weapon of choice of celebs requiring an edgier image. Stick it on your average non-celeb though and you can assume she's a girl of dubious sexual intentions. Never assume this is an inked flirt signal to attract the gents. It's more likely to be something tribal to ward off the girls and warn that she's well-hard, y'know?

Precious Tattoos

This girl has only one, possibly two tattoos and they're safe designs like stars or small hearts. This girl likes to believe she's as daring as hell but in reality she's a bit of an attention-seeking perfectionist rather than a binge-drinking harpy. Nice enough to take home to meet the parents.

Sailor Tattoos

Is it ironic or symbolic? Well, it's probably a bit of a fashion statement but more and more girls are getting it done. Explain Mermaid titties when you're in your eighties? The point about this girl is that she's saying she doesn't care what you or anyone else thinks, she's just doing her own thing. So fill up your pipe and get into some sea shanties or leave the deck free for a real man.

Sex Signals

This girl sports the sort of tattoos you'd only really get to see while you were having sex and they act a bit like a sat-nav with things like snakes pointing the way to her crotch or ladders creeping down towards her bottom. She clearly has a liking for thick blokes who are too dense to find their way without a map. Impatient, demanding and scornful of a bad performer in bed. Any takers?

Blokes' Names

Look at the list and then place it under close scrutiny. Any sign of skin grafts? Additions of letters to change one name to another? Wrongly spelled names? Because this girl will be a complete pain in the neck, falling in love with you utterly and completely but only until the next guy comes along, plus you also need to wonder why the need to prove her love with the Banksy-body defacing thing. If she can only say it by a taty she clearly has no mechanism for saying it in words or deeds. This is an 'I love you, okay?' kind of a girl. Romantic she ain't.

Once you're down to the tattoos you're very likely to be one step away from his or her underwear. The gift-wrapping of their naughty bits, the pants and panties, may be small items of clothing but their implications are huge.

What woman hasn't secretly crossed her fingers and held her breath hoping and praying that he'll take his socks off first and not have a lurex thong lurking underneath his combats?

WHAT HIS PANTS TELL YOU

Most men feign nonchalance when it comes to pant-purchasing but believe us, in actual fact anxiety and hysteria are bubbling beneath that seemingly indifferent surface. Otherwise why is it so many guys stick to the one style and colour throughout their adult lives while others pick the same style pants they wore as nippers: white Y-fronts? Male-pant role models are so rare that the sight of David Beckham lolling in them on a billboard (no prizes for guessing that they were pseudo white Y-front nipper pants) induces waves of almost tearful relief as men can sleep safe in the knowledge that their pants are 'normal'.

For pants read penis, as the vulnerability factor is similar – they tend to get revealed last to a date pre-sex and can easily lead to responses like giggling, disgust, ridicule or complete turn-off from the woman. Currently there are more 'wrong' pants for a guy to choose (like thongs, comedy and bloomers) than 'right ones', as opposed to women's knicker-buying decisions, where only the infamous big knickers or maybe a pair with the wrong day of the week on them might remotely be thought of as a turn-off.

Boxers

In years gone by the boxer was first employed in public during that outdated theatrical comedy the Whitehall farce. Actors, such as the likes of Brian Rix, were called upon to drop their kecks every night on stage without scaring the matrons in the audience. Hence the billowy great things still beloved by bankers to this day that show no outline of the meat and two veg when they drop their pants at the annual Christmas bash.

Boxers are the pants-next-door of the pants world: safe, unsexy, presumably uncomfortable stuffed into tight jeans but (allegedly) good for the old sperm count. Boxer man likes to hedge his bets and really does think about things like getting run over by a bus and being seen wearing the right thing for a stint in A&E.

He's not necessarily very clever and he's not very sexy but he is your man in an emergency or when you're looking for a chum with whom to marry and breed. If they're silk he's a weird mix of down-to-earth and pretentious, if they're plain or stripy cotton he's a child in a man's body and if they're festooned with a comedy print you should make your excuses and leave because laughing at a man's underwear is really destructive to the seduction process. He must know this, meaning he's not really that into sex.

White Pouch Hugging Pants

These are the über-trendy pant of choice at time of going to press, so this guy is canny and a keen seducer with a nice line in persuading and influencing. The white lets you know he's clean, which can in turn imply good health (note the use of the word 'imply' – in reality white pants only mean good washing powder, not germ-free sex bits) and the link with a toothsome-looking Beckham suggests fitness plus fashion-nous. This guy might have the pants of a nine-year-old but he's probably a vain but prolific seducer.

Thongs

The ultimate deal-breaker, thongs tend to be worn by guys keen to look like your ultimate dream lover but who are in reality well into the male andropause – the male menopause – and want to recapture all their lost youth. They do bum-crunches and sit-ups in a bid to get a six-pack but unfortunately Thong Man nearly always sports bum-flab and an over-hanging gut. This is the guy who believes women will be attracted by power and money (they could be right) and that the sexy underwear will be seen as an added bonus (they're wrong).

Tight-leg Pants

Tight-leg pants man will either have well-honed thighs, in which case he's sexy, clever and a bit of a man's man, or he's got weedy legs, in which case he's a bit of a twerp with the pant legs flapping a bit in the breeze. Longer legs suggest a longer penis and the tight cut of the leg accentuates the package between, meaning a nice-but-naughty effect from a man who knows he's good and has no need to boast.

Retro Pants

Yes, it's the old Y-fronts in those ghastly prints and colours of the seventies and only guys born well after programmes like *The Sweeney* hit the screen should ever be viewed as having sexual potential in pants like these. Any older and the pants are likely to be original, which is neither funny, clever or hygienic. If he's young, then he's ironic, groovy and too clever for his own good, probably a uni student who thinks he is so adept in bed that he no longer needs to advertise his sex appeal.

WHAT HER PANTS TELL YOU

Vampish Red Undies

She should know that they're a bit of a sexual cliché, which means she's either a massive man-pleaser, naïve or someone who likes to think she can shock by showing she's up for it once the lights are dimmed and the smoochy love tunes are playing in the background. By wearing red knickers she's showing you weren't the first one that thought about having sex and this probably makes her feel stronger, naughtier and more in control in bed. She's letting you know she's not a push-over although her rather 'Carry on Camping' choice hints that in reality she might be. She definitely sees sex as a bit of an occasion and an occasion that she will rise to with energy and enthusiasm, at least for the first few times. A woman who wears these sorts of undies could be a born mistress, a high performer who likes to please older guys and/or guys for whom sex with the wife has become a bit of a chore. Red is allegedly the colour of passion but beware: it also signals aggression and conflict.

Comfy Briefs

Bridget Jones-woman might arrive clad in comfy knicks but only if she had no intention of having sex with you, so consider yourself way down the food chain when it comes to her seducing you. To put it another way, no woman would go out on a date with Brad Pitt wearing a pair of these. If you've talked her into sex with you she's either had one too many Babychams or she glimpsed her ex with someone else while you were out and decided to get revenge in any way possible. Every woman has a pair of these comfy briefs somewhere, but if you find her whole knicker-drawer is full of them you could be looking at someone who is genuine, honest, thoughtful and warm-hearted and who rates comfort as one of her key values. She loves nights in cuddled in front of the TV, and although you should never expect waxed bikini-lines and spray-on tans she will at least be a good laugh in bed.

Sexy Thong

Girls who expose these poking above trouser-tops might look like sex kittens but it's primarily an assertion gesture, placing her in control by baring her underwear and then daring you to look and therefore define yourself as a lech. Thong Woman might enjoy sex but only on her own terms and although she might appear to be suffering for her art (thongs are like dental floss for the bottom) she's unlikely to make too much effort to get it. Thong Women like partying with their mates and will tend to mock men on a regular basis. Toothsome but tough she will be the least likely to settle down, unless you're a premiership footballer.

Frilly Knickers

These retro-pants might look a bit old fashioned, suggesting a frothy, giggly, soppy traditionalist who likes her men to take charge, but frilly wearers can also have a bit of a superiority complex. Retro can mean clever and ironic and you might have to keep your wits about you dating this girl. Frillies aren't only worn by curvy types keen to ape the likes of Kelly Brook, they can also be the knicker of choice of post-modern intellectuals who amuse themselves using the 'popsie' look to lure men into their world of seduction. Assume cute and ditsy at your peril.

Novelty Undies

When you blend comedy with underwear you're probably talking suppressed insecurity and borderline shyness because choreographing laughter once the kecks come off will normally only be a defence mechanism: she's getting the first laugh in before you laugh at her. This girl might seem happy-go-lucky but in fact she's likely to be sensitive to criticism and prone to mood swings.

Boy Pants

These resemble tight-fitting hipster shorts and tend to be worn by androgynous skinny types who are nevertheless sufficiently confident in their sexuality to go like a stoat in bed. Not your average sex kitten but don't be put off, this girl has hidden depths.

Power of pants

According to a survey by Match.com a third of women and 28% of men say they never go on a date without wearing their lucky pants.

Once the first date is over and you've agreed a second and third you're into a relationship faster than a barrel over the Niagara Falls. Love is a form of madness, albeit a very nice (if sometimes painful) madness, meaning your critical faculties numb to the point where you find him or her better-looking than Pitt or Jolie, wittier than Eddie Izzard and that knuckle-cracking habit is totally endearing. But before this dumb stage kicks in, take some time to question even the most seemingly innocuous behaviours, like:

WHAT HIS ROMANTIC GESTURES SAY

A romantic gesture is really something of a self-stroke. It stokes your own sense of self-adoration as much if not more than it induces fond feelings in somebody else. We like to use these gestures to measure our own attractiveness through the noble act of giving. However, givers are also receivers and so there will often be some sort of strategy lurking behind each and every one of these acts. Often the romantic act will be a face-saving ploy, aimed at delegating all the real effort we would have to put into loving acts or communications through things like 'saying it with flowers'. Romantics are often in love with love rather than actually in love and the overly romantic gesturer has quite possibly never been in love in his or her life. You'll often see a guy carrying the bunch of flowers he's just bought back to his car with a self-satisfied smirk on his face. He's just affirmed himself as a romantic lover in his own eyes, as well as in the eyes of the world. And do remember that romantic gestures are often easily transferable. If you're out when he calls he might easily give them to his mum instead.

Couriered Flowers

He's displaying a cool, remote form of passion plus showing you that he has the power to delegate by sending the courier to do his courting. This makes him an odd fish because you'll end up thanking and smiling at another man as you clutch the blooms to your chest. This means he knows that you will have to call him to thank him, which must be his turn on, rather than the sight of your little face lighting up.

This is the most uninvolved form of romantic gesture: one quick call from him (or his PA) and a florist makes up the bouquet and another chap gets into his van to deliver it. It's love and sex by proxy and this sums up his attitude to life. It's quite possible he chose your bouquet on price alone. It's also possible he sent the flowers out of guilt to make up after a row and say sorry for his own bad behaviour. Reciting the number on your credit card is hardly an act of atonement though. Ruthless, controlling and remote.

Petrol Station Flowers

Life really did roll over the top of his head, didn't it? Any man who looks on forecourt flowers and considers they will charm any woman apart from an elderly, partially sighted gran is truly deluded and lacking in all the finer graces in life. However besotted you might be, never go overboard in your praise for this 'romantic' gesture or next time it will be a sackload of charcoal briquettes and a tree-shaped air-freshener. This guy is a thick-skinned optimist who believes women will love him for his scampish charm and sense of irresponsibility. If he gets a night of sex out of these blooms he must either be a veritable stud-muffin or dating the world's most desperate woman.

Dinner Out

He's a traditionalist without an ounce of creativity and has a taste for the classical things in life. He's also a bit of a control-freak because he knows it's hard not to end this type of date without sex. It shouldn't escape notice that his 'romantic' gesture is a treat for two that can be enjoyed by him as well as you and if he likes his scoff then it's a good bet he's rather self-centred. There's something of the primate about this guy who revels in his ability to do the hunter–killer thing and bring food to the table for his woman. On a more strategic note remember he'll also be busy sizing up the way you eat to see whether you're a goer back in the bedroom or not.

On a visual note he's likely to be vain, as the meal will involve a lot of face-watching although he's deleting any competition by getting you all to himself. He clearly rates his verbal skills too as there will be a lot of chatting or listening going on.

Dinner At Home

Oh dear God, not the paper napkins and the floating candles and the red wine casserole and the profiteroles again! As he puts the Chris Rea on the CD, plugs in the ambient air freshener and uncorks the Frascati he really does think he's God's gift to the seduction game. He probably spent the afternoon shaving his chest and plucking his nose hairs, and now he waits for his victim to get home from a long hard day playing Solitaire on the office computer. Although he's making out this is a romantic gesture secretly he's riddled with glee, less at the thought of the surprise you're going to get than at the forgone conclusion that there will be sex after the meal. And you'll have to mask the expression of suppressed horror on your wan little face as you realise that instead of a quiet night in front of *Top Gear* or *Strictly Come Dancing*, you're going to have to muster up the energy for a night of fake debauchery. He's too mean to pay for a meal out or he's a fan of the Ken Barlow school of seduction or he's a stranger to the joys of spontaneous sex.

Diamonds

He's astute, intelligent, manipulative and successful. He knows what he wants and he knows how to get it, and although people he works with fear him for his buccaneer-style ruthlessness and directness he will have absolutely no trouble when it comes to finding a mate. In fact, he probably has queues outside the door to rival *The X Factor*. He's not a bluffer or a game-player and he has no qualms about the fact that his wallet is part of his charm. He will also have a possessive streak. When his girl wears diamonds he gave her, the message to outsiders is the equivalent of a dog spraying its territory: hands off.

Handwritten Poems

He's truly one of life's innocents, a naïve optimist who wears his heart on his sleeve and will happily give it away, even if it's only to get it broken. Which it does. Regularly and often. In the age of text when a romantic message amounts to 'Gt yr pnts off im cming hm now' his penned sonnets mark him out as an old-fashioned soppy. Remember what happened to the last guy who emailed his heart to his girl in verse? It ended up on the Internet with comments like 'I'm puking' and 'Poor sod' affixed under it but this won't put him off. This man is determined and he knows the right girl is out there for him somewhere. Break his heart if you feel like it because it's there for the breaking. Sadness and pining are well within his comfort zone.

The Weekend Away

One thing about this guy is that he has no trouble getting to the point. No matter how thatched the cottage or scenic the view we all know that the sole objective of this romantic gesture is getting his end away, as often as possible in the time available. He's an opportunist masquerading as a romantic. While you're busy packing silken nighties and a range of designer clothing he's sticking a toothbrush, vibrator and pack of 'buy one get one free' condoms into a small plastic carrier while on the phone checking the room is soundproof, bombproof and not overlooked.

The Grand Gesture

He employs football stadium tannoys, aeroplanes with streamers, hot-air balloons or even banners on motorway bridges to make his romantic gesture and to impress you but, more importantly, the rest of the world too. Why be subtle when you can make the big statement? For him sex and love are all about having fun, and a romantic gesture is something to tell his mates about down the pub, whether it worked or not. When he spray-wrote 'Will you marry me, Angela?' across the M25 flyover it was adventure he was after, not your hand in marriage. In fact he probably spelled your name wrong. He does nothing by halves and friends know him as a party-loving extrovert. This guy will have a soft heart deep down inside somewhere but by making grand and wacky gestures like this he makes sure he keeps it well protected. He's frightened of getting hurt which is why sitting down in front of you and quietly telling you he loves you fills him with dread.

Once the seduction is in the bag it's all about the two 'S's: Shagging and Sleeping. It could be argued that the sex bit is easy compared to what inevitably follows. Sleeping together is the ultimate bonding exercise, and also the ultimate deal-breaker if you're the 'Now shut up and go to sleep' type while your partner's more into professions of undying love . . .

SNOOZE WHO: WHAT THEIR SLEEPING POSITION REVEALS

The way we sleep tells us a lot – both when we're alone and together as couples. Sleeping has to be the most subconscious act of all and therefore our personality is allowed to roam free under the covers. You might think that we simply sleep in random positions every night. In fact we do move around a lot – between 40–60 times a night on average. But people do fall into very particular categories of posture that they favour when they're between the sheets and psychologists believe that it's the position that we go into just as we go off to sleep that's the most revealing, as it's the one we're most comfortable in. Here's our guide to what some of the classic positions identified by psychologists reveal . . .

Foetal

The position we adopted in our mother's womb with legs and arms drawn in tight to our body. This and the semi-foetal positions are the most popular.

What it says: Foetal sleeps are shy people who can feel vulnerable. The drawn-in position – guarding the heart – shows that they want to keep things close and don't open up easily. They'll be wary of quick commitment in a relationship but tend to have intense liaisons once they do. They are likely to be highly emotional and artistic people.

Pillow talk

In a study Professor Chris Idzikowski, director of the Sleep Assessment and Advisory Service, discovered that 41% of us adopt the foetal position when asleep.

Sleeping On the Side with Both Arms Out In Front with Knees Slightly Bent

What it says: Those extended arms display an open nature – these are people prepared to adapt to change and able to compromise. They are sociable – in fact they look to others to define themselves. Easy going but likely to avoid conflict and to feel easily hurt. If the arms are down by the side they can lack creativity and be a touch gullible – they're happy to blend into the background.

Face Down with Arms Above Your Head

What it says: An outgoing, successful type who is verging on the brash – but their bravado tends to be an act. Quite nervy underneath, they don't react well to criticism and could be controlling in a relationship and tend to be a stickler for things like punctuality at work.

Lying On Your Back with Both Arms By Your Sides

What it says: This is a revealing position, related to a high degree of mental toughness. Confidence is high and these characters verge on the arrogant. The showy position means that they are happy with their image and likely to be into flaunting wealth and snappy dressing. Being centre of attention is second nature. There is a selfish streak here and you'll have to love them for who they are rather than the compliments they will lavish on you.

It's also possible to read a lot about your relationship from the kind of posture you adopt as a couple.

Turn your back on your lover!

A recent study for the hotel chain Travelodge found that the most common sleeping position for British couples was to sleep back to back, though not touching.

WHAT YOUR SLEEP-TOGETHER POSITIONS SAY ABOUT YOU

Her Head On His Chest

This is early days in a relationship stuff, when passion is so intense you giggle about the fact that your bodies appear to have been hand-crafted for one another as every sleep/cuddle position feels wonderfully comfortable. And indeed his bony chest does feel like a pillow and you barely notice those chest-hairs tickling your face or the wax-stubble exfoliating your forehead. This is Alpha male, frontiersman stuff with the compliant little woman safe against her man's heart.

His Head On Her Chest

Done purely for sexual and/or pseudo-infantile gratification. Either he's using your boobs as a water-bed or he likes the nurturing feel. Either way, not the most adult bloke in the box.

Back to Back

Not as unhappy as it sounds, as long as the spines are close and there is some touch involved. This position suggests a couple who watch out for and protect one another against the world, literally watching one another's backs.

Back to Back – Apart

This is less encouraging in relationship terms, especially if you're hanging in that hammock that's created where the sheet tucks into the mattress, which implies you're trying to get as far away from one another as possible.

Star Shapes

You're both hogging the space in the bed, meaning you could well have status issues in real life. Did you measure your side of the bed yet? You will, believe us. Thinking your partner has an unfair share of the mattress displays a competitive and argumentative streak in your relationship.

Face to Face

Curled up like two little dormice, with hands linked and heads close suggests childlike trust and shared values. You want your partner to be the first thing you see when you open your eyes and will happily put up with morning bear-breath to achieve this, which has to mean unconditional love.

Spoons

The most sexual pose as it means most of the main sex bits are in contact throughout the night, meaning you do like to be in tune with one another's sexual needs. A protective role for the guy as well, curling his little sex goddess up into his body where he can watch over her all night or at least until she pops out to the loo.

Having spent many years analysing celebrity power-couple poses it would be unfair, if not impossible, to write this book without setting out the same set of rules for more normal humans who are not cosying up on the red carpet in front of a wall of press cameras. For the rest of us then here's . . .

WHAT YOUR PARTNERSHIP POSES SAY ABOUT YOUR RELATIONSHIP

When you're out with your partner you will have your own rituals of touch and contact as you walk along the road. These gestures can have an evolutionary development, changing as both you and your relationship matures, although not necessarily as some elderly couples will still hold hands like teenagers. Whether they vary or not though, these rituals will reveal much about the emotional and status-state of your relationship, from the way you hold hands to who takes the lead.

Mutual Hand-holding

This is an adolescent ritual that suggests a youthful approach if it continues through a longer-term relationship. It's practical, easy-going and fun, although the hand-clasp retains a valuable method of exchanging quite intimate information using subtle tie-signs like squeezing or pulling, plus a snapshot of mood via tension, heat or even sweat-levels.

Hand-holders retain the right to express individuality as there is little scope for actual body-touch with this clasp. The hand that is on top usually denotes where the power and leadership lies in the relationship and entwined fingers suggest even closer ties than a simple clasp.

Arms Round Waists

This much less practical gesture (it makes normal walking difficult) creates an emphatic level of physical intimacy via torso-touch, suggesting that sexual closeness is more important than sociability for this couple.

Arm Around Shoulders

The 'top' arm in this mobile cuddle belongs to the dominant, protective partner and the amount of congruent snuggling from the other partner shows whether this dominance will be accepted or cause long-term conflict.

Arm or Hand Around Neck

This gesture is less about affection and more about play-wrestling as it can feel threatening for the 'victim'. Neck-clasps suggest ownership and marking one's territory. The 'grapple' implications suggest sexual experimentation and testing, which is what most play-fighting among couples amounts to.

The Bicep Grip

When a girl holds her guy's arm around the bicep she's signalling an old-fashioned 'You Tarzan – Me Jane' approach to the relationship. This gesture accentuates the bloke's manliness and strength and makes him look like a physical trophy.

The Gap

When a couple walks with a gap in between them you can assume this relationship is well past its prime. If the gap is emphasised by the carrying of a bag, phone or car-keys or the shoving of one hand in a pocket there is a desire to create even further space by the use of barriers.

So now that you've sussed him or her out via the state of their bathroom cabinet or their pizza order you can turn your thoughts back onto 'You' again, as we use Part Three of *The You Code* to study different strategies when it comes to image management. How do you *want* to be seen? What kind of date do you want to be? And what promotion are you after at work? Part Three of *The You Code* contains the key steps to successful image tweaking, meaning those small but high-impact changes to your choices and behaviours will make essential differences to the way you are seen by those around you.

PART THREE: HOW TO TWEAK YOUR HABITS TO GET WHAT YOU WANT

8

BEING LIKED

How important are the instant impressions you make on other people? Bestselling author and cultural commentator Malcolm Gladwell describes the process of first impressions as 'thin-slicing' – our ability to make sense of complicated situations and information in a flash, while Professor Frank Bernieri of Oregon State University says that 'First Impressions are the fundamental drivers of our relationships . . . A first impression is your initial condition for analysing another human being.'

His students videoed job interviews and found they could predict whether the candidate would be offered a job from the first 15 seconds of the tape, based on handshakes and instant appearance and behaviours. One of the problems with this kind of instant decision-taking process is that although we might like to think we're subsequently being fair and keeping an open mind about a person, the likelihood is we're more likely to look for confirmation that those first impressions were right, even if it means our judgements are biased. It's a useful process to keep this bias in mind and rock and roll with it rather than fighting it, learning to play other people like a mandolin by tweaking your behaviours, rather than falling foul of the traits of 'just being myself'. In any event it's not exactly cheating, just enhancing what is already there.

THE REAL 'YOU'

And if the above doesn't persuade you to start tweaking, keep in mind theories about self from the likes of Carl Jung. The 'real' you could well consist of a darker side or 'shadow self' that we'd do well to hide from public view as it can be rude, intolerant and aggressive, especially when you feel stressed or threatened. If all your niceness and good manners are just a front to help you survive in society, how helpful can it be to be 'yourself' during that important job interview or impressing a new partner on the first few dates?

Can image tweaking make you more popular? Back in the 1930s a hugely popular book was published called *How to Win Friends and Influence People*. Over seventy years later it still sells in the millions because it provided what seemed like a textbook guide to popularity and people realised that these are skills that can be learned. Why be a Billy-no-mates or the one sitting home alone on a Saturday night when all it takes is a few sociable techniques? Today we tend to flounder every bit as much, thinking popularity or unpopularity are just a case of getting life's long or short straw. We all strive to be successful, yet success tends to lead to isolation and unpopularity. Name one celebrity or famous name who hasn't suffered from the Tall Poppy Syndrome (the name given to the moment when their head appears above the balcony because they have become successful and is lopped off by the public, effectively cutting them down to size). No wonder that psychologists have searched for a 'likeability' blueprint. We expect people to like us and are confused when they don't. When parents smother their child with attention and affection or give unconditional love they often scupper a child's ability to take active steps to foster affection and 'like' in others. Why would you bother to learn something that's always been there on tap?

PRACTICAL TWEAKING

So now that you've undergone some behavioural analysis and learned how to suss out that date via the evidence of his sock drawer or her bathroom cabinet it's time to look at personal modifications. Now, before you start quoting the J.B.Y. rule of life-skills at us (Just Be Yourself) it would be wise to take stock of what a Tom Cruise movie once famously referred to as collateral damage. Has your life been one long happy-ever-after fairy tale in terms of career success and meeting/dating/mating? We suspect not or you wouldn't have picked this book up in the first place. No, like the rest of the universe your life is less than perfect and your behaviours could do with a bit of a reboot. Especially if you're older, in which case you will have acquired several tastes and habits along the crazy-paving path called life that need to be changed or shucked off if you are to avoid being forced into a cave like a hermit.

If you've read through the rest of the book with an air of mounting horror and have come to the conclusion that there's so much about you that is wrong that even starting to make improvements seems beyond you then don't worry because we're here to hold your hand and make things as easy as possible. There is nothing truly chaotic or Herculean about changing the way other people see you. The good news is that the smallest of tweaks can have the greatest effect overall.

Rule Number 1: Know Your Aims

It's amazing how many people change their image or behaviour without knowing what effect they're trying to achieve. Hairdressers in particular are well aware of the 'Do what you like but just make me look different' syndrome where we go into the salon expecting that a mere haircut will change the entire direction of our lives.

Knowing what you're striving for in terms of ideal image and perception is vital. Imagine you are writing a script and that your body and your behaviours are the lines of that script. And remember that it can often be the odd word or two of that script that can make all the difference in terms of the message received by other people.

The 'attribution effect' defines the way we tend to judge other people according to what can be one-off random behaviours. We feel impelled to sum people up in a very short space of time and will be heavily swayed by these fleeting events. One scowl, sigh, yawn, smile or nervous twitch and we feel we have the 'handle' on that person's personality and future behavioural patterns, especially when that person is a colleague or employee in the workplace.

If we have low expectations of that person we will employ negative attributions, looking at even the smallest hint that things might not be right and taking it as evidence to endorse our assumptions. Or we can use positive attributions, which mean we might even take a negative and turn it into a positive to suit our own needs and desires. It's common for people falling in love to use 'love goggles' when they judge their new partner, reading positive messages from negative signals. If they are always late turning up for dates or forgetting to phone, the loving partner is tempted to read this as a sign of eccentricity rather than indifference, or when the partner fails to get in contact after the first night of sex the besotted partner might tell themselves they might have been frightened by the intensity of their own emotions rather than that they just didn't rate them in bed.

Static v Dynamic
The signals you send out to others, especially through your body language, daily choices and behavioural patterns will

fall under one of two headings: your Static Cues, which are essentially the way you behave normally and your Dynamic Cues, which are speedier acts or emotions that may appear out of character. If you start to make sudden and dramatic changes in your behaviour and choices then it will be seen as irrational changes in your Dynamic Cues, with people around you expecting your habits to go back to normal after a while. Make gradual and more natural changes though and people will begin to see you in a new light.

Rule 2: Plot Your Strategies Using Cognitive Algebra

It's important to understand that other people read you according to clusters of behaviour that occur at any one given time and that they evaluate one against another to come to their conclusions. This process is called Cognitive Algebra and the term describes the process of adding together information suggested by certain traits or behaviours then subtracting any opposing signals to come up with an overall conclusion about someone. So if they see you jogging into a health food shop and coming outside to light up a fag they will read a whole host of very small, often subliminal signals to judge whether you really are a health nut – or just a nut. Do you look otherwise fit? Are your clothes suitable for exercise? Did the cigarette come out of a packet and was it lit by a lighter or had you perhaps just begged one off a friend and lit it with a match, suggesting it's a habit you're seriously fighting to quit?

So you need to be aware of your current signals before you learn to balance them or swing them into a different direction. If you can do this any changes you make will look congruent and authentic rather than part of some huge devious plot to spin yourself in a way that could be perceived as manipulative.

Rule 3: Look At Your Four Key Impacts

There are four key ways that you can begin to make a difference that works:

1. Selling You to You

Your intrapersonal impacts, that is, the messages in your own head, will affect your external image. So it's important to begin by selling yourself to yourself. Do you have self-belief? Do you have inner confidence? If not your negative thoughts will leak out via your body language and behavioural signals.

2. Interpersonal Impacts

This is the way you communicate with other people. Are you able to get your messages across verbally and visually?

3. Performance Impacts

There are times in your life when you are called upon to step up to the plate in terms of image and impact: job interviews, dates, presentations or speeches, difficult one-to-one discussions etc. Does the way you put yourself together enhance or conflict with the message you're trying to impart?

4. Environmental Impacts

This is how you behave in different circumstances with different people.

So when you start to plan your Cognitive Algebra you should take your current impact or image, then set it against your image goals. In mathematical terms this means starting with your solution, or ideal image goal and then working through the mathematics backwards to discover how to get there. Which, in turn, means studying existing behaviours to see how they currently affect that solution.

To put it simply it could look something like this:

AIM: I want to come across in the next weekly team meeting at work as keen, positive and confident.

- I currently find I tend to be seen as quiet or reluctant to make a point.
- This is because I arrive looking nervous, sit without doing introductions, take the seat furthest from the front and fold my arms and legs and only speak if I am asked a direct question.
- I need to deal with all the negative voices in my head that tell me to keep quiet, or that my ideas are worthless or will be ignored anyway.
- I need to look at practical ways of making more impact, like walking in looking relaxed and sitting in a more prominent seat.
- I need to change other visual habits like chewing on an old biro, doodling or wearing a colour that suggests I want to be ignored.
- If I get the balance right without looking too dramatically different I should be able to change people's perceptions about me in a way that has an air of authenticity.

Am I Being Phoney?

Given the tools to enhance your lot in life it's blisteringly common to hear people complain that working their image and impact will somehow make them a phoney, or that they will be compromising their personal integrity.

Well, impression management is only like learning or honing any other skill. If you wanted a job as a chauffeur you'd go on an advanced driving course and if you needed to work abroad you'd learn a foreign language. So why not bother to take a few steps back to see how you project to others around you, especially potential partners, clients and bosses, and then either tweak or extend your skills to enhance your chances of success? You weren't born with the body language you use now, nor were you born with your tastes in food, wine, music and interior design. These are all learned behaviours so why not learn a few more as you work your way through life?

US President Barack Obama is a great example of a man who gets his image right. Transforming himself from someone with little voter recognition to a man who has have achieved wide admiration that even borders on hero-worship took him a little less than a year. Did he do this by 'being himself'? He certainly did it by appearing to be himself but it would be foolish to imagine he discovered the knack of wandering out on stage in front of millions of people and speaking in a powerful and convincing manner just by chance. Or that he was simply born with the skills of oratory and persuasion.

In many ways President Obama has created the ideal blend of traits for success: he is not a sham, he is known to be a clever and intellectual man, so his image isn't a pretence. But there have been many other brilliant minds throughout political history who never won the people over in the way that he has.

President Obama has three key psychological impacts and selling points, all of which work as well as the other:

1. He projects an air of leadership and control. When he speaks he has a knack of raising his head, narrowing his eyes and gazing off into the middle distance, portraying himself as a man of destiny. In photographs he was looking like a president well before he set foot inside The White House. He is a smart but

unobtrusive dresser and good-looking enough to cash in on the phenomenon in which good looks are normally assumed to be a sign of a good personality and niceness.

2. He projects paternalism. There is always a subliminal desire for our leaders, bosses and coaches to take on a quasi-parental role in our lives, even on a fitful or temporary basis. This makes it easier to accept their authority and creates an air of safety, which is especially seductive when times are hard. President Obama is a relatively young man and yet his appearances with his daughters give him an air of idealised fatherhood that appeals to old and young alike.

3. He projects as a lover. A subtle and special form of sex appeal will have similar across-the-board appeal for voters. Many politicians have tried and failed at this technique, either indulging in exaggerated displays of touching and kissing with their partners before being found out as cheats, or making such clumsy and awkward attempts to look loved-up that they end up looking as though they and their spouses had only just met. The Obamas are relatively cheesy in their portrayals of love, respect and attraction for one another but so far it has always worked. He manages to gaze at her from the stage as though she is the only person in the audience and she responds with realistic looks of pride and humour.

Getting your words, thoughts and image to match up like this is called creating congruence, which, in turn, leads to a look of authenticity.

The good news is that you can also create congruence in your own image and impacts even when you're under pressure to 'perform' for occasions like dates, interviews and first meetings.

TAKING STOCK

Once you've begun to get some idea of how you want to be perceived by one significant person or many people you will need to do a quick self stock check. This means YOU looking at YOU, which in turn means some very honest and objective thinking.

How do you think people who know you currently see you? And how do you think people who have met you for the first time tend to judge you via first impressions?

To work out the answers to both these vital questions you'll need to remove two types of unhelpful thinking from your assessment:

1. Intentional thoughts
2. Sick notes

Your intentional thoughts are to do with all those things you meant to change or get right, like intending to polish your shoes/tidy your bedroom/get rid of a couple of pounds in weight/clean out the car/be on time for a date.

Your sick notes are all the excuses you make to yourself for not 'performing' or behaving well. Sick-note dialogues include lines like: 'I wanted to talk but I was too shy', 'I'm confident with people I know well, but . . .' 'I didn't know they would ask to come back to my place for coffee', or 'How was I to know that other guy in the lift while I was slagging off the firm would turn out to be the one that would be conducting my interview?'

The problem with both these sets of thoughts is that they only exist in your head. Other people can't see them or hear them.

You can't argue with other people's perceptions of you. If you come across as boring, vain, dumb, lazy, scary, obsessive, superficial, snobbish, unreliable then it's up to you to create a better impression of yourself, even if you know you are none of the above.

Or in other words: If the cap doesn't fit, don't wear it.

9

CHANGING THE WAY OTHERS SEE YOU

Once you have your aims in mind and know your current image, as well as what is provoking those perceptions, you can begin to make what we call critical tweaks. These 'choice changes' will affect your daily impacts, making your boss, colleagues, clients and dates see you in the way you want to be perceived. Taking a random approach to your key impacts means letting fate control your future. If this has always created success in your life then get out your inflatable lilo and float along with fate for as long as suits you. But if you prefer to believe you could do better in terms of winning business, getting jobs, being popular and bagging a partner then take your destiny into your own hands and therefore make it objective-focused. After all, would you feel happy getting into your car and just driving around the streets in the hope you will arrive at a destination that you haven't decided on? No, you pick your destination first then you plan the best route to get you there, even using sat-nav to ensure you get there as efficiently as possible. So why not apply the same process to your own life? And here's your image sat-nav guide to help you achieve those goals:

Most people arrive at work every day without any idea exactly how they make their entrance and what impact it has on everyone they work with. Everyone who works with or studies animal behaviour knows that the first impression is vital for survival and acceptance. How one animal approaches a pack, group or herd can be a matter of life and death. How you approach colleagues or clients in the workplace might not be literally lethal but even with a group you work with on a regular or daily basis the way you define your mood and approach as you arrive in the morning will have the most tremendous effect on your longer-term impacts. The following is a guide to tell you how to make an instant impact at work.

Hard day's night

A study revealed that workaholics could, in fact, be the best lovers. Jonathan Schwartz, a professor of psychology, studied the sex lives of 100 sexually active couples over the space of a year and found that women with partners who worked long hours were happier with their sex lives.

Undoubtedly the arena in which most of us have to create the right impression every single day is the workplace. But forget donning shoulder pads or having an expensive haircut. You may be able to change the whole way that you are perceived by others simply by swapping your pen.

PEN PORTRAITS

The famous phrase goes: 'The devil is in the detail' and never has this been as true as at that moment when the pen comes out during a business meeting, sales pitch, or even noting down of a mobile number. Forget all the conscious image effort of suits, smiles and aftershave, it's the small nibbed object that reveals all about his or her genuine levels of class, wealth and self-esteem. Pens come and go throughout our lives at an alarming rate but every one we buy, save and use takes on the shape of our own little image-offspring, joined to use by ink if not blood and telling everyone who sees it exactly what type of parent/owner you really are. Prepare to make excuses about your own pen ('My best ones get stolen', 'I picked this up in a hotel', 'I never saw it before' etc) but prepare to understand that if it followed you home like an unwanted stray it is still your pen and therefore a chip off the old block. If you hated it you would have thrown it out. You adopted it just as much as it adopted you. The fact you allowed it desk space, bag space or pocket space means it has some symbiotic meaning that you can never effectively deny.

The pen is both a writing implement and a gestural weapon. The writing usage falls a very poor second to the weapon usage in most offices. Anything that gets held in the hand in the workplace will automatically qualify as a prime mover in the Deferred Gesture arena, meaning what you do with that pen, cup or paper is often seen as what you would secretly like to do to the person you're speaking to. All inner emotions get a public airing when we clasp a pen in our hands . . .

The Ballpoint

This is the plat du jour of the pen world, something so achingly plain, dull and functional that it defies all attempts to apply a style or taste tag on it and the same applies to anyone owning one. These pens come in boxes of twenty or more and never get nicked because no one ever wants them. They do nothing to either harm or enhance your handwriting but do considerable damage in terms of kudos if discovered lined up like anorexic soldiers in the shirt breast pocket.

Ballpoint owners will have absolutely no memory whatsoever how – like wire coat hangers and plastic forks – they came to be in their possession but they also make no move to dispose of them once they are discovered, which only proves that the ballpoint owners have an affiliation with something so undeniably naff. Ballpoint owners are stingy, anal and practical and stupefyingly boring. Only ever bring one out of your pocket if absolutely everything else about you screams 'über-cool style legend'. If you do then it will be seen as something akin to performance art. Gilbert & George could manage a biro and get away with it and so could cerebral actors. If you do use a ballpoint it must look pristine and still have its cap on. Keep it in a stupidly expensive pen-holder or – even better – a box.

The Chewed Ballpoint

Chewing a pen is a sign of frustration but rarely sexual frustration so don't think you're a coiled spring in the bedroom department. Boring but stressed would be words that would define you perfectly. Get out of the habit and never own, get close to or even touch a chewed ballpoint. Bargepoles come to mind regarding these pens.

Designer Pens

A perfect purchase that says all the right things, especially if the rest of your image is more random and chaotic. A designer pen that looks, smells and writes good is a sure sign of a successful person and someone who self-rewards on a regular basis. There's a degree of low self-esteem lurking insofar as you might need an astronomically priced pen to prove your worth and your place on this planet but it's sufficiently well hidden, meaning the cracks rarely show. This pen defines you as someone who likes subtler displays of status and worth and that you are capable of quality work and thinking.

The Hotel Pen

This pen might look like a small whoopsie: you spent the night in a hotel and the pen that you picked up in an emergency to write down a phone message somehow made its way home with you. Don't forget that the implications are greater and a tad more sinister. People who take pens from hotel rooms are avid hunters, craving any 'kill' from an expedition, no matter how small and symbolic. They travelled, they trekked and so they needed a souvenir. Did you pocket the small notepad as well but then see sense and put it down at the last minute? This item will make you look thoughtless and non-strategic, blundering your way through life with a half-baked smile of apology, and with faintly dangerous overtones of kleptomania. Hotel Pen Man/Woman is not seen as someone to either trust or rely on. Bin it.

The Coloured Pen

Of all the childish ways to stand out and define yourself as a 'special' person the coloured-ink pen has to be the dumbest. The coloured pen will show you up as someone who adores signing cheques, documents and letters in green/purple ink and then shrugging and smiling as though to say 'what am I like?' Are you an eccentric wannabe, liking to see yourself as crazy, fun and totally different from all their colleagues at work? This pen only displays superficial and contrived eccentricity. Colleagues will see that deep down you are still governed by the coloured ink at school culture, where red or green were used as an evaluation and a reward. This pen suggests you achieve very little in life but that you like to mark your own small achievements with a mental 'tick'. This means you will look sad, defensive and hostile in the face of teasing or criticism. Only use this pen if you really do need to create a 'Not waving but drowning' form of action to attract attention in your business. Although being memorable for purple ink alone is questionable.

The Fun Pen

Of course there are loads to choose from and these pens do tend to be gifts, meaning that if you own one of these, someone close to you decided you would suit a pink pen with flashing lights, a gigantic, tasselled biro or a pen with kittens or cartoon animals portrayed along the length. The fact you accepted and then used the pen means you took a conscious decision to *like* the image message being sent out by it. So inside that pin-striped/unsmiling/dour/ professional exterior you adopt for work lies a fluffy little bunnykins or a veritable funster. This is peek-a-boo politics, implying a hint of something you aren't showing on the outside. You think this rounds you out as a character, we think it means you're spooky. Move away from the pen. Get rid.

The Fountain Pen

This is the King Canute of pen ownership, suggesting you're someone who wants to hold the tide progress that is coming in on a wave of ballpoints and felt tips. You're into quality and class but also inky fingers and Jack the Ripper-style script writing. The pen is heavy enough to suggest you're someone who otherwise travels light and you're so full of your own self-importance that you feel everything you write deserves some kind of ritual attached to it, like removing the cap first and blotting or waving the writing afterwards to avoid smudging. You're someone who's heavily into quality performance and happy to work hard behind the scenes to back that performance up (did you ever see someone refill a fountain pen? It's not a pretty sight).

If the pen is the tool or weapon of choice then the font is the flourish that defines your written communications. How often do we deny all choice in the matter of PC font styles, claiming it was the setting you inherited and never bothered to change? Image is all about perception though, so if your font style is too baroque or too out-of-date there's no excuse in the world that will erase the signals that have been transmitted by it . . .

BE THE FONT OF ALL KNOWLEDGE

As far back as the 1500s graphologists made a business out of analysing our handwriting and showing what it revealed about us. They believe that certain styles and stroke structures can be related to certain personality traits. But these days many of us don't write almost anything longhand. We have to choose a style. Some of the fonts we choose are chosen for us by the programme or application we use. But whether it's personal correspondence or a business email most of us have a favourite style of typeface, even if we don't necessarily know its name. We use these things every day – we have to live with them. We also know that others are going to have to see them – especially in emails, CVs and letters. And psychologists believe that which font you use can make a difference to how others perceive you as a person, though they may never have met you, making it all the more important that you get it right. A 2001 study called 'The Psychology of Fonts', revealed some of the personality traits behind fonts and its author,

Dr Aric Sigman, believes a typeface can significantly influence what the reader thinks.

It appears that typefaces do have inherent personalities. What you choose may reveal yours, but by picking another you can subtly alter the messages you want the reader to get. So you might choose one type of font to write a CV for a job in a bank, another for a job in TV. Here are the kind of messages we believe you're sending out by using some of the most popular fonts.

Times New Roman

By using this hugely popular typeface you feel you're showing that you are a pretty weighty type with something important to say by choosing it. It's likely that you favour classic choices in other things too but the words you use are important – you're saying that issues are more important than style. You consider yourself trustworthy and respectable as well as formal and stable. This is a choice for a solicitor or a newsreader. If you're any further down the food chain in terms of intellect this is the typeface for you as this Burberry raincoat of fonts will add gravitas to anything you write. (We hope!)

Arial

Seen as the choice of someone who wears sensible shoes, according to Dr Sigman. It's a font that leaves people guessing. However its simple, straightforward style doesn't mean that you're dull. It's a typeface that concentrates on the message, not the writing itself. So it's someone who isn't bothered about the peripheral or image. You want to honestly reveal yourself, which is helpful in business. With Arial, people think that they're getting the real deal and that you're an easy-going, helpful kind of person.

Courier

Small, straight fonts like this hark back to a golden age. It might be the choice of the grumpy old man or woman. It's a typeface of someone who resents the computer age and would rather be back drinking whisky hunched over an old typewriter. There's a lack of imagination here. A reader might infer that you're a stubborn type, unlikely to be open to change.

Helvetica

Said to be the world's most popular font and has been famously used by phone giant Orange. This is a modern reassuring font, a smooth font without too many flourishes. You're saying you don't want to stand out by using this, but you're also showing that you're a safe pair of hands, if verging on the dull. It's a typeface that shows you're happy to be corporate fodder and won't rock the boat but you're also a contemporary, forward-thinking type and can adapt to change.

Comic Sans

A typeface that's attention-seeking and ever so slightly goofy. A study by Wichita State University shows that people who use flowery fonts in their email are less likely to be taken seriously by readers. Fine if you're designing a fun website; not so good for a CV. There's an element of not living in the real world here. You could be a genius but you'd want a boss who was going to want to give you free reign. You probably think you've got a sense of humour but readers can be scared. They think you're the type of person who spells crazy with a K. It comes across as overly friendly so use it only to write to a pal who already knows your foibles.

Georgia

Curvy shapes suggest a bit of a 'designer rock-chick' personality. The fashion-conscious style of this font suggests someone who is into design and who dislikes compromise, while the very rounded emphasis hints you're sexy, sensual, an extrovert and a bit of a sexual adventurer.

Impact

Modern Display fonts like this are most associated with masculine traits. The word 'Impact' suggests assertive or even aggressive when applied to a font, rather like capitals signal you're shouting or angry. If you use this font you could appear rude and bossy, with your emails demanding to be read in a way that will get most people's backs up.

Calibri

In a survey done at Wichita State University, Calibri was the most popular font for email, instant messaging, and PowerPoint presentations. It also ranked highly for use in website text. Safe if a little bit anorexic.

Insult a man's font and you question one aspect of his taste but insult a man's tie and you insult his penis, which is why most married men claim their wives chose their ties for them . . .

WHAT YOUR TIE SHOULD SAY ABOUT YOU

Where did ties come from? Historians claim men started wearing strips of red fabric around their necks to appear macho by mimicking blood drawn during battle, hence the reason why the classic tie colour is claret. The tie is an attention-grabbing piece of theatre that men use to liven up the bland and dour work suit. It waves 'personality' like a banner of war and is often the only outlet for eccentricity, charisma, personal taste and narcissism. Odd then that so many men claim their wives buy their ties for them, suggesting they're allowing themselves to be paraded as some form of 'ideal' representation of their partner rather than having the balls to make their own selection down at Tie Rack.

Of course we have to mention the Freudian role of the tie, as referred to in the section on fiddling. The tie has been refined into something shaped like an arrow, with the point of the arrow resting just above the crotch. Therefore size is everything and the length and width of the tie is as revealing as the pattern of the fabric it's made from.

Thin, Dark Plain Colour

This is the cool choice of tie, implying you are only visiting the world of classical work-wear, rather than residing there. This tie implies moodiness and a degree of edginess, especially if it's black, which you will have chosen because you are a fan of *Reservoir Dogs*. Trendy you might be but generous you ain't. This is a mean person's tie, suggesting you could be less than giving with your emotions, making you a bit of an enigma. Enigmatic might sound like a plus point for business but beware the more staid corporate environment. By refusing to join in tie-wise you could find yourself the object of something bordering on fear, which can in turn lead to isolation or aggression. Wear this to look like something of a maverick or even to intimidate. Avoid it if you're keen to integrate. Plain, average-width ties look safer when you're dealing with clients or trying to look like one of the team.

Diagonal Stripe

This is a UK classic, reminiscent of schooldays and private members' clubs. It's a security tie, worn by someone who wants to conform and be accepted. It's bought to look grown-up but it really signals 'schoolboy', suggesting that despite your aspirations to look like a captain of industry and exude power and status you are a potential push-over for anyone who has the energy to stand up to you. Under pressure you will revert to childlike behaviours, including comfort eating, sulks or silly humour. Pick this tie to look 'right' in terms of conformity but remember the clubbish signals and do make sure you don't accidentally wear a 'wrong way' stripe or something that implies you went to Eaton. Best worn with a Ralph Lauren swagger.

Paisley

This is the gentleman's classic print, a confusing and buzzy little pattern that manages to blend into something virtually anonymous. This tie implies your father is your role model in life and that you hold old-fashioned values and tastes. Paisley also has a look of self-justification too, implying you are stubborn when pushed and love pointing out rules and regulations to prove points, although you might also present an alternative air of laid-back rebellion at times, smoking the odd fag or buying jazz music. If you're aiming for a look of calm security in a 'chap next door', retro rather than wiz-kid way then this is the tie for you. If you're trying to look creative and cutting-edge opt for something more geometric or brightly coloured.

Animal and Cartoon Prints

A comedy phallic symbol? Wearing a tie like this will imply you clearly believe you can laugh a woman into bed, although no one has pointed out to you that the girl is supposed to laugh with you, not at you. This desire to flag up your sense of humour suggests a deep-rooted insecurity about whether anyone would get it otherwise. There could also appear to be more sinister reasons behind your advertised humour. Humour is a form of attack, albeit masked. You will therefore appear to have problems making direct criticisms or giving feedback at work, preferring to use jokes and sarcasm, which you can then deny if the victim complains, saying you were 'only joking'. It would be good to say there is a comedy tie out there that will point you out as something other than a sad case but unfortunately there isn't. Keep your most outrageous version for fancy dress parties where you want to look like an eighties throwback and burn the rest.

Spotted

Spots have genuine comic potential and suggest an optimistic, attention-seeking type. Circular shapes imply a cheerful personality, albeit rather self-centred. You adore the ability to show off or perform and hate criticism or attacks by people who accuse you of being allergic to planning, preparation and detail, preferring to fly by the seat of your pants at times. Wear large spots to raise morale and create positive energy in your team but avoid spots if you are asked to attend a disciplinary or present tragic half-year figures or even speak at the funeral of the CEO.

Satin

Your gleaming tie will suggest a strong streak of vanity and a rather smooth charm which could mean you're self-centred. If you wear a satin tie you'll be the one they like but don't trust at work, not a team player but competitive enough to make alliances for personal gain. You have potential as a perfectionist, because this fabric is the most unforgiving when it comes to creases or stains. This will suggest you can be confident and also strategic.

Flowers

Flowered fabrics will define you as earthy, warm but immensely dull at times. This tie will suggest you approach work with a very non-combative air and will do all you can to avoid conflict or open disagreement. Flowers bear the whiff of either a muesli-munching family man or a retro-loving sixties fan with a hint of irony about your approach to other people. If you're deeply competitive and Machiavellian this tie could help you get under the radar with colleagues assuming you're 'nice' rather than a chancer. If not, give it a wide berth.

While business clothing for men is mainly about the tie colour for women it's often about block colours that will help define you in the context of status and projected personality.

WHAT COLOURS REVEAL

Colours have their own psychology that can affect us in and out of the workplace. In terms of perception here's how you're likely to be seen:

Red

This is the classic attention-seeking colour, making you appear loud to the point of disruptive. Red sends out signals of confidence and positivity but it also connotes war and aggression. In business it will often imply you've come to do battle or, at least, to make your presence felt.

Grey

Charcoal is a business classic, implying gravitas and experience, plus a whiff of financial wealth. Paler shades can tend to suggest weakness though, especially with decision-taking.

Pale grey is draining too, making the wearer appeal more frail and likely to blend into the background.

Black

This is the colour of cool, except that black dye doesn't take too well on cheaper fabric, meaning it will show up a budget suit quite easily. Black implies individualism and mystery, making it seem you are confident and assertive but not loud or pushy. It's a choice that is no choice, an easy option that reveals only what you want it to but without making you look like a push-over.

Beige

Although this colour drifts in and out of fashion it always risks being seen as the ultimate in bland, especially if your colouring is equally dull. Beige can even suggest depression and negativity. People with strong amounts of *joie de vivre* are rarely described as wearing beige.

Brown

This is the colour of integrity in the way that soil is honest. Earthy, non-showy and with a hint of a dour or grumpy side lurking beneath a kind exterior.

Yellow

This is seen as the colour of naivety, creativity and optimism, so a good colour to wear to all those creative 'blue sky' meetings at work. People will assume you're jolly if you wear this colour, which could in itself ensure your mood remains buoyant.

Green

This colour tends to shy away from the fashion profile apart from the odd brief appearance. Green can even be seen as an unlucky colour by some people. It can suggest a lack of creativity or desire to change. Green clothes can give out an old-fashioned vibe.

Navy

This is the ultimate good-guy colour, non-controversial, safe and reassuring it has undertones of school uniform but not in an odd way.

Blue

Blue is the most universally acceptable colour because of its calming effect, meaning very few, if any, people will ever claim to dislike it. This means that wearing it suggests you are a rational, reasonable and empathetic human being. Blue is the safe option, albeit not the most memorable choice. Excellent for client meeting or job interviews where image flexibility is important.

Purple

Purple is full of blue notes, meaning it has similar calming and rationalising values but it is also a very vivid and memorable choice, historically linked to royalty, status and even death! This is a very flattering colour but also a slightly risky one: if people dealing with you are reminded of their favourite bar of chocolate they might warm to you, but if they see subliminal connections with ermine-clad royalty they might be turned off by your status posturing.

Overall colours might say one thing but we're talking blends in most outfits, meaning your cognitive algebra applies to your clothing combinations as well as your behaviours and body language . . .

WHAT YOUR SHIRT SHOULD
SAY ABOUT YOU

'When in doubt, opt for white' is the mantra of the work-place. Gleaming, snowy white shirts are flattering as they reflect light upward to your face taking a few months, if not years, off your age, and demanding of trust and even affection as a man who wears a white shirt is clearly healthy, clean and knows about good hygiene. Remember though that white must mean white so bin any shirts that have acquired that tinge of grey or other hues from the washing machine and only sport white shirts that are perfectly ironed and pristine. Once the collar begins to curl or the seams begin to grumble you will look like a man who wants to be seen as clean and safe and optimistic and successful but who has somehow gone down the tramp route of life – a scruffy sham and a charlatan.

The collar of your shirt should reflect your lapel and tie width and they in turn should reflect that funny old thing called 'fashion'. Always look like a man in control of his life and his destiny by binning any shirts where the neck is too tight or too large or the collar curling. Never wear a tie with the top shirt button undone. This will only say one of three things: either you're too stingy to buy a shirt that fits; you've suddenly put on weight a la Incredible Hulk, or you don't care. None of these statements work in the workplace.

Do invest in collar-bones as these will make your shirt collars lie flat. Plastic ones are fine but Tiffany silver ones can induce spontaneous orgasms in women once they clap eyes on them.

Chambray Blue

The second-best choice of business shirt as it has the ability to mask hangovers and make you look preppy-fresh. A man in a soft blue shirt and deep red/maroon tie is a man who will be trusted, right up to the point where he is found to have lost his company $6 trillion on the stock market.

Pink

Is an odd one. Pink man looks like statement man. He seems to say: 'I am so comfortable with my sexuality that I can wear a pink shirt without compromising my hetero-sexuality'. Because even in the twenty-first century there are still grown men who will snigger about or refuse point blank to wear a pink shirt.

Stripy

Are a classic although anything too wide can look borderline clownish or Beach Boy. Stripes will make you look assertive and challenging but can also be rather irritating, as there's something about striped shirt plus a striped or otherwise patterned tie that can make you look like the TV test card. Wear cautiously to avoid giving your colleagues migraines.

Check

Have the look of graph paper about them, suggesting your head is full of dull statistics and other maths-teacher type facts. The check will make you look boring.

Short-sleeve

Yuk. You look like a clip-on-tie-wearing repair man from the seventies. So what if it's hot? Any amount of suffering is worth avoiding looking like you wear nylon trousers. And we don't think a few inches of cotton sleeve really rates as 'suffering' anyway.

The Hawaiian

A classic for overweight/ageing comics or DJs who are aware the ageing/fat process is rendering them in danger of looking like a boring old fart and so believe that by sporting a hideous shirt they will still be part of the 'yoof' circus. Even Roland Rat looked wrong in one of these. Don't go there. Ever. Even on holiday in Hawaii.

Neither clothing nor actual accessory, your business cards tend to lurk around in the pockets of your clothing, trying to join in with the sartorial style. The fashion for cards is slightly less fickle than the fashion for clothing but only marginally . . .

WHAT YOUR BUSINESS CARDS SHOULD SAY ABOUT YOU

In one gesture of neat formality the exchanging of business cards makes or breaks your image in the workplace. Unlike the Japanese who cherish their cards as a sign of status and character, or the Americans who shove them around regardless of hierarchy or income, the Brits offer cards furtively, pulling a card out of the inner reaches of our deepest fluff-lined pockets and apologising for the fact that it's dog-eared and a little stained.

The best business cards come on good quality paper (white) with your name and contact details in clear, un-fussy print. There should also be a line explaining your role in your business but avoid all those euphemisms like 'sales executive' or 'communications manager' as they make it sound as though you're ashamed by your real job.

Photos

Photos are a very bad idea on a business card as they only tend to come in two types: either the passport snap variety that makes you look like a serial killer or the flattering variety that will make you appear to be a vain, deluded fop. Photos can also imply that you realise you are not visually memorable. Cards do tend to be handed out in person and at quite close quarters. Have the confidence to believe that anyone that close to you would find you memorable in the long-term.

Embossed

Embossed cards used to be the bees-knees in the days when people were expected to work for a company for longer than a couple of years. Now they will tend to appear over-stated and a little fusty.

Drawings

Your company logo is a likely necessity on your card but anything else should be discouraged. Cartoons, animal pictures or other 'meaningful' or symbolic artwork like Greek columns, motor cars or weighing scales will imply some degree of desperation to impress.

Front and Back Cards

Okay, so you noticed there is a blank back to your card meaning there's an extra opportunity to plug your business. Wrong. Printing things on the back looks mean and long-winded. Keep it simple.

Cheap Cards

Why bother getting cards printed if the only message they will ever carry is exactly how stingy you are when it comes to business? Once upon a time there were DIY machines in railway stations and – okay – we all had a go at printing our own even though it took twenty attempts and even then there would be some major spelling error that you missed and which the first potential client you handed one to would pick out like a hawk in bi-focals. ('I thought you said your name was James? It says Jomes on your card.') Even if your card has been spell-checked the paper and print quality will be sub-standard. Don't go there.

Outsize Cards

Oh how funny! You have just presented me with a card that is too big to place in my pocket, my Rolodex or the business card section of my wallet! Three points for impact, minus ten points for annoyance factor. Check out the bins or the recycling boxes because that's where your cards will invariably end up.

Your card is produced to create a long-lasting visual memory of YOU, being stored longer in clients' desks or briefcases than your words might be stored in their heads. Some words have a longer shelf life in people's memories than others though and not always for the right reasons.

WHAT YOUR BUZZWORDS SAY ABOUT YOU

People profess to hate them. But they still use them. And people are sure to make judgements about your place in the business hierarchy depending on those you use. So let us lob a 'thought grenade' into your workplace as we unlock the secret messages in the most pervasive examples.

'Thinking Outside the Box'/'Blue Sky Thinking'

You're like an annoying, bounding puppy who keeps trying to hump people's legs. Your enthusiasm knows no bounds and you love to call yourself a creative thinker, but sadly your buzzwords prove you're a phoney and a hypocrite. If you really could think in a 'different', creative way you'd never be using these tired old clichés that are as stale as week-old focaccia.

'Down-sizing'

What you mean is sacking, firing, making redundant and other versions of the Night of the Long Knives only you're too much of a scaredy-cat to admit it so you hide behind nice-sounding euphemisms like this. Your life's aim is to do nasty things but still be liked.

'At the End of the Day'

Even sports stars and commentators have got over this one and all it really shows is that you are desperately unoriginal and dull. You're sociable but keen to blend into the background as much as possible, meaning you fear ridicule to the point that you end up creating it.

'JoinedUpThinking'

This phrase went around the public sector a few years ago like a dose of dysentery. It's smug and scornful, using a childlike term to pour ridicule on anyone who isn't behaving in the same way the speaker is. This is the sort of person who will laugh at their own burps or farts as though they've produced something clever.

'Going Forward'

Hey, let's not get into blame culture or dwelling on the past! Let's move on into the future! This comment is almost always used on behalf of the speaker who has clearly screwed up to an almost illegal degree and wants everyone to forget what they've done. By not looking back they absolve themselves of all crimes, describing horrendous behaviours like losing the company squillions of pounds as being 'on a learning curve'. What they should learn is what the end of a dole queue looks like. Selfish, irresponsible and arrogant.

'Back in the Day'

Whose day? This is a favourite phrase of recessionary times, when nostalgia rules okay. This is the phrase of someone wanting to look experienced and superior when all they're really feeling is old.

'Singing From the Same Hymn Sheet'

If ever there was a phrase guaranteed to make you become allergic to team-building and like-minded agreement it's this one. This person sees themselves as intellectually and morally superior by their use of religious imagery to make their point.

Plain speaking

Tamsin Constable, a Plain English consultant, says; 'Unnecessary business jargon shows, however unintentionally, that someone's not really that bothered whether you understand or not. They've done their expert bit, now it's up to you, the layperson, to make sense of it. It's lazy, it's disrespectful, it's discriminating. Sometimes, if a client or patient doesn't understand, it can be dangerous. I would even say that jargon, sometimes, amounts to bullying.'

'Cherry-picking'/'Thought Shower'/ 'Nailing Jelly to the Wall'

Post-modern irony? No, charisma bypass because anyone who uses these phrases is a stranger to cool and style. If they wanted to be ironic and clever they'd make up their own pieces of nonsense as a gag, like 'You might as well push a donkey round a theme-park' or 'He made All-Bran of that idea'. Anyone in a leadership or management role using any of these or similar should be sent home without pay.

We've covered food and its consumption in previous chapters but in terms of individual impact it's easy to overlook that humblest item of snacks, the biscuit. However the devil is always in the detail and this is as true in reference to cognitive algebra as it is to any other aspect of our lives . . .

WHAT YOUR BUSINESS BISCUIT SAYS

In the past two decades it has become a cliché of interviews and job assessment forms: 'If you were a biscuit, what biscuit would you be and why?' The humble snack also plays an important role in business meetings. What a biscuit lacks in size it more than makes up for in psychological evaluation because that little lump of sweetness that you use to bridge the food gap between brekkie and lunch reveals a whole host of secrets about your behaviours and self-esteem, so much so that businesses had such a thing about them in the eighties that interviewers would often wait to see which one an applicant selected from the plate offered with the Earl Grey and then judge whether they were a suitable prospect for employment.

In many ways that plate of assorted biscuits was like the earliest form of psychometric testing so here's how you would come out according to the one you dunked or nibbled . . .

Jammy Dodger/Funny Face

A competitive attention-seeker with a childlike streak. Unsophisticated and unashamedly spontaneous.

Crumbs of comfort

Of 1,000 professionals questioned, an astonishing 80% felt that the outcome of a meeting could be directly influenced by the range and quality of biscuits on offer according to a survey by the The Holiday Inn chain.

Bourbon

Self-centred but strategic and can come across as charming. They like to get their own way and can be smoothly devious to ensure they do.

Rich Tea

Dull, self-sacrificing, lacking in innovation or creativity. A plodding, thorough employee rather than imaginative or ambitious. Can be stubborn or pedantic.

Custard Cream

Shy but optimistic and polite, they will blend into the background or hide initially but can be groomed for a more independent role if they are praised and motivated.

Digestive/Hob Nob

Quality but not showy and a good team player. Thorough without being boring or tiresome.

Pink Wafer

All style and very little substance and rather superficial.

Foil-wrapped chocolate

A 'doer', as Sir Alan Sugar would say. Ambitious, greedy to succeed and with a level of confidence bordering on arrogance. Into status and individual praise and recognition.

Fig Roll

Tendency to be anal.

No amount of impression management will produce results in the workplace if you're simply not very good at your job or just make yourself unpleasant to your colleagues. What we're saying is know the limits of how much your work will impress and how much people are making judgements about your abilities from the smaller details. It's these they often remember and play a big part in affecting their subconscious when they are thinking about pay rises and promotion.

10

PULLING POWER

In many ways the same is true of impression management in the meeting/dating/mating process as it is in the workplace. Centuries ago people lived in smaller communities and travelled less, meaning you probably got to know everything about your future mate as you grew up alongside them. Now we have access to the rest of the world via Internet dating or travel and it is deemed unusual or even 'weird' to pair off with a guy/girl that you've known for longer than six months or so. We have become risk-ready in our approach to sex, finding it perfectly normal (if naughty) to have sex with someone on the first date and equally happy to seek a life partner through five minutes of speed-dating. What this means is that you need to keep your 'sales' signals – the image messages you send out – set to warp speed most of the time because unless you're meeting your partner in the workplace (therefore having time and opportunity to get to know him or her and to allow them to get to know you properly) that Mr or Ms Right might not end up stopping around for long enough to realise you're the Mr Darcy to her Elizabeth Bennet or vice-versa.

Love at first sight

The importance of making the right impression is shown by a study from Ohio State University that seems to prove love at first sight exists. Professor Ramirez who conducted it says: 'Earlier research had assumed there was a cumulative effect that happens in the first days of meeting that helps determine how relationships will develop. But we're finding that it all happens much sooner than that – literally within a few minutes.'

So, let's say you have got your first date with a prospective life-partner. How do you go about ensuring you are vivid, salient, charismatic, authentic and nose-bleedingly wonderful in that small space of time that is referred to in business as a 'window of opportunity'?

And while you're busy peddling all your wares of fabulousness, how will you go about hiding what Carl Jung referred to as your Shadow Self – the dark side we all try to keep hidden from the public, those rude, intolerant, aggressive and otherwise unpleasant behaviours that normally only emerge either three months after you've been selected for that new job or your sales pitch has been successful, or you are nearly down the end of the aisle in church and about to emerge into the sunlight to have the dreaded wedding photos taken?

DATING AND MATING

You have no real idea how you select a mate but psychologists conclude that it was down to more than just his aftershave. There's a whole load of subliminal connections linked to childhood role models, rewarded behaviours and social and economic factors plus a heady brew of matching levels of beauty and attractiveness, sexual preference signals, not to mention the assault of senses like smell, touch, hearing and sight. So, given the fact that you look a bit like his mum, have matching working-class roots, are in the same ball park in terms of looks and earnings, smell of vanilla (it will remind him of breast milk – that is, comfort and safety), can answer the same amount of questions right on *Who Wants to be a Millionaire?*, have the same place in the family pecking order (some psychologists claim we are attracted like for like, that is only child/only child, second born/second born etc) and you dress alike, smile in a way to suggest you share the same sexual perversions and touch him back when he touches you, you should be in with a chance of a second or third date.

Confused? Perhaps this simple quiz will help.

ARE YOU SET TO GET THAT SECOND DATE?

Although many aspects of attraction might appear random there are certain behaviours that will tend to help or hinder your chances of hitting it off with a new partner and getting hooked up for a second or third date. We've taken what might seem like luck, chance or chemistry and analysed the processes to help you understand if you're scuppering your own dating effectiveness.

1. DO YOU TURN UP FOR YOUR DATE . . .
A) Early so I can have a look at him/her as they arrive.
B) A few minutes late. I believe in keeping them waiting.
C) Very late. Treat 'em mean, keep 'em keen.
D) I'd plan to be punctual, but not arrive first.

2. YOUR CHOICE OF OUTFIT IS . . .
A) I tend to show off my best points and look sexy: tight clothing with a lot of flesh showing.

B) Something smart/casual unless I know we're going somewhere more formal.

C) I like to make an instant impression. Bright colours or high fashion styling makes me memorable.

D) I'll often wear something that goes with his or her sense of style to make us look more like a couple.

3. YOU LIKE A DATE WHO . . .

A) Isn't *too* pretty/handsome as they tend to be less vain and more appreciative.

B) Has a great personality. I'm not interested in looks in the slightest.

C) Is drop-dead gorgeous. Looks matter and it doesn't bother me if a guy/girl is much better looking than I am.

D) Is roughly as attractive to look at as I am. It makes us more of a pair.

4. YOU WOULD CONSIDER A DATE A CATCH IF . . .

A) They were a bit less knowledgeable as I like to impress people.

B) They were better educated. I like to listen to intelligent people.

C) They were loaded and successful.

D) He/she shared the same background and type of upbringing as me.

5. YOUR MAIN TOPIC OF CONVERSATION ON A DATE TENDS TO BE . . .

A) I'm a bit of a smooth-talker. I like to pay compliments and keep the chat-up going.

B) I crack a lot of jokes and get a bit of verbal diarrhoea

C) Me. I love explaining who I am and what I do and I go

through my dating history. I believe in being up front about past relationships, especially painful experiences.

D) I'll chat to discover things we have in common then focus on those.

6. SEX: YOU TEND TO . . .

A) Seal the deal on the first date. If you fancy someone why wait?

B) I tend to play it by ear.

C) I let them know I'll need to get to know them first, even if I am a bit flirty.

D) I'd always wait until the third or fourth date or even later if necessary.

Mostly A

You try so hard to impress your dates that it could be possible you're driving them away. This is looking like the passive option. In other words, putting your date's needs first instead of making the date a mutual event. Selective modesty is a successful ingratiation technique but overall compliance might be seen as desperation. By looking too keen and eager to please you can spark suspicion in your date. Exactly why are you so eager to impress? They'll worry there's a flaw somewhere and often set out to discover what it is. Opting for a date who is equally desperate (less attractive, less intelligent etc) you think you'll get instant approval but that view is patronising and superficial. Instead of boxing below your weight in a bid to score some hits why not examine and work on your own behaviour and techniques to make yourself more of a catch? Dressing too sexily will easily repel a date and by rolling into bed on the first outing you lessen your chances statistically of having a long-term relationship.

Overall: Anxious and with issues.

Mostly B

Your techniques should earn you a second and third date as you're coming across as nice, warm, friendly but flexible enough to bond without too much trouble. Your casual, subtly sexy dress style is ideal and although you tell yourself off for talking too much and getting nervous your date could easily find this adorable, as long as you don't let it get too out of hand. You come across as practical rather than romantic and will probably appeal to a date with marriage in mind, rather than one looking for fireworks.

Overall: safe rather than sexy.

Mostly C

You are confident, egocentric and a dating game-player, coming across as noisy, sexy and dominant. Your 'in-yer-face' style might make you feel happily in control of your dating destiny but did you ever study the amount of relationship disasters you've left in your wake, counting them off to the fact that he or she must have been commitment phobic/dead/secretly into sex with otters? The fact is that a date with you is like a date with a steamroller. Your confidence is likely to be a sham but waiting and hoping for someone to spot the real, charming, sensitive you behind the façade could well be a fruitless exercise unless you change your techniques to get past first base.

Overall: Scary. Stop swinging from that chandelier and try some rapport-building instead.

Mostly D

If you're not getting a second date you need to check your deodorant because your dating techniques are as sound as a pound. You opt for manners over game-playing by arriving on time, you employ mirroring techniques to create strong instant bonds by dressing in a way that makes you look like a matching pair, you prefer men or women with similar social-economic background, which is pegged by the psychologists as being the ideal formula for a long-term relationship, you chat in a way that pares back to similarities and shared interests via your directional small-talk techniques and you make your date wait for sex, which has been statistically proven to ensure stronger long-term relationship bonding.

Overall: Psychologically sound.

DATE DRESSING

Ever wondered why, when you go out dressed up to the nines no potential date will come within a mile of you, yet dress plainly and more casually in something like jeans and a T-shirt and you suddenly get approval signals and chat-ups?

When you're out on the pull your overall impact will largely depend on your body language and your dress/ grooming signals. Keep in mind that there is no such thing as an ugly ape when it comes to sex. Animals tend to send out signals that they are up for it and then – depending on prior ownership or commitments – they get hit on.

Your pulling clothing and grooming choices and techniques are very likely to be sending out the wrong signals and therefore undermining your success rate. To get the idea, take a couple of what Desmond Morris would refer to as Naked Apes like David and Victoria Beckham. They are both good-looking and both have a habit of dressing up to the nines. Imagine David Beckham walking into a club near you wearing the kind of fashion look he's known for, with a sharp suit, waistcoat, spats, diamond studs etc. Then imagine him wearing an overtly sexy outfit with a satin shirt slashed to the waist and tight trousers and shades. Lastly see him in casuals: well-fitting denim jeans, a clean white T-shirt and a battered leather jacket. (Straight men might like to work down the same scenarios with Victoria Beckham as their heroine!)

Now – although you might be more than happy to be approached by the Becksmeister in any of these get-ups, which one would make you feel most comfortable and confident if it was you making the first move?

Sexy or dressy clothes only really add to our attractiveness on paper. In reality, though, it's a flawed logic. Although your low-cut top/tight skirt/low-slung jeans might act as a useful display tool for attracting a prospective partner's attention it could also be making you look daunting in terms of an actual approach. Someone walking about in a vividly sexual outfit will be seen to be going for a splatter gun display ritual, meaning lots of potential mates will be attracted, which in animal terms means fights with other suitors, possibly even to the death. It can also signal 'difficult' status signals that put the booted and suited person on a higher status level, making them potentially unobtainable, and it can make them appear easy or desperate.

Most of these 'rules' will occur when there are lots of other people present, at a club or bar or other crowded place where 'pack' thinking is dominant. In a more intimate setting there is less pressure caused by potential rivals so the turn-off effect might be less obvious. However even long-term couples can feel threatened when one of them makes a special effort to look sexy in public, even when it's done in a bid to boost admiration and attraction from the existing mate. The notion of threat and fight can be so intimidating, even subliminally, that a partner will often get annoyed or even angry to be accompanying someone who should make other males or females jealous, and comments are often made about a partner looking better without make-up or when casually dressed.

Apart from the 'I can approach you without getting into a punch-up' appeal of clean casuals, they also transmit good, solid messages in terms of breeding. That nice white T-shirt not only shows off your muscles, body shape and posture it also suggests that you are clean and therefore germ-free, while a naturally groomed approach without layers of make-up and products allows a potential partner to assess other signs of health and breeding-potential like a clear skin, bright eyes and glossy hair. With the absence of strong perfume or cologne he or she can also get subliminal signals about your health and desires from your body scent, which is why perfumiers spend money and time searching for scents that mimic natural human musk.

BASIC ATTRACTORS

The main things a potential partner will be checking out or looking for consciously or subconsciously on a first date will all come under five key headings:

1. WEALTH SIGNALS

It can be easy to up these but do use your impression management equations before you do. The key wealth indicators when you're out on a date are your jewellery, the wallet or purse you carry and your car. Before you set about image-managing this it might be wise to remember that we tend to prefer someone in the same economic league as ourselves. Or if you want to impress by illustrating you dun good then refer to your humbler roots if it creates a stronger sense of rapport with your date.

WALLET/PURSE SIGNALS

Watch their eyes when this comes out (or not if you're too mean to pay your way).

The Leather Wallet

Women like a nice leather wallet that looks neither too new nor too exhausted or tatty and they also like to see a healthy number of notes in there but not all crispy and in military order.

The Money Clip

Money clips look a little effete, as though you're too flash or precious with your cash.

The Man Purse

Forget a man purse with coins in it as they have to be one of the biggest turn-offs in the history of dating. If you own one of these, especially the little money sacks that look like something Jack would keep his beanstalk beans in, or those ghastly little leather sporran jobbies with a lift-up lid then you should be seriously considering castration, as no girl is ever going to have sex with you.

The Gran Purse

The female equivalent is probably the mum-purse, those huge, clutchbag-size clip-top things in faux leatherette with pockets for your bus-pass and sections for food stamps. Unsexy doesn't even begin to describe it.

The Girlie Purse

Random by purse, random by nature. If you want a man who will be a provider then pull out something silly and sparkly that you bought from a teenage accessory shop. Then go through all the cards that tumble out, giggling over club cards, Top Shop cards and student union cards until you finally find one shabby credit card that you then spend ages peering at to check the expiry date. By that time he will have paid the bill.

The Girl Wallet

If you pull something more androgynous – slim, dark leather and containing a small selection of credit cards you set your stall out as an Alpha rival to his hunter–provider crown in which case he will either be mightily turned on by the sight of an assertive/dominant female or will feel threatened, owing to low self-esteem.

JEWELLERY SIGNALS FROM A WOMAN

Large, Expensive Jewellery

This flaunting of wealth can produce an impression of existing high status or career–life success plus you're happy to flaunt your status, which makes you come across as daunting and possibly difficult with a huge hunk of low-self-esteem lurking behind all this amount of self-endorsement. Or it can imply you are sponsored by others, that these are gifts from parents or partners and that you are pampered, spoilt and high maintenance.

Now, although like might attract like and your goal could be to attract the type of male who will enjoy squandering lorry-loads of dosh on you, it has to be said that males like this are rather thin on the ground.

Subtle But Real Jewellery

There's a strong look of confidence about this type of adornment unless it comes under one of two sub-headings:

Wannabe Jewellery

This is a habit often acquired by girls in their late teens/early twenties, when they start to wear what look like wedding/engagement rings, either on the right hand or even on the traditional ring finger. This tends to signal a huge desire to get engaged and married and – if they felt they could get away with it – these girls would be pacing around in wedding-style dresses to drop even more hints that they're dying to be next up the aisle. What makes this worse is that the hint is not specific. They're rarely even dating, so this is a general signal, not just aimed at an existing boyfriend.

Trophy Jewellery

Girls tend to collect things on chains around their necks like notches on a bedpost. Hearts, lockets, names and initials, these very intimate-looking items will display the fact that you have an emotional and sexual history. This also suggests that you have rather low expectations of getting a partner in the future and are clinging to the memory of old ones, like Miss Haversham clung to her wedding dress. There's something forlorn about jewellery that looks as though it's come from previous loves. Did they die, in which case are you a tragedy queen? Did they vanish, in which case are you like Sarah Woodruff in *The French Lieutenant's Woman*, waiting for him to return? Or did they just dump you, in which case why didn't you rip it off and grind it into the dust with the heel of your boot? This is such an obvious, unsubtle statement as you sit grinning at your potential date, waiting for and almost challenging him to either ask you the story of your trinkets or risk marinating in suppressed jealousy for the rest of the relationship.

Cheap Jewellery

Fun but tacky, cheap jewellery gets less fun and more tacky the older the wearer gets. While there's nothing wrong or odd about a teenage girl getting her supplies from a cheap accessories shop, there is something intrinsically sad or even worrying about an older woman wearing plastic hair bobs, glittery drop earrings with froufrou on them or plastic bangles. If you think she looks like the type that ends up stalking celebrities you're probably not far wrong. If her eyeshadow matches her necklace perfectly rest assured this is more than mere hunch and that you are almost certain to be right.

Noisy Jewellery

This is a rather sad attempt to attract sexual attention via the clanking and rattling of chains and baubles. This is not a positive, optimistic impact but rather the desperate behaviour of a woman who hopes men have a Pavlov's dog response to bells and other sound signals and that the charms she wears around her neck are like a summons to your attention: 'Hey, look over here, cleavage and tits!!!'. Any man who finds clanking jewellery charming and pretty should be warned that making assumptions about these items being removed during sex is dodgy. If the idea of mating with a woman sounding like a chain-gang trotting to work doesn't float your boat then don't go there as many of these items might well have been welded on.

JEWELLERY SIGNALS FROM A MAN

Women are very tuned into jewellery and will manage to read signals there that you probably had no idea you were transmitting. Whereas women are expected to wear jewellery, for men it's less compulsory and therefore more ritualistic. The watch and wedding ring are bog-standard but other items worn regularly by a guy are assumed to have meaning – in the bloke's life. Something is being marked by the wearing of it.

Parental Purchases
Anything that bears the sticky paw-marks of Mum or Dad, like a neck-chain with '18' on it or some kind of football logo will mark you out as a doughnut of the lowest order.

Holiday Trinkets
You went somewhere hot. You came back and dressed for work. But you still wore the bangle or neck-beads, not to signal that you're in touch with your feminine side, but to show you have another life that involves sand deposits in your pants and being sick on sangria. They're there to show girls you look neat in a pair of Speedos and that you do have friends, because bead-wearers tend to hang around in small tribal groups. The mates thing is an advantage as, although it's unlikely to suggest you're a reliable life partner, it does hint that you're not weird.

Heavy Metal
If you purchased some of the über-macho trinkets on the market, like death's head necklaces, skull and crossbones earrings or leather thong wristbands you'll come across as someone who likes to advertise his masculinity and sexuality but – as most heavy metal giants spend all their times on stage simulating various acts of masturbation – it's unlikely that any girl will see this as a direct benefit to her.

The Signet Ring
This ring should look like an heirloom, that is, it should be forged out of a richer shade of gold than the paler

stuff currently on sale, and be worn on the little finger. If it is you will convey the impression that you are loaded, or at least impoverished landed gentry, which is almost as good as long as the woman you're after likes cold draughty houses in need of roof repairs. If it's the paler type of gold it's likely to look like a more recent acquisition which will give the impression you're aspirational-rich or that someone bought it for you for your eighteenth birthday.

The Ring On A Chain

Is it a girl's ring? If so you will look like a Mr de Winter (don't bother reading *Rebecca* – it's a girls' book but the hero was eerily attached to his dead wife's clothing and portrait) that is, haunted by, mourning and hating in turns, his ex. Don't go there unless you're seeking a girl who is a fan of blokes that come with old emotional baggage.

Bling

This trashy flashy stuff signals you're into clubbing, laughing and having a whale of a time but not in the way that includes cosy night in watching *Sex and the City* for the fifth time.

2. YOUR HEALTH SIGNALS

Yes, these are all to do with breeding stock and about as subtle as checking a horse's teeth or looking for fleas on a kitten but what nature has created we ignore at our peril, even when we have no conscious desire to breed. Health signals are primarily natural although we all know nature is only there for the meddling with but make sure your tampering is working in your favour before you check into that tanning salon or go on that vegan diet.

Subliminal health signals tend to come from:

TEETH
Which is why your smile is important, so that he/she can take a stab at your age and health history.

SKIN
We all know zits are random but for many centuries spots and pustules were seen as early warning signs of disease so keep that spot cream on hand.

HAIR
Too many products create a sticky or lank look that conceals natural attractors like glossy, clean-smelling hair.

POSTURE
Which is why we prefer a nice upright stance, suggesting all your muscles are trim and raring to perform.

SMELL
Fresh-smelling suggests clean and healthy. Too much scent masks the cleaner smells, suggesting you've got something to hide.

CLEAR EYES
Which is why getting an early night before the date may help.

3. MIND FACTORS
Showing off your brain cells on the first date might depress rather than impress your date, according to your perceived compatibility. While it's okay to be physically impressive the intellectual stuff works best if it's seen to lie around a mutual level.

When you're in the rapport-building stage many of the small-talk topics are all about feeling one another out in terms of interests and intellect. Discussions of favourite books, films, TV shows will all form part of an intellectual foreplay designed to reveal compatibility levels.

Line on chat

Researchers at Edinburgh and Central Lancashire Universities investigated what the world's best chat-up line is. Two hundred female students were given a questionnaire containing 40 lines taken from the Internet, films and television series such as *Sex and the City* and asked to rate them. The result? 'It's hot today, isn't it? It's the best weather when you're training for a marathon.' Believe it or not psychologists reckon the line is a winner because it's an ideal way for a man to display both his intelligence and his athletic abilities!

FILM CHOICE

When in doubt always say your favourite movie is *The Shawshank Redemption*. This film seems to be above negative criticism and so will you be for liking it. Watch *The Green Mile* as well and compare the two to develop the discussion.

Only discuss your liking for cult classics if you're sure they share your taste.

Remember that a lot of work on the first date is being put into discovering whether you are normal enough to be safe, so do avoid discussing the merits of *Friday the 13th* or *Henry: Portrait of a Serial Killer*.

Soppy is as soppy does. Only rave about *Four Weddings and a Funeral* if you're sure he's looking for an über-girlie girl or if you feel your normal role as council enforcement officer might otherwise be off-putting. If you're a guy avoid the trap of pretending to have loved all these films in a bid to portray yourself as her ideal life-mate. The straight guy who loves *Sex and the City* is a mythological beast, like the man who enjoys shopping. Women claim to love the idea of him but even if their brains said 'yes' their loins would be screaming 'no'.

BOOK CHOICE

Similar rules apply to the type of book you profess to reading. Many have died at the altar of literary pretentions simply because they boasted about a book they had never so much us blown dust off the cover of, only to be revealed as a liar from the moment they made their first guess at the plot as their potential partner liked it so much they had it memorised word for word. Books you have devoured and loved might be a problem unless you have a photographic memory as it is easily possible to read *The Da Vinci Code* and forget who dunnit or to confuse the plots of the *Gormenghast* trilogy or forget whether Scarlet and Rhett did end up married or forget whether Harry did kill Voldemort or not. Unless you would consider yourself something of an expert on your chosen tome it might be wise to avoid in-depth bookish chats like this:

'My favourite book is *The Oxford Murders*.' (A solid safe choice, combining academic pretentions with a good solid plot.)

'Why's that? Should I read it?'

'Yes it's great and very original. It combines mathematical theory with murder and crime.'

'Really? How does that work then?'

'F**k me, I don't know. I read it but I can't really remember. It was good, though.'

Men also need to be aware that – unlike TV shows and films – there is a very strong sexual bias when it comes to literature. Although girls might swoon over romantic heroes like Heathcliff and Darcy their lips tend to wrinkle in disgust over guys who claim to have read those books themselves. On the whole they prefer men brought up on *Treasure Island* (suggestions of masculinity and adventure/daring), weaned on *Lord of the Flies* (hints at a deeper understanding of psychology and the human psyche) and maturing via Richard Yates (signals you're cool, as his books are retro, full of boozing, smoking, cutting-edge blokes like Don Draper from *Mad Men*) or Nick Hornby (funny, warm, normal and good father material).

TV CHOICE

Letting slip your favourite choice of TV programme on a first date can have long-term consequences, as every woman knows that – if the relationship has legs – at some stage you'll both be sitting on that Land of Leather settee with the kids gone to bed and fighting over the remote control to see if you're watching David Dimbleby or Dale Winton.

Beware going for the instant-bonding/rapport hit by trying to choose a programme that you believe your date might like too. Although a woman might be welded to her soap it's not always a world she will have been itching to share with her sexual mate, and professing to be a huge fan of *Hollyoaks* or *Emmerdale* might raise eyebrows of disbelief rather than smiles of delight.

TV choices need to reflect your ideal image rather than your ability to bond via similar tastes. When a guy says he likes cop shows he'll go up a notch in the macho stakes, and if he claims to enjoy *Newsnight* he'll seem intellectual and deep-thinking.

Girls can get away with reality TV shows as long as they don't then try to talk about or explain them at length (or even at short, come to that) as it can make drying paint sound fascinating by comparison.

Saying you like quality dramas should be a green light choice although keep in mind that there aren't any on TV at present and, if there are, they tend to be long and drawn out, meaning you'll sound like a bit of a couch potato. (An intellectual couch potato, but a couch potato nevertheless.)

And avoid enthusing over daytime TV: a) it tends to be bland and girlie in the worst way, and b) it will imply you're unemployed.

4. BODY

For an in-depth analysis of your own sex signals look no further than the 'eating' (pages 187–98) and 'bedroom' (pages 97–103) sections of this book.

5. SOUL

Were any words more heart-sinkingly scuppering of first-date potential than 'I'm a white witch actually' or 'Can I give you this pamphlet about God?' Your soul should have little place on a first date and is better left at home with a mug of tea and packet of HobNobs to appear much later in a relationship when trust and even love have been confirmed. However, spiritual leanings do have a tendency to leak out, even during what you might consider innocuous conversations like . . .

STAR SIGNS

This quasi-spiritual topic of conversation should be banned from the dating circuit on the grounds of death by boredom. You might think the phrase 'What star sign are you?' is a good small-talk ploy and all we can say is that the other person will always feel obliged to join in whether they want to or not. This enquiry comes masked as a request to discover more about the person you're considering at best spending the rest of your life with and at least shagging the once, but if you really wanted to know all about the subtler depths of their personality why stick with the following conversational format:

'What are you then? No, no, no, let me guess . . . Pisces! . . . no? Then you have to be Aries? . . . no? Am I close? . . . Taurus then? . . . No, I know, I know . . . you must be Sagittarius! No? Not Cancer? No, no, of course not . . . Leo? No? Libra? Yes! I knew, I knew you were Libra the moment I met you! I'm never wrong you know!'

Did you want to project yourself as empathetic, interested and deep? This is never the way to do it.

GREEN ISSUES
The newest ethical/moral plat du jour and a very safe way to make yourself sound and look responsible, clever and forward-thinking. Avoid going through the ins and outs of the food/waste recycling process while your date is eating, though.

POLITICS
No.

RELIGION
No.

WHAT A CHAT-UP LINE SHOULD SAY

Very few things in life are as mind-bogglingly, toe-curlingly, projectile-vomit-inducingly awful as a bad chat-up line. Get it right and you could pull the partner of your dreams but get it wrong (and most do!) and you could wreck your chance with the person who might just have been 'the one'.

So why the need for chat-ups at all? Why not just engage someone in a series of non-verbal signals that seal the deal before one word has been exchanged? In fact, this is how most of the pulling groundwork is done, hence that classic girl's line: 'Oh look, he's coming over'. Like other animals we share a capacity for spotting and signalling approval to a potential mate from distances that make verbal foreplay a challenge. But unlike other animals we also have to survive the verbal broadside, that opening gambit that can make or break all the groundwork that has been done non-verbally.

So what makes a good chat-up line?

The first rule of thumb is that if you are in possession of what can only be described as drop-dead good looks then it's likely anything you say will be classed as a good chat-up line. For the rest of us though it is all too easy to end up looking and sounding like a prat. Over-rehearsal will kill the funniest line stone dead as it will reflect in your tone but allowing yourself to be too spontaneous could mean you end up with a poke in the eye rather than in the bedroom.

Clichés

Using lines that come complete with the mould of age, like 'Do you come here often?' or 'What's a nice girl like you doing in a place like this?' will single you out as being either older than an episode of *Columbo* or über-ironic with a nice line in cynical humour. Unfortunately for you it isn't you who gets to decide which you are, it's the recipient of the line. Which means you're taking quite a risk unless you are happily ancient but also ironic, in which case go right ahead.

Using a cliché can mean more complex communication issues though. The best answer to a cliché is a matching cliché, therefore the pressure on any woman asked 'Do you come here often?' is to retort the scripted response: 'No, only in the mating season.' But that would leave her sounding like a very elderly trollop. Which means your comment is compromising to both her age and integrity. Or she's left with little else to do but giggle in which case you have compromised her emancipated status.

Avoid clichés unless you have the confidence and apparent air of spontaneity to carry them off.

Direct And To The Point

If your pet chat-up is along the lines of 'Get your coat you've pulled' or 'I suppose a shag would be out of the question?' or even 'Do these look real?' (in the case of a woman hitting on a man), you're showing off your Alpha hunter–killer side by opting for the short, sharp shock treatment to land your prey. There's no going back after these opening gambits as you're offering sex on a plate, meaning your sexual confidence levels are high but your morals are low.

Of course you could shelter behind the 'ironic' cloak. Either way though you're testing the sexual waters in a subtle or less than subtle way meaning you see yourself as being a bit of a serial shagger who considers long slow seductions a waste of good drinking time.

Romantic/Slushy

If you're able to wax on about 'Heaven must be missing a star tonight' and other such Mills & Boon romantic guff then it could be you strive so hard to be seen as smoothly seductive that you end up coming across as seriously sleazy instead. There's a difference between simply telling a girl she's beautiful and going all poetic and comparing her to the night sky. One is called flattery and the other risks sounding sarcastic. Lines like this should make you sound caring and sensitive but a genuine-sounding delivery is so hard to pull off that you could end up sounding like a Billy-no-mates loner.

Suave

Telling a girl that her dress will look nice on your bedroom carpet will give you the air of someone who aims for quantity rather than quality with their shagging. This is the 'cold-call' of chat-up lines, cheeky, persistent but relentlessly up-beat in the face of defeat and able to move on to the next victim without as much as a shrug or a sigh. Lines like this suggest it's all about the chase for you, with short sprints being more your thing than marathons. It suggests the same about the quality of your relationships, too, meaning a long-term love affair for you is probably one that lasts beyond the second bottle of wine.

Smart

Telling a girl her eyes match the colour of your Porsche brings a competitive sense of strategic cunning to your image, suggesting you're a confident and optimistic go-getter who will be ruthless when it comes to achieving his goals in life. Unfortunately, it also implies you have assumed the girl in question to be avaricious and slutty, someone who can be seduced into sex by the waggling of a set of car keys. It also implies that she will be unduly impressed by the type of car you have chosen and that she can therefore stand no chance of owning anything similar or better. Meaning you think she's cheap. If she is impressed by your line at least you will know that she *is* cheap, which could constitute a hit in your book at least.

Simple

'Can I buy you a drink?' or 'Have we met before?' might sound glaringly obvious but they will make you look confident but not sleazy as long as your follow-up isn't weak:

'Can I buy you a drink?'

'No thanks I've already got one.'

'Well, would you like to buy me one then?'

Lines like this aren't pointedly sexual, meaning you're not putting your victim on the spot by demanding an instant sexual response, plus you get to change your mind if you find your target has got a laugh like a wart-hog. Girls using the chat-up line 'Can I buy you a drink' can make a man go weak at the knees as many men fantasise about a woman who gets the first round in.

What not to do

If you want to put your date off your personality completely then be rude to the waiter. A poll of 3,000 people for www.OnePoll.com found 63% of people said it was the thing that most put them off a person while sharing a romantic dinner. Drowning a dish in salt before tasting it came second.

Of course there are many more people you will want to impress in your life than a hot date but that date might just be around for longer if he or she is a possible life-mate, so any time spent on analysis and personal presentation has got to be a worthwhile investment.

Keep in mind that nothing in this section of the book is intended as a suppression or masking of YOU. Although we've advocated presenting your ideal image to the significant people in your life it should work as an enhancement of your best bits rather than a burying of your worst.

And when you're choosing other people to spend your life with why stick to a selection process that is probably less thorough than choosing a puppy at a pet shop: if it looks cute and wags its tail a lot it must be okay? Knowledge is always power. And although we can't guarantee you'll find everlasting love by reading potential mates' traits choices and behaviours, or by enhancing how you project your own, we reckon you will improve your odds. And even if you decide to make no changes, at least you will know how those choices affect what the people in your life see when they assess, look at and judge the person called YOU.

CONCLUSION

WHAT READING THIS BOOK SAYS ABOUT YOU

You might think that this book has been an exercise in narcissism with a heavy helping of paranoia. And, up to a point, you'd be right. But deep down everyone knows that talking and thinking about themselves is their biggest hobby.

By reading this book you should have realised a little more about yourself than before.

So what exactly?

1. That it's not always the big decisions you make in life that reveal the most about you.
2. That your choices reveal not just your style, but what's going on in your inner psyche.
3. That those choices are not just down to obvious things, like how you dress, but there to be analysed in everything from the pictures you hang on the wall to the way your desk is organised at work.
4. That by studying these you can come to a better understanding of yourself and, crucially, how others see you.
5. That you need to go and change your computer passwords and make the bed.

With *The You Code* as your guide, you'll begin to understand other people better too, whether you want to date them or work for them. Once you know the rules there's a lot of fun to be had in spotting that little habit and having your own personal 'lightbulb' moment as someone inadvertently reveals their 'inner self'.

You'll have discovered:

1. That knowing your boss's habits can be useful in the workplace.
2. That we all have certain friends for a reason.
3. That what a prospective partner wears, owns and even jokes about provide signals that you can analyse to find out whether they are the right person for you.

And, when it comes to you, our aim hasn't been just to get you to be honest about your habits or to shock you into changing them. Because once you know yourself you'll be in a better position to understand the decisions you make and with a little effort, tweak them to make yourself into the person you want to be – or the person that you need to be.

Once you know The You Code and start using it, you can save a lot of time. It can help you avoid dating the wrong person, allow you to perform better at work – or even simply realise that the job you're in doesn't fit your personality.

While fashions do change the core values and personal interactions between people don't alter that much over time. Even our ancient ancestors would have made assumptions about each other based on the cut of their loincloths. And what you've learned in *The You Code* can be applied to pretty much any future situation in which you find yourself.

CONCLUSION

So be proud to pass on what you've learned to others. They might think you're self-obsessed but, secretly, they are too.

Headings Index

Subject Index

THE YOU CODE

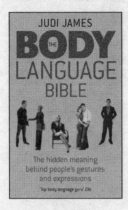